BLACK SPHINX

ON THE COMEDIC IN MODERN ART

jrp|ringier

Black Sphinx: On the Comedic in Modern Art

Volume 4 of the SoCCAS
[Southern California Consortium of Art Schools] Symposia

Edited by John C. Welchman

jrp|ringier

TABLE OF CONTENTS

John C. Welchman

PREFACE

Black Sphinx: On the Comedic in Modern Art is based on the fourth annual symposium of the Southern California Consortium of Art Schools (SoCCAS), programmed in partnership with the Hammer Museum of Art, Los Angeles. Our thanks go first, then, to the energetic and creative curators and staff at the Hammer, including Director Ann Philbin, Senior Curator Gary Garrells, Russell Ferguson, and James Bewley. Generous support for this event was also provided by the art departments of the SoCCAS member schools (Art Center, Otis, UCI, UCLA, UCSB, UCSD, USC); by the University of California Institute for Research in the Arts; and the Center for the Humanities, UCSD. Thanks also to Meg Cranston for interviewing Los Angeles artist John Baldessari for the live event.

The symposium was only the centerpiece of three programming initiatives. The second was an evening of live entertainment, *Live Sphinx: An Evening of Stand-Up Comedy* (May 21, 2007), curated by James Bewley, which featured host Murray Hill and appearances by Jessi Klein, Al Madrigal, Michelle Biloon, and Patton Oswalt.

A few nights later the Hammer put on *Video Sphinx: An Evening of Funny Films* (May 29, 2007), at which we screened videos and excerpts by Paul McCarthy (*Painter*, 1995); Yoshua Okon (*Coyoteria*, 2003; *Parking Lotus*); João Onofre (*Untitled [Vulture in the Studio]*, 2002); Ryan Trecartin (*A Family Finds Entertainment*, 2004); Alex Bag (*Untitled*, 1995);

Mike Kelley (*Day Is Done*, 2005); Bryan Boyce (*State of the Union*, 2001); The Yes Men; Skip Arnold (*TV Shorts*, 1980); Martin Kersels (*Pink Constellation*, 2001); B&T (*Ultimate Champion*, 2006); Susan Mogul (*Take Off*, 1974). Special thanks to Sara Hunsucker who gave generously of her time to make this event possible.

As ever, I'd also like to thank the art departments of the consortium members, their chairs, deans, faculty, and student representatives: the four University of California schools, UCLA, UCI, UCSB, and UCSD, as well as the University of Southern California, Art Center Pasadena, and Otis College of Art and Design. Every year someone steps up to lend crucial advice and assistance, and this year it was Andrea Fraser from UCLA, who, even though she had only recently arrived in town to take up her new position, gave generously of her time and expertise throughout the programming of the event and moderated the panel discussion on "Women's Laughter" at the conclusion of symposium. Thanks also to others who worked with the consortium in 2006, especially Julia Dzwonkoski and David Mather, among many others.

Finally, we are entering a sixth year of collaboration with our publisher, JRP|Ringier in Zurich, Switzerland. This book and the series of which it is a part would not be possible with out the vision, support—and necessary good humor—of editorial director Lionel Bovier, and the diligence (and patience) of others at the press, Clare Manchester and Salome Schnetz. I would also like to thank those responsible for the design and layout of the book, Gilles Gavillet and Nicola Todeschini.

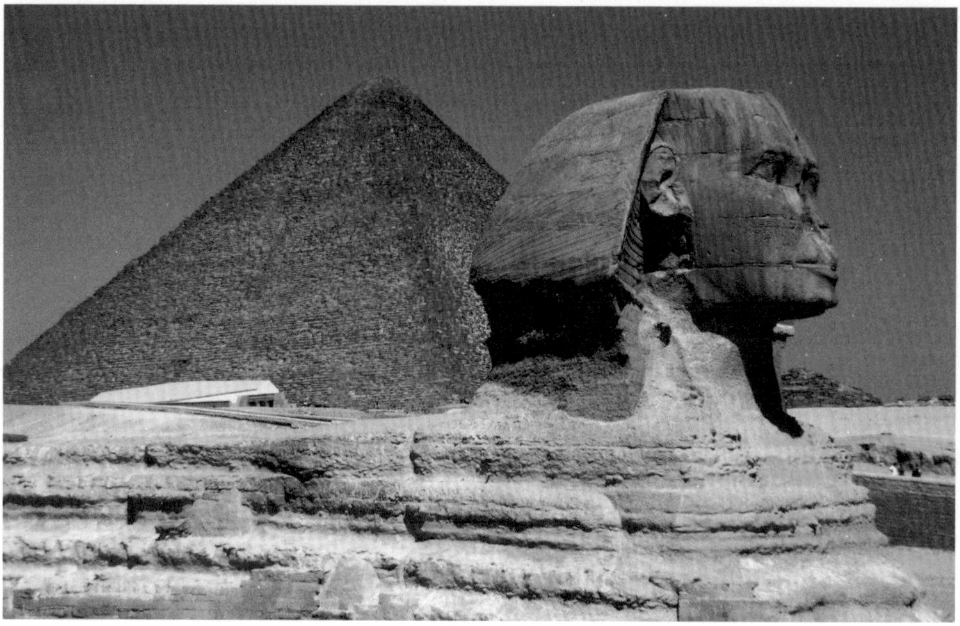

Marcio Ruiz
The Great Sphinx, 2008
Photograph

John C. Welchman

INTRODUCTION

Having programmed events around such potentially serious topics as "Institutional Critique and After" (at the Los Angeles County Museum of Art in 2005) and "The Aesthetics of Risk" (at the Getty Museum in 2006), we thought it was time to create an occasion that was a little more lighthearted—though serious, worthy, and, above all, darker issues will crop up here and there. We took our title from a telling phrase used by Surrealist kingpin André Breton while he was preparing his famous anthology of Black Humor, a decade-long endeavor which was finally published in French in 1939, but only translated into English in 1997 by City Lights in San Francisco.

In his preface, "Lightening Rod," Breton offers what appears to be a rather cryptic remark, which he cites from his own earlier essay "Surrealist Situation of the Object" (1935): "the black sphinx of *objective humor* cannot fail to meet along the dusty road, the road of the future, the white sphinx of *objective chance*, and ... all human creation after that will be the fruit of their embrace."[1] Breton himself traces the "objective humor" he couples with "the black sphinx" back to Hegel, who noted the formation in the Romantic period of a unique compound of humor and objectivity ("*Objektiver Humur*"), which offered what little hope he appeared to have for art in the wake of Romanticism. In a wider frame, the compound of human and beast, woman and lion, represented by the sphinx and its encounter with Oedipus, symbolized for Hegel the struggle and potential triumph of rationality, or at least the awareness of the rational faculties, over animality and instinct—or the pre-rational.[2]

Breton's collection of "humour noir" features tart and salacious extracts from such writers as Jonathan Swift, Franz Kafka, Arthur Rimbaud, Edgar Allan Poe, Lewis Carroll, and Charles Baudelaire, as well as passages from relatively lesser-known figures including Xavier Forneret, Alphonse Allais, Jean-Pierre Brisset, Jakob van Hoddis, and the sometime Dada pugilist, Arthur Cravan. While he doesn't quite offer a theory connecting the two, Breton clearly saw the creation of Black Humor by what he termed its "true initiator," Swift, and the incorrigible legacies to which it gave rise, as a crucial product of the rise of a general modernity that was somehow clinched by the Surrealist movement he so zealously defended. In the head texts and mini-essays that preface his selections, Breton gave vent to an elaborate chiaroscuro predicated on gradations of *noir* that ranged from the deep and morbid blackness of the Marquis de Sade or the savage, gallows humor of Swift, to the lighter shades of gray made up by the not-quite-innocent whimsy of Lewis Caroll, the almost benevolent humor of O. Henry, or what Breton termed the "genial buffoonery" of Christian Dietrich Grabbe.

In the mid-1960s, Black Humor had come into vogue in the US and was busily correlated with another generation of dark and sardonic authors, from William Burroughs and the Beats to Thomas Pynchon. One of the signposts of this interest was another anthology bearing the title *Black Humor* published in 1965 with an excerpt from *The Ginger Man* by J.P. Donleavy and short pieces by Pynchon, John Barth, Joseph Heller, Céline, Terry Southern, Vladimir Nabokov, Edward Albee, and others.[3] It was during these years, of course, that Marcel Duchamp, whose moves across the fields of black and white took in chess and urine-resistant porcelain, offered another reflection on the origins and importance of noirist wit. "Humor," he observed in an interview in 1960, is "a great power ... a sort of savior so to speak because, before, art was such a serious thing, so pontifical that I was very happy when I discovered that I could introduce humor into it. The discovery of humor was a liberation. Not humor in the sense of comedy ... Humor is something ... profound and serious and more difficult to define. It's not only about laughing. There's a humor that is black which doesn't inspire laughter and doesn't please at all. It is a thing in itself, a new feeling so to speak, which follows from all sorts of things that we can't analyze with words."[4]

When is humor black? he was asked. "Black, that's a way of speaking, since it was necessary to assign a color. Obviously there wasn't a more explicit color because black is somber, the somber of this humor makes it a thing almost mean instead of friendly and dangerous. It's almost like a sort of dynamite, of the spirit, isn't it? And that's why we call it black. Black doesn't have any meaning but it's a little like the black curtain of anarchy, if you will, things like that."[5]

One of our main aims at the symposium and in the present publication is to add some before and after hues to this constellation of blacknesses in the form of a few of what Duchamp himself referred to as "invisible colors." The notion of the sphinx itself grants some of this permission, with its intimations of enigma, unknowability, and mythological pastness which leaven the black ground of noirist humor with different shades and figures. The old theory of the four humors already opens onto this wider palette of colors, for the black bile of melancholy was caught up in a matrix of associations that posed it with and against the blood-red of the sanguine, the yellow of choleric, and the green of phlegm.

Breton himself participated in the prismatic splitting of the blackness that cloaked his anthology. For on their journey into the inky depths of dark humor many of his noirist consorts could only be apprehended only in the light of other colors. Baudelaire's dandyism was defined by sartorial affectations that organized his triumphs over the vicissitudes of fortune "from the pale pink gloves of his luxurious youth," writes Breton "through the green wig exhibited at the café Riche, to his scarlet chenille boa and the supreme finery of his declining years."[6] With Isidore Ducasse or the Comte de Lautréamont, Breton's chromatic reveries are even more intense. For his "fierce melancholy" can only be approached by passing though a double rainbow of colors, first "the colors that Lewis used in *The Monk*" to paint his apparitional spirit; and then "the colors with which Swinburne captured the true appearance of the Marquis de Sade"—his "veins swollen with divine blood" and his body cavities "kneaded with Azure."[7] Only thus could Lautéamont's prismatic sublimation of modernity be apprehended ... in a scenography of sapphire floors, silver-beaked gas lamps, the green membranes of space, and the white-hot heart in an asbestos cage that beats in the middle of it all.

Reflecting on the wider contexts of Breton's ideas, Michel Carrouges shakes out his propositions through a centrifuge of color separations: "Black humor has nothing in common with Rabelesian good humor, nor with Voltaire's intellectual wit, nor with the red humor that marks the robust health of the masses, nor with the rose humor of elegance."[8] His is just one of several dialogues with Breton's anthology that attempt to open up new spectral possibilities for its variegated darkness. Discussing Kafka's humor, Jean Collignon notes that "This is no longer 'black humor' as Breton tried to illustrate it in his *Anthologie de l'humour noir*, but to coin a term suggested by the French phrase 'rire jaune,' a sort of 'humour jaune.' Black humor might be reserved for those who are either cynical or desperate; 'yellow humor' remaining the last chance of those on the verge of despair, but not yet altogether immersed in it."[9]

Breton's essentially literary fancies were offered both social and visual correlates a few years earlier as the light black humor practiced in café concerts such as the famous Chat Noir in Paris in the 1880s and 1890s exploded into a spectrum of dissident colors. Beginning in 1882, Alphonse Allais made an extraordinary series of works activated entirely by the extramural or parergonistic text of their titles and driven by the anarchic combustibility of color-assisted humor. In addition to their schoolboy humor and ironic self-reflexivity, they are, at the same time, the first monochromes in the Western tradition. The red work was titled *Récolte de la tomate par des cardinaux apoplectiques au bord de la Mer Rouge* [*Apoplectic Cardinals Harvesting Tomatoes on the Shore of the Red Sea: Study for the Aurora Borealis*]; the blue, *Stupeur de jeunes recrues en apercevant pour la première fois ton azur, ô Méditerranée* [*Stupor of Young Recruits Perceiving Your Azure for the First Time, Oh Mediterranean*]; the green, *Bande de pochards dans le brouillard* [*Band of Boozers in the Fog*]; the yellow, *Partage d'un apéritif anisé entre asiates ictériques dans un champ de blé* [*Sharing an Anise Aperitif Among Jaundiced Asians in a Cornfield*]; and the white and empty piece of commercial white Bristol paper *Première communion de jeunes filles chlorotiques par un temps de neige* [*First Communion of Anemic Young Girls in the Snow*].

Humoristic color takes on a set of wider implications at the end of the 19th century as it is reallocated in a new set of national and social symbolizations and allied with color-cued stereotypes and colonial-era clichés. The artist, T. Bianco, one of the leading satirical illustrators of the era, for example, made a series of postcards depicting the six grave dangers facing France around 1900—many in surprising continuity with popular xenophobic conceptions at the beginning of the 21st century. One of the heirs of the tradition of tapered and contaminated produce that flared most recently in the 2008 Chinese powdered milk scandal, *Le péril blanc: le lait falsifié*, points to the effects of earlier batches of contaminated milk that endangered the lives of babies. *Le péril bleu: le papier timbre*, skewers the bureaucratic over-coding of commercial life as French business is strangled by paperwork and regulations. *Le péril jaune* refers specifically to China, the so-called "Yellow Peril" that threatened Europe through immigration and economic competition. Another dose of contemporary resonance is supplied by *Le péril noir: le mauvais prêtre*, an anti-cleric jab against corruption and exploitation by priests and the Church. And finally, the *Le péril rouge: la révolution sociale* points to the wars, conflicts, and revolutions wrought (or willed) by socialism.[10]

As witnessed by the final danger (*Le péril vert: l'absinthe*) and numerous humorous attacks on the influence of alcohol on art, such as an elaborate caricature published in *Le Rire* in 1904 (*Absinthe: influence de l'alcoolisme*), the green-hued dangers of absinthe occupied a special place in this palette of perils, becoming a kind of roguish indicator for the delirium-induced stylistic experiments of the modern movement. The color coordination which linked laughter and danger in these years also precipitated another, more confounding, aspect of humorous relationality—the reflex association of color and comedy with national, ethnic, gender, and other social stereotypes ... as set out in the yellow peril of China. There is, of course, another set of associations caught up in the reduction of the monochrome to a racialist identification. The work of Alphonse Allais was bound into this system of assumptions, especially the monochrome in his series to which I haven't yet referred, *Combat de nègres dans une cave pendant la nuit* [*Combat of Negroes in a Cellar After Dark*]. Breton was also party to it; for in the 1966 preface to the Black Humor anthology, he noted that when they first appeared (in 1939) the words "black humor" "made no sense (unless to designate a form of banter supposedly characteristic of 'Negroes')." Even though he capitalizes Negroes, puts the word in scare quotes, and plants an exclamation point after it as if to signal his distance from someone else's word, Breton reminds us that Black Humor has cultural ramifications outside its superficial descriptive neutrality.

Indeed with the Civil Rights movement in train in the US as Breton was writing in France, another round of attention to the idea of Black Humor had already arrived. Of course, theorists of humor and comedy have long wrestled with the dependence of so much in the world of jokes and laughter on the ethnic stereotype, and many have concluded that this correlation itself constitutes one of the foundational ways in which humor might always have in it a trace of blackness (or redness, or yellowness ...).

Black Sphinx commences with Sigmund Freud's brief essay "Humour," written in 1927, more than two decades after the publication of his longer and better-known study *Jokes and Their Relation to the Unconscious* (1905). For many years one of the more obscure of Freud's works,[11] "Humour" offers a succinct summary of his understanding of jokes and laughter and the dispositions that produce, manage, and receive them; and at the same time reconsiders several of his earlier contentions in light of revisions made during these years to his theory of the structure of the psychic economy. Freud argues that humor can be conceived as a strategic defense against the depredations of traumatic reality. Humorous exchange or perception acts as a solvent for the psychological outcropping of anxiety, a non-pathological defense against its unwanted and potentially harmful incursions. In this sense, the ego acts to repackage traumatic events as occasions for its own pleasure.

As with Hegel, the sphinx played a signal part in Freud's social, aesthetic, and professional life. As early as 1885 Freud wrote to Minna Bernays, the sister of his fiancée, that he was "under the full impact of Paris and, waxing very poetical, could compare it to a vast overdressed Sphinx who gobbles up every foreigner unable to solve her riddles."[12] Several decades later, at the height of his career, he was presented with a medallion on the occasion of his 50th birthday. Featuring a "design of Oedipus answering the Sphinx" it was "inscribed with the words 'Who knew the famous riddles and was a man most mighty.'"[13] With the possible exception of the influence exerted by Ludwig Laistner's *The Riddle of the Sphinx: Characteristics of a History of Myths* on the composition of *The Interpretation of Dreams*,[14] references to the part played by the sphinx in the story of Oedipus are conspicuous by their absence in Freud's writings. This has led some to conclude that he thereby "erased the Sphinx, the tricky, troublesome feminine."[15] But whatever its eventuation in his theoretical writings, the hybrid creature was something of an obsessional object for Freud. His personal collection of antiquities, already extensive by the late 1930s at the time of his move from Vienna to London, featured several examples, including a terracotta from Southern Italy (late 5th or early 4th century BC).[16] In addition to the small sphinxes on his desk, his consulting room was furnished with a print of Jean-Auguste-Dominique Ingres' *Oedipus and the Sphinx* (1808), hung "near the couch, where he could contemplate it as he decoded his patients' conundrums"[17]; while the design of Freud's *ex libris* featured a rendering of the same subject done in a style somewhere between neo-Greek and Art Nouveau.

Jeffrey Minson's "Resonances of 'Raillery'" takes us back to one of the origins of civil society in the writings of Anthony Ashley Cooper, the 3rd Earl of Shaftsbury, particularly his "Sensus Communis: An Essay on the Freedom of Wit and Humor." His argument traces the origins and implications of Shaftesbury's historically important contention that humor is both a catalyst and a symptom of the conditions of freedom defined by the polite and rational discourse that underwrote the emergence of truth-seeking selfhood in the Enlightenment. What Minson defines as Shaftesbury's heartfelt plea for reflective playfulness is both a community ideal and a cultural tactic. But it is also a digressive zone within which the claims of dissent can be tested in the belief that truth and justice will not only survive this process intact but also be somehow improved: so that "the laughter in just raillery is the soundtrack to a higher truth." Minson investigates several roadblocks on the hard—but sometimes amusing—journey to truth, including the challenges posed to aesthetic taste by the category of the "ugly" and its relation to the prevalent anti-aestheticism of much modern and contemporary art.

In "Irreverent, Illicit, Incoherent: Belle Epoque Comedy," Janet Whitmore discusses the extraordinary unfolding of wit and comedic irreverence concentrated in the bars, cafes, and café-concerts of Montmartre in Paris in the 1880s and 1890s. The habitués of these bohemian enclaves—a seething mix of artists, musicians, Symbolist poets, chanteuses, actors, anarchists, decadents, and sundry hangers-on—produced some of the most uproariously humorous and dryly ironic products of the modern era. Ricocheting between literary obscurantism and slapstick immediacy, from political satire to smutty innuendo, Belle Epoque wit adapted itself to the graphic languages of caricature as well as finding unique precipitates in objects realized (or just imagined) through the provision of verbal puns.

David Robbins gives us a name for the new form of comedic collision, or something like it, that was developed in the next generation, especially by the Bavarian-born comic and performer Karl Valentin (1888–1948): "Concrete Comedy." For Robbins, Valentin's wittily resourceful creation of comic objects and contexts gives rise to nothing less than a new language of comedy organized not around the traditional parameters of language, narrative, and illusion, but by the pull of the comedic gravity of objects themselves. Materialist, actual, and actionist, concrete comedy begins when the experience of mass production and abstraction are understood as neutral "facts." Robbins suggests that the major proponents of this new comedic mode, including Valentin and Marcel Duchamp, were committed to a physical comedy predicated on gesture and real-time site-specificity.

In his essay "Bataille's Laughter," Louis Kaplan attends to the part played by wit, humor, and eruptive laughter in the writings of Georges Bataille. These experiences, particularly the burst or explosion of laughter, point to one of the limit-terms of rational, philosophical discourse, and can be apprehended only through what Bataille terms "the practice of intellectual scatology." Arguing that "Bataille put laughter (rather than the formless) at the center of both his philosophy and the problems that occupied him throughout his life," Kaplan examines how embodied humor informs Bataille's thoughts about death and non-knowledge. This analysis has two parts. The first traces the relation between the development of Bataille's ideas and the place of humor in the writings of Friedrich Nietzsche and Henri Bergson, which he took up in his wartime essay "Nietzsche's Laughter" (1942) and a lecture, "Non-knowledge, Laughter, and Tears," delivered in Paris in 1953. The second discusses Bataille's essay "Max Ernst, Philosopher!" published in 1960, just two years before his death. Prompted by Ernst's dissident visual cosmologies, Bataille speculates here on the presence of a darkly forceful humor that might lead to the death of thought.

Jo Anna Issak's reflections on the relations between humor, gender, and recent art practices, "Whoever Wants to Understand Is Invited to Play," also have a point of commencement in Surrealism. Issak argues that "while Surrealism invested its faith in the revolutionary potential of repressed (male) desire, the role for women was that of sexually liberal muse, not fellow revolutionary." She extends her critique to the writings of Freud, including his 1927 essay on humor, noting that women are corralled with criminals and comedians by virtue of the "primary narcissism" they all—purportedly—share. Isaak connects the pleasurable rebellion of Freud's view of humor to Mikhail Bakhtin's understanding of the carnivalesque, and sets both in relation to the forms of humor and laughter originated by and shared among feminist artists and critics beginning in the early 1980s, including work shown in two signal exhibitions she curated, *The Revolutionary Power of Women's Laughter* (1983) and *Laughter Ten Years After* (1995).

Developing some of the ideas first set out in his book *On Humor* (2002), Simon Critchley's "Laughing at Foreigners: A Peculiar Defence of Ethnic Humor" takes on the *bête noire* of jocular culture noted above: its tendentious fixation on racial and ethnic stereotypes and not occasional unapologetic xenophobia. Rather than offering a moralizing corrective to that class of humor predicated on the reflex nationalisms of the Polish or Irish joke and their myriad variants, Critchley contends that in its widest frame humor is a "form of critical social anthropology" that defamiliarizes the familiar, demythologizes the exotic, and inverts the world of common sense with its provision of an "oblique phenomenology of ordinary life." By returning those that deploy it to their *ethos* or locality, humor also touches on the constitution of an *ethnos*; and it is here that the retrograde stereotypicality of vernacular jokes kicks in. Critchley admits the centrality, even dominance, of this type of humor, but refuses to become subject to it; or, rather, he argues that the prevalence of ethnic jokes, which has surely touched or implicated us all, offers a salutary reminder of the recalcitrant kernel of potential prejudice that dwells in each of us. In this sense humor offers a short circuit that exposes our discomfort, which Critchley also links to the critical function of art and Freud's theory of repressive discharge.

Each of the remaining five chapters of *Black Sphinx* examines the production of comic and humorous effects in the work and its contexts of artists and movements active during the last 40 or so years in Europe and the US. We begin in West Germany before the fall of the Berlin Wall in the 1980s. In "Retreat to the Private Sphere: In-Jokes in West German Art of the 1980s," Gregory H. Williams discusses the social and cultural conditions informing the irreverent and not occasionally hermetic wit of a loose group of male artists including Werner Büttner, Georg Herold, Martin Kippenberger, and Albert Oehlen active in the Rhineland city of Cologne during these years. Williams carefully situates the humorous work of these artists in the contexts formed by the "hangover" climate of the 1980s in the wake of the chancellorships of Willy Brandt and Helmut Schmidt, and the intellectual and cultural debates occasioned by the writings of Theodor Adorno, Peter Bürger, and others. He sets this group in apposition to another—even looser—Cologne cohort comprised by artist Rosemarie Trockel and dealers Monika Sprüth and Esther Schipper, whose interests lay more in what Williams terms "stealthy irony" than clamorous "bar humor." Looking across to an interest in the outmoded shared by US artists such as Richard Prince and Mike Kelley, Williams suggests that jokes furnished the grounds for "an appealing inappropriateness ... that made them suited to the obsessive, postmodern recycling of the past."

The Los Angeles-based critic Jan Tumlir guides us through the high energy situational pranksterism of the performance artist Skip Arnold. "Your Confession Booth Is My Soapbox" takes as its point of departure one the most physically traumatic of Arnold's works, *Marks* (1984), in which the artist, wearing nothing but an old motorcycle crash-helmet, hurls himself against the walls of a small room until he collapses with exhaustion or passes out, at which point the performance ends. Tumlir connects the dark humor that underwrites the ironically entropic self-defeatism and existential mockery of this performance with the larger debate about mark-making after Abstract Expressionism; and sets both in relation to the recalibrated slapstick that attends Arnold's voluntarily impulsive subjection to physical limitations and social constraint.

In "V-Notes on Parody," Jessica Chalmers reflects on the witty interventionism of the V-Girls of which she was a member (along with Andrea Fraser, Marianne Weems, Erin Cramer, and Martha Baer) for a decade between the mid-1980s and mid-1990s. Her overview of the changing relation between feminism and laughter over the last two decades passes through several of the discussions mapped out already (including Hélène Cixous' "The Laugh of the Medusa" [1975] and the comedic theories of Henri Bergson and Georges Bataille). Thinking through the questions of anger and outrage, femininity and authenticity that had preoccupied the preceding generation, Chalmers examines how the V-Girls took up postmodern tactics of parody, impersonation, simulated pomposity, and deconstruction in order to regenerate the critical power—sometimes disturbing, sometimes uproarious—of comedic intervention. Of one of the signature performances by the group, *The Question of Manet's* Olympia*: Posed and Skirted* (1989–1992), for example, Chalmers notes that the range of discursive materials it addressed included "elegy, poetry, lists, opera summaries, and analytical critique."

Michael Smith muses on another group performance, this time made up of his own histories and alter personae, including Baby Ikki and "Mike" (aka "Blandman"). Based on the script for his live talk at the Hammer Museum, "The Nut Doesn't Fall Far From the Tree: A Piece of Work in Progress" layers offbeat autobiography with comedic improvisation and bundles both in a rhetorical web of spot-on, matter-of-fact irony. Art figures in all this as a kind of off-stage step sibling, collections of children's drawings, family photos, maps, and miscellaneous snapshots that meter out the disarming inevitability of Smith's life and times. The jokes, one-liners and sundry asides set out between these visual records, add up to a kind of delirious giant caption annotating "Mike's" always emerging but never-quite-coming of age.

In "'Don't Try for Laughs': John Baldessari and Conceptual Comedy" I outline some of the elements of the humor—both explicit and implied—at work in and around a movement long considered one of the driest and most serious in the 20th century. One of the central contentions of many revisionist histories of the Conceptual art movement, I suggest, foregrounds the various forms of irony, absurdity, and even mild buffoonery manifest not only in the work of artists such as Baldessari and Douglas Huebler (where they might be expected), but also in some of the projects and writings of Joseph Kosuth, Robert Barry, Seth Siegelaub, and others (where one might not expect to find them). My main focus, however, is on Baldessari's career-long commitment to droll and off-beat humor, and a disarming and uniquely sustained comedy of para-formal relations. I argue that a key figure for these interests can be found in the comedic metaphor of "deadpan," more commonly associated with a particular humorous disposition in film or theater. It is on the site of this exchange that Baldessari's organized interruption of code-based practices meets Bergon's notion of "mechanical elasticity," generating a new model for the comedy of deferral.

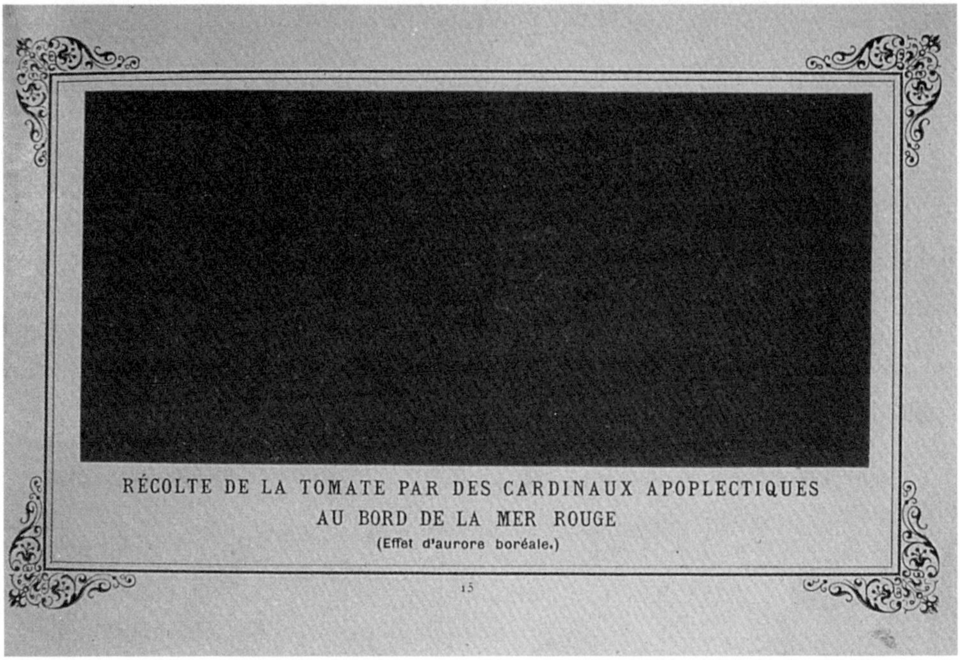

Alphonse Allais
Monochromatic image from *April fool-ish* Album (Paul Ollendorff, Paris 1897): *Récolte de la tomate par des cardinaux apoplectiques au bord de la Mer Rouge*

NOTES

1
André Breton, "Lightening Rod," in *Anthology of Black Humor*, trans. Mark Polizzotti, City Lights Books, San Francisco 1997, p. xvi. "Surrealist Situation of the Object" was published in *Political Position of Surrealism* (1935); and trans. in *Manifestoes of Surrealism*, University of Michigan Press, Ann Arbor 1969.

2
Laura Mulvey discusses this symbolization in "Netherworlds and the Unconscious: Oedipus and *Blue Velvet*," in *Fetishism and Curiosity*, Indiana University Press, Bloomington and Indianapolis 1996, p. 145–146. Hegel's discussion can be found in Georg Wilhelm Friedrich Hegel, *The Philosophy of Art: Being the Second Part of Hegel's Aesthetic*, trans. William M. Bryant, Kessinger Publishing, Whitefish, Montana 2006, p. 192. See also Kirk Pillow, *Sublime Understanding: Aesthetic Reflection in Kant and Hegel*, MIT Press, Cambridge, Massachusetts 2003, esp. chapter 7, "Aesthetic Unity in the Hegelian Context," p. 197–230; Stephen C. Law, "Hegel and the Spirit of Comedy: Der Geist der stets verneint," in *Hegel and Aesthetics*, ed. William Maker, SUNY Press, New York 2000, p. 113f.; John D. Erickson, "Surrealist Black Humor as Oppositional Discourse," *Symposium*, vol. 42, 1988; and Doug Haynes, "The persistence of irony: interfering with surrealist black humour," *Textual Practice*, vol. 20, issue 1, 2006, p. 25–47.

3
Black Humor, ed. with an intro. by Bruce Jay Friedman, Bantam Books, New York 1965.

4
"To Change Names, Simply," Marcel Duchamp interviewed by Guy Viau, Canadian Radio Television, July 17, 1960 [trans. Sarah Skinner Kilborne]; http://www.toutfait.com/issues/volume2/issue_4/interviews/md_guy/md_guy.htm.

5
Ibid.

6
Breton, *Anthology of Black Humor*, p. 98.

7
Ibid., p. 132.

8
Ibid., p. 15.

9
See Jean Collignon, "Kafka's Humor," in *Yale French Studies* 16 ["Foray Through Existentialism"] (1955), p. 53–62.

10
Le Musée virtuel de l'absinthe (at http://www.museeabsinthe.com/) reproduces each of these cards and their original wrapping.

11
This was certainly the opinion of Ernest Jones, as reported by James Strachey in his introduction to *Jokes and Their Relation to the Unconscious*, Penguin, Harmondsworth 1976, p. 24.

12
Cited by Peter L. Rudnytsky, *Freud and Oedipus*, Columbia University Press, New York 1992, p. 9.

13
Rudnytsky, *Freud and Oedipus*, p. 174.

14
On the influence of Ludwig Laistner's *Das Rätsel der Sphinx: Grundzuge einer Mythengeschichte* (*The Riddle of the Sphinx: Characteristics of a History of Myths*) on *The Interpretation of Dreams*, see Robin N. Mitchell-Boyask, "Freud's Reading of Classical Literature and Classical Philology," in *Reading Freud's Reading*, eds. Sander L. Gilman, Jutta Birmele, Jay Geller and Valerie D. Greenberg, NYU Press, New York 1995, p. 23–46.

15
See Janine Burke, *The Sphinx on the Table: Sigmund Freud's Art Collection and the Development of Psychoanalysis*, Walker and Company, New York 2006; cited in Kerryn Goldsworthy, "Old and Grubby Gods," *Australian Book Review*, no. 286 (2006), p. 34.

16
See also Lynn Gamwell and Richard Wells (eds.), *Sigmund Freud and Art: His Personal Collection of Antiquities*, State University of New York, Binghampton 1989.

17
Janine Burke, *The Sphinx on the Table*; cited in Kerryn Goldsworthy, "Old and Grubby Gods," p. 34.

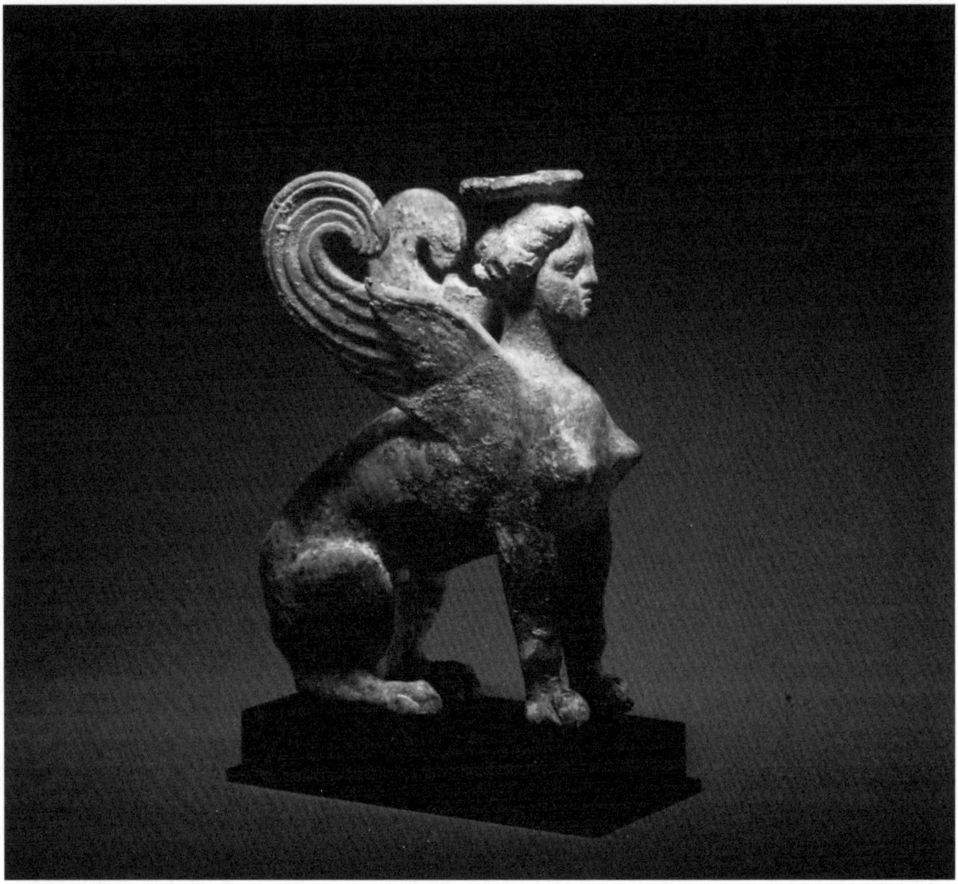

COURTESY OF THE FREUD MUSEUM PHOTO LIBRARY

4387, Sphinx
Late 5th–early 4th century BC
Culture: Greek; Southern Italian
Material: Terracotta
Dimensions: h. 7 in /18.5 cm

Sigmund Freud

HUMOUR*

Der Humor

Freud wrote this paper in five days during the second week of August, 1927 (Jones, 1957, 146), and it was read on his behalf by Anna Freud on September 1, before the Tenth International Psycho-Analytic Congress at Innsbruck. It was first published in the autumn of the same year in the psychoanalytic 'Almanac' for 1928.

The paper returns, after an interval of more than 20 years, to the subject discussed in the last section of the book on *Jokes* (1905*c*). Freud now considers it in light of his new structural picture of the human mind. Some interesting meta-psychological points emerge in the later pages of the paper, and for the first time we find the super-ego presented in an amiable mood.

—James Strachey

In my volume on *Jokes and their Relation to the Unconscious* (1905*c*), I in fact considered humour only from the economic point of view. My object was to discover the source of the pleasure obtained from humour, and I think I was able to show that the yield of humorous pleasure arises from an economy in expenditure upon feeling [*Standard Ed.*, 8, 236].

There are two ways in which the humorous process can take place. It may take place in regard to a single person, who himself adopts the humorous attitude, while a second person plays the part of the spectator who derives enjoyment from it; or it may take place between two persons, of whom one takes no part at all in the humorous process, but is made the object of humorous contemplation by the other. When, to take the crudest example [ibid., 229], a criminal who was being led out to the gallows on a Monday remarked: 'Well, the week's beginning nicely', he was producing the humour himself; the humorous process is completed in his own person and obviously affords him a certain sense of satisfaction. I, the non-participating listener, am affected as it were at long-range by this humorous production of the criminal's; I feel, like him, perhaps, the yield of humorous pleasure.

We have an instance of the second way in which humour arises when a writer or narrator describes the behavior of real or imaginary people in a humorous manner. There is no need for those people to display any humour themselves; the humorous attitude is solely the business of the person who is taking them as his object; and, as in the former instance, the reader or hearer shares in the enjoyment of the humour. To sum up, then, we can say that the humorous attitude—whatever it may consist in—can be directed either towards the subject's own self or towards other people; it is to be assumed that it brings a yield of pleasure to the person who adopts it, and a similar yield of pleasure falls to the share of the non-participating onlooker.

We shall best understand the genesis of the yield of humorous pleasure if we consider the process in the listener before whom someone else produces humour. He sees this other person in a situation which leads the listener to expect that the other will produce the signs of an affect—that he will get angry, complain, express pain, be frightened or horrified or perhaps even in despair; and the onlooker or listener is prepared to follow his lead and to call up the same emotional impulses in himself. But this emotional expectancy is disappointed; the other person expresses no affect, but makes a jest. The expenditure on feeling that is economized turns into humorous pleasure in the listener.

It is easy to get so far. But we soon tell ourselves that it is the process which takes place in the other person—the 'humourist'—that merits the greater attention. There is no doubt that the essence of humour is that one spares oneself the affects to which the situation would naturally give rise and dismisses the possibility of such expressions of emotion with a jest. As far as this goes, the process in the humourist must tally with the process in the hearer—or, to put it more correctly, the process in the hearer must have copied the one in the humourist. But how does the latter bring about the mental attitude which makes a release of affect superfluous? What are the dynamics of his adoption of the 'humorous attitude'? Clearly, the solution of the problem is to be sought in the humourist; in the hearer we must assume that there is only an echo, a copy, of this unknown process.

It is now time to acquaint ourselves with a few of the characteristics of humour. Like jokes and the comic, humour has something liberating about it; but it also has something of grandeur and elevation, which is lacking in the other two ways of obtaining pleasure from intellectual activity. The grandeur in it clearly lies in the triumph of narcissism, the victorious assertion of the ego's invulnerability. The ego refuses to be distressed by the provocations of reality, to let itself be compelled to suffer. It insists that it cannot be affected by the traumas of the external world; it shows, in fact, that such traumas are no more than occasions for it to gain pleasure. This last feature is a quite essential element of humour. Let us suppose that the criminal who was being led to execution on Monday had said: 'It doesn't worry me. What does it matter, after all, if a fellow like me is hanged? The world won't come to an end because of it.' We should have to admit that such a speech does in fact display the same magnificent superiority over the real situation. It is wise and true; but it does not betray a trace of humour. Indeed, it is based on an appraisal of reality which runs directly counter to the appraisal made by humour. Humour is not resigned; it is rebellious. It signifies not only the triumph of the ego but also of the pleasure principal, which is able here to assert itself against the unkindness of the real circumstances.

These last two features—the rejection of the claims of reality and the putting through of the pleasure principal—bring humour near to the regressive or reactionary processes which engage our attention so extensively in psychopathology. Its fending off of the possibility of suffering places it among the great series of methods which the human mind has constructed in order to evade the compulsion to suffer—a series which begins with neurosis and culminates in madness and which includes intoxication, self-absorption and ecstasy.[1] Thanks to this connection, humour possesses a dignity which is wholly lacking, for instance, in jokes, for jokes either serve simply to obtain a yield of pleasure or place the yield of pleasure that has been obtained in the service of aggression. In what, then, does the humorous attitude consist, an attitude by means of which a person refuses to suffer, emphasizes the invincibility of his ego by the real world, victoriously maintains the pleasure principle—and all this, in contrast to other methods having the same purposes, without overstepping the bounds of mental health? The two achievements seem incompatible.

If we turn to the situation in which one person adopts a humorous attitude towards others, a view which I have already put forward tentatively in my book on jokes will at once suggest itself. This is that the subject is behaving toward them as an adult does towards a child when he recognizes and smiles at the triviality of interests and sufferings which seem so great to it [ibid., 223–224]. Thus the humourist would acquire his superiority by assuming the role of the grown-up and identifying himself to some extent with his father, and reducing the other people to being children. This view probably covers the facts, but it hardly seems a conclusive one. One asks oneself what it is that makes the humourist arrogate this role to himself.

But we must recall the other, probably more primary and important, situation of humour, in which a person adopts a humorous attitude towards himself in order to ward off possible suffering. Is there any sense in saying that someone is treating himself like a child and is at the same time playing the part of a superior adult towards that child?

This not very plausible idea receives strong support, I think, if we consider what we have learned from pathological observations on the structure of the ego. This ego is not a simple entity. It harbours within it, as its nucleus, a special agency—the super-ego.[2] Sometimes it is merged with the super-ego so that we cannot distinguish between them, whereas in other circumstances it is sharply differentiated from it. Genetically the super-ego is the heir to the parental agency. It often keeps the ego in strict dependence and still really treats it as the parents, or the father, once treated the child, in its early years. We obtain a dynamic explanation of the humorous attitude, therefore, if we assume that it consists in the humourist's having withdrawn the psychical accent from his ego and having transposed it on to his super-ego. To the super-ego, thus inflated, the ego can appear tiny and all its interests trivial; and, with this new distribution of energy, it may become an easy matter for the super-ego to suppress the ego's possibilities of reacting.

In order to remain faithful to our customary phraseology, we shall have to speak, not of transposing the psychical accent, but of displacing large amounts of cathexis. The question then is whether we are entitled to picture extensive displacements like this from one agency of the mental apparatus to another. It looks like a new hypothesis constructed *ad hoc*. Yet we may remind ourselves that we have repeatedly (even though not sufficiently often) taken a factor of this kind into account in our attempts at a metapsychological picture of mental events. Thus, for instance, we supposed that the difference between an ordinary erotic object-cathexis and the state of being in love is that in the latter incomparably more cathexis passes over to the object and that the ego empties itself as it were in favour of the object.[3] In studying some cases of paranoia I was able to establish the fact that ideas of persecution are formed early and exist for a long time without any perceptible effect, until, as the result of some particular precipitating event, they receive sufficient amounts of cathexis to cause them to become dominant.[4] The cure, too, of such paranoic attacks would lie, not so much in a resolution and correction of the delusional ideas as in a withdrawal from them of the cathexis which has been lent to them. The alternations between melancholia and mania, between a cruel suppression of the ego by the super-ego and a liberation of the ego, after that pressure, suggests a shift of cathexis of this kind;[5] such a shift, moreover, would have to be brought in to explain a whole number of phenomena belonging to normal mental life. If this has been done hitherto only to a very limited extent, that is on account of our usual caution—something which deserves only praise. The region in which we feel secure is that of the pathology of mental life; it is here that we make our observations and acquire our convictions. For the present we venture to form a judgment on the normal mind only in so far as we can discern what is normal in the isolations and distortions of the pathological material. When once we have overcome this hesitancy we shall recognize what a larger contribution is made to the understanding of mental processes by the static conditions as well as by the dynamic changes in the *quantity* of energetic cathexis.

I think, therefore, that the possibility I have suggested here, that in a particular situation the subject suddenly hypercathects his super-ego and then, proceeding from it, alters the reactions of the ego, is one which deserves to be retained. Moreover, what I have suggested about humour finds a remarkable analogy in the kindred field of jokes. As regards the origin of jokes I was led to assume that a preconscious thought is given over for a moment to unconscious revision [ibid., 166]. In just the same way, *humour would be the contribution made to the comic through the agency of the super-ego.*

In other connections we knew the super-ego as a severe master. It will be said that it accords ill with such a character that the super-ego should condescend to enabling the ego to obtain a small yield of pleasure. It is true that humorous pleasure never reaches the intensity of the pleasure in the comic or in jokes, that it never finds vent in hearty laughter. It is also true that, in bringing about the humorous attitude, the super-ego is actually repudiating reality and serving an illusion. But (without rightly knowing why) we regard this less intense pleasure as having a character of a very high value; we feel it to be especially liberating and elevating. Moreover, the jest made by humour is not the essential thing. It has only the value of a preliminary. The main thing is the intention which humour carries out, whether it is acting in relation to the self or other people. It means: 'Look! here is the world, which seems so dangerous! It is nothing but a game for children – just worth making a jest about.'

If it is really the super-ego which, in humour, speaks such kindly words of comfort to the intimidated ego, this will teach us that we have still a great deal to learn about the nature of the super-ego. Furthermore, not everyone is capable of the humorous attitude. It is a rare and precious gift, and many people are even without the capacity to enjoy humorous pleasure that is presented to them. And finally, if the super-ego tries, by means of humour, to console the ego and protect it from suffering, this does not contradict its origin in the parental agency.

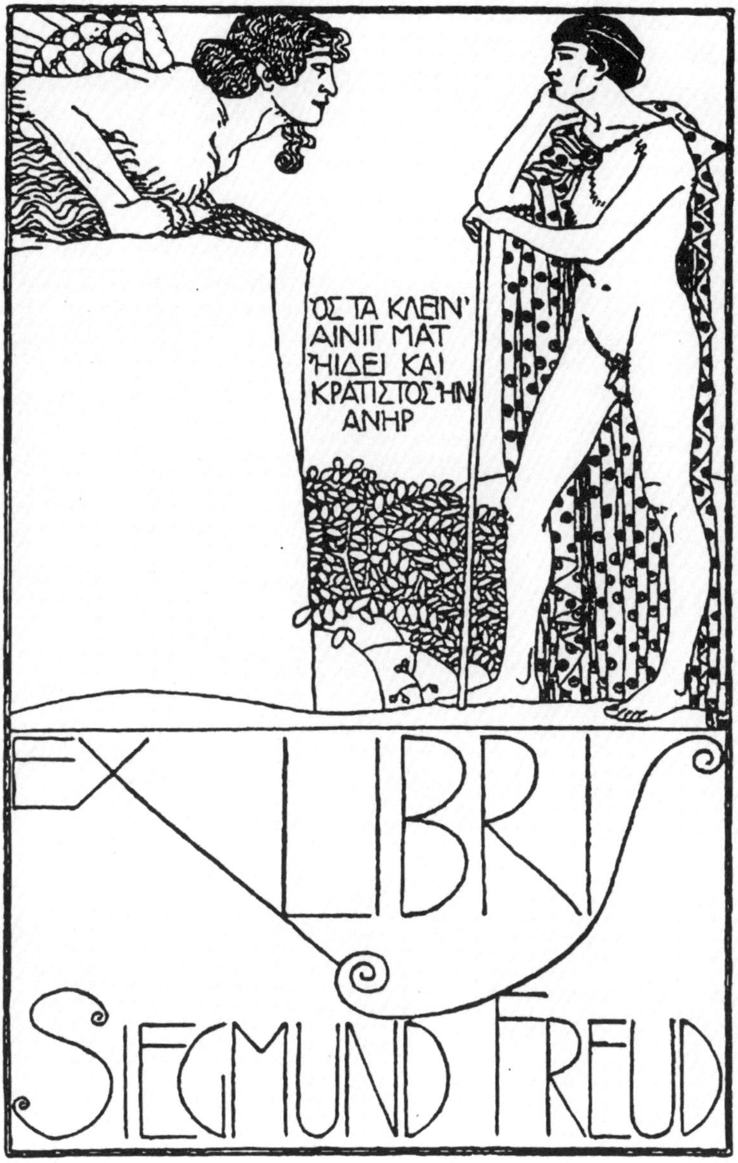

Sigmund Freud
Ex Libris

(A) GERMAN EDITIONS

1927 *Almanach, 1928*, 9–16.
1928 *Imago*, 14 (1), 1–6.
1928 *G.S.*, 11, 402–408.
1948 *G.W.*, 14, 383–389.

(B) ENGLISH TRANSLATIONS

'Humour'
1928 *International Journal of Psycho-Analysis,* 9 (1), 1–6 (trans. Joan Riviere).
1950 *C.P.*, 5, 215–221 (revised reprint of above).

* We reprint the text of "Humour" as it appears in *The Standard Edition of the Complete Works of Sigmund Freud*, vol. 21, trans. under the general editorship of James Strachey, The Hogarth Press and the Institute of Psychoanalysis, London 1953–1974, p. 159-166; with kind permission of The Marsh Agency, London.

NOTES

1
Cf. the subsequent long discussion of these various methods of avoiding pain in Chapter II of *Civilization and its Discontents* (1930*a*), p. 77 ff. above. But Freud had already pointed out the defensive function of humour in *Jokes* (1905*c*), *Standard Ed.*, 8, p. 233.

2
It may be remarked that in a footnote at the beginning of Chapter III of *The Ego and the Id* (1923*b*) Freud says that 'the system *Pcpt.-Cs* alone can be regarded as the nucleus of the ego', (*Standard Ed.*, 19, p. 28.

3
See Chapter VIII of *Group Psychology* (1921*c*), *Standard Ed.*, 18, p. 112–113.

4
See Section B of "Some Neurotic Mechanisms" (1922*b*), *Standard Ed.*, 18, p. 228–229.

5
See "Mourning and Melancholia" (1917*e*), *Standard Ed.*, 14, p. 253–255.

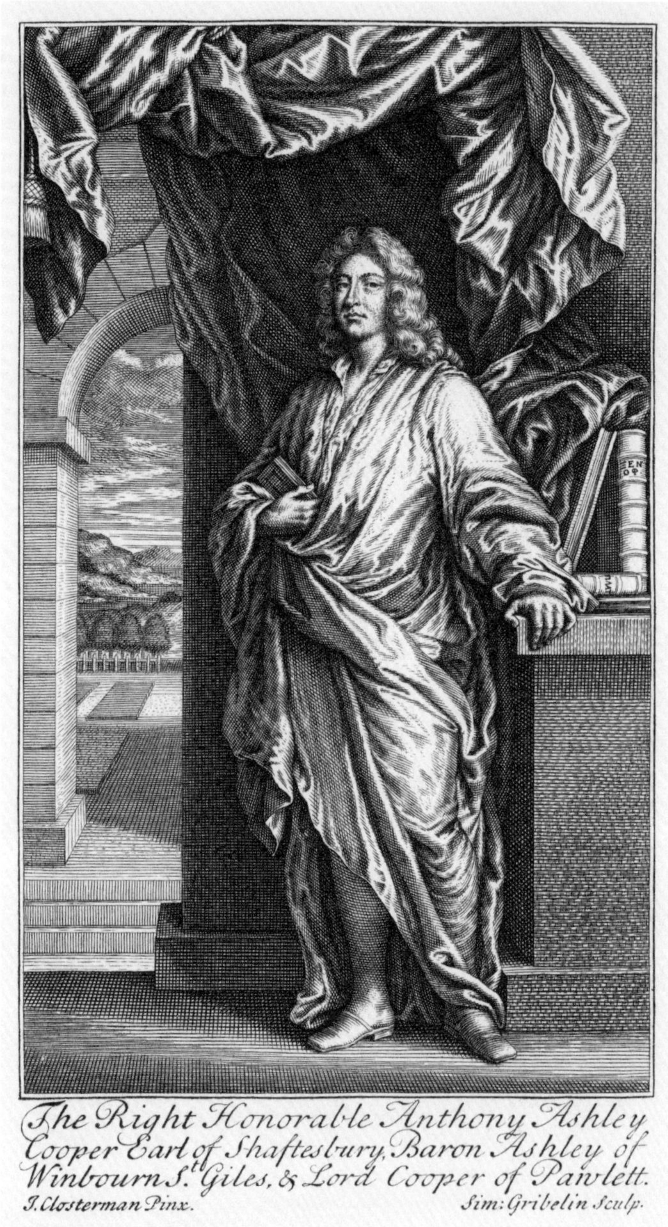

Anthony Ashley Cooper
Third Earl of Shaftesbury (1671–1713)
Engraving by Simon Gribelin, after John
Closterman, published 1723

Jeffrey Minson

RESONANCES OF "RAILLERY"[1]

Introduction: "Merdedelamerdelamer ... de l'amerique!"[2]

1961: In a now canonically rude gesture toward the art market, Piero Manzoni offers for sale in Rome, at the going price of gold, 90 personally signed 30 gram-sized cans of his own shit. By no means past their use-by date, Manzoni's cans of institutional critique exemplify the use of humor in contemporary art to challenge the aesthetico-moral sense of what's *civil* (though as we'll see, Manzoni's gesture is neither simply the opposite of civil, nor merely critique).

Merda d'artista clearly alludes to the excremental dissidence of the Dadaists as set out by Tristan Tzara, brandishing a roll of paper inscribed with "merde" at the end of a performance at the Cabaret Voltaire in 1916; in Marcel Duchamp's *Fountain* (1917); or Francis Picabia's *L'Œil cacodylate* (*The Cacodylic Eye,* 1921). But it was made in the wake of a wider anti-aesthetic avant-garde program that infected more mainstream practice (Jean Dubuffet, Francis Bacon) giving rise to works which were "not afraid to look ugly"[3]—that vaunted the aleatory, the childishly lumpish or form-less, the monstrously misshapen or comically incongruous, the offensive or disgusting, and the abject. In more recent times, both the cachet and distribution of an anti- (or "post-" or "outside") aestheticism dedicated to outrage and moral perturbation have accelerated—not just in the art world, but also in literary and theoretical writing, architecture, and on TV comedy. What is to be made of this "triumph of the ugly"[4] and what role does humor play in relation to it?

I want to approach this question by looking back to a remarkable early modern interweaving of the (anti-)aesthetic, the politico-ethical, the humorous, and the (un)civil in the work of Anthony Ashley Cooper, third Earl of Shaftesbury (1671–1713). Shaftesbury put into play an intellectual and political program for bringing the ethical and the aesthetic together so as to make philosophy more "polite"—an intervention which also injected "raillery" into philosophical, political, and religious controversy. While in some respects his polite aesthetic ethos stands at the farthest remove from artistic raillery such as *Merda d'artista*, his influence has been such that we have to take account of a "Shaftesbury effect" in modern intellectual culture. From this angle the third earl appears as an unexpected ancestor in the family tree of the anti-aesthetic disposition. His voice resonates with current concerns and even vocabularies while conjuring some unexpected associations. As a way of coming at the question of continuities and disjunctions between Shaftesburian aesthetics and contemporary art and culture of the ugly, I want to reflect on the problem of delineating ugliness outside aesthetic terms of reference (drawing on the work of Mark Cousins); and conclude with some examples of artistic raillery which variously contest or evoke Shaftesburian aesthetico-moral senses of ugliness.

Shaftesbury's Program: Metaphysical Aesthetics and Polite Sociability

> [T]o interrupt the long-spun thread of reasoning, and bring into the mind, *by many different glances and broken views*, what cannot be so easily introduced by ... one continued stretch of sight ... raillery and humor ... and flights, sallies, and excursions of every kind are found agreeable and requisite.[5] (*C*, 433)

In order to sound out the implications of this attempt by Shaftesbury to account for the philosophical gravity of humor, I want, first, to make some remarks about his overall project.

Born in 1671, Anthony Ashley Cooper was the namesake, grandson, and protégé of the First Earl of Shaftesbury (1621–1683), a prominent English political insider who became Charles II's most important radical republican Whig opponent. Due to ill health, the third earl's involvement in English parliamentary politics, though serious, lasted only a few years. Most of his short life was expended in intense ethical, spiritual, cultural, and political studies. His reputation rests mainly on one published (and much revised) work, *Characteristics.*[6] By virtue of his influence on Johann Joachim Winckelmann (1717–1768) (and on garden design), he is often portrayed as a precocious pioneer of modern aesthetics. And so he was, but Shaftesbury's aesthetics—including the part assigned to humor—are inseparable from his cultivation of a political and ethical spirituality.

While the third earl owed his early intellectual formation (and much else) to the philosopher John Locke, he charged his "old tutor and governor" with having "struck at all fundamentals," throwing "all order and virtue out of the world, and made the very idea of these (which are the same as those of God) unnatural, and without foundation in our minds."[7] These charges against Locke for not being a moral absolutist contradict a still influential anglophone view of Shaftesbury as a "moral sense" theorist and philosophically unserious apostle of politeness. While the moral role of sentiment is crucial ("It is not merely what we call a principle, but a taste which governs men" [*C*, 413]), a *faculty* of moral sense is not the foundation of his ethic. Another tradition of commentary (which I broadly follow here), however, sees Shaftesbury's thought as grounded in a Neoplatonic supposition of a *rational* order of moral-aesthetic realities; these being accessible especially, if fleetingly, to those who cultivate a mix of autonomous reason and sensibility.[8] So understood, Shaftesbury's "rationalist sentimentalism"[9] is a *metaphysics* built around a veritably *sacralized* ideal image of the free person as a creative, i.e. undetermined, intelligence. How, then, does this spiritualized ethic inflect the seemingly more worldly philosophy of polite sociability, leavened by humor, for which he is better known?

Josef Chytry argues that, uniquely in his time, Shaftesbury "posed the task of aesthetics in terms of recuperating the ideal political community of the ancient Greeks and Romans, according to the leitmotif of the aesthetic state." Shaftesbury was heir to and recombined three utopian Renaissance traditions and their "energies": a Neoplatonism running back to Renaissance magical thought, allied to artistic symbolizations; a civic humanist ethos of the "Commonwealthman" acquired from his grandfather (and associated with idealizations of Renaissance Italian republics as premised on "persuasion"); and the "courtly-aesthetic" ideal of polite society famously sketched by Baldassare Castiglione in *The Book of the Courtier* (*Il Cortegiano*, 1528).[10]

However, not all philosophical advocacy of polite sociability was of an aesthetic or aristocratic ilk. Shaftesbury's attack on Locke rehearses a long-running European polemic between "metaphysical" philosophies—especially significant for modern thought are precursors and legatees of Immanuel Kant—and "civil" philosophies (e.g. those of Samuel von Pufendorf, Thomas Hobbes, and David Hume) committed to promoting peaceful and tolerant law-states and polite, sociable citizens, neither states nor citizens as such being guided by thoughts of personal or social redemption, aesthetic or otherwise. One way in which the self-consciously anti-metaphysical thrust of civil philosophies expressed itself was in "desacralizing" characterizations of ethical distinctions—holding that they were based only in socially or legally enforced conventions and training or in natural sentiments, precisely the view of morality Shaftesbury attributed to Locke.[11]

The atmosphere and rivalries associated in Britain with 17th-century "polite" versions of Enlightenment constitute an important backdrop to Shaftesbury's program. Unlike many of their French counterparts, British polite philosophies were rarely hostile to organized religion as such. They were woven out of a mélange of statist, religious, aristocratic, party-political allegiances and, not least, aesthetic strands. "Politeness" then was an umbrella term covering a vast range of concerns and objects.[12] In the late 17th century, centuries-long, pan-European religious strife was no distant memory. British polite philosophical concerns about religious zealotry were personified in the figure of the religious or philosophical "enthusiast." Yet some enthusiasm had to be legitimate. Few Enlightened Christians wanted to be likened to the apocryphal Anglican clergyman "whose tombstone declared that he served his Maker for 50 years without the smallest sign of enthusiasm"[13]: hence the frequent symbioses between polite philosophy and the redemptive thinking it sought to contain. Shaftesbury was no exception.

Shaftesbury is unusual, however, in his express insistence that philosophy should not be a search for systematic foundations but rather about the cultivation of a distinct kind of self. This is to be constructed in the image of a freethinking philosopher seeking truth and self-mastery through dialogue while also being attuned to human affective dispositions, and capable of cutting a plausible figure in "polite society." Standards of morality and good taste cannot be set by English aristocratic custom and practice, readily corrupted by courtly "dazzle"[14]—or by any local moral conventions. In keeping with his faith in an objective moral and spiritual reality, Shaftesbury contends to the contrary that an absolute "measure" of justice and merit, harmonious social cooperation and virtue, has been naturally imprinted in human minds. However, we initially glean these moral standards only through aesthetic prefigurative *sensings of moral distinctions*, that is, by glimpsing *the beauty or ugliness of character or conduct*. Further reflection, he supposes, will connect these intuitions to a harmonious cosmos presided over by its Creator. So Shaftesbury's Neoplatonic aim is "to assert the reality of a beauty and charm in moral as well as natural subjects and to demonstrate the reasonableness of a proportionate taste and determinate choice in life and manners" (*C*, 446). But the point of the demonstration is to build a personal disposition: "*to discover how we may to best advantage form within ourselves what in the polite world is called a relish or good taste*" (*C*, 404, emphasis in original).

Shaftesbury's ideal of the human person is thus constructed in the image of an artistic God, a notion that is pagan as much as Christian: a well-cultivated person is "a second maker," "a just Prometheus," "the architect of his own life and fortune"—who "can ... give to an action its just body and proportion." Virtuous character is "the harmony of parts," while "knavery is ... dissonance."[15] The locus of beauty lies not in the artistic object, but rather in the "forming form" or "forming power" of the artist's mind and sensibility (*C*, 322–323). To approximate this self-ideal you need an ascetic regimen. You must learn to "divide yourself, or be two," then to practice an "art of self-dissection" in the form of quoting out loud ("apostrophising") your passional impulses as a prelude to according them their "just body and proportion" (*C*, 77, 89).

If philosophy were to break out from the cocooned condition of the formal treatise-dominated philosophy of his day—"immured, poor lady, in colleges and cells" (*C*, 232)—it had to be given a more affectively charged bodily presence and to find a wider audience in the domain of polite society—while at the same time attempting to *elevate* it: "To philosophize in a just signification is but to carry good breeding a step higher" (*C*, 407). In such passages Shaftesbury affirms his commitment to recasting and disseminating higher philosophy beyond academic bowers, political courtesy beyond courtly circles, and the "energies" of the art beyond religious and hermetic milieus.

These rhetorical concerns are part of the reason for the multi-generic and digressive character of *Characteristics*. But, for all its *Tristram Shandy*-like meanderings, it does not lack logic and sequence. It has a centerpiece, a treatise-like text, "Inquiry Concerning Virtue or Merit," which is book-ended—and its humourless *modus operandi* thereby critically qualified—by texts written in a variety of informal genres: letters, soliloquy, dialogue, friendly counsel, miscellany. Yet its core philosophical themes are not rejected but rather subjected to studiously informal re-elaboration, supplementation, and critical modification in these other texts. Unlike in "Inquiry," a certain tension between the forces of reason and sociability is quietly acknowledged as something requiring mutual adjustment. And staging the "soliloquy" essay's injunction to self-division, the five "Miscellaneous Reflections" successively discuss each of the preceding essays, referring to their author in the third person.

The head text of this section sets out one of his most telling "miscellaneous" considerations. We are now in a position to see why humor and digression are necessary "to interrupt the long-spun thread of reasoning, and bring into the mind, *by many different glances and broken views*, what cannot be so easily introduced by ... one continued stretch of sight" (*C*, 433). The programmatic significance of this plea for reflective playfulness lies in its implication that Shaftesbury's resort to a multi-generic and informal form of presentation is driven not only by rhetorical calculation—the incapacity of abstract philosophical contemplation to reach a wider public or to have practical effects—*but also by his Neoplatonic metaphysical philosophy itself*. The problem is the incapacity of formal philosophical discourse or ever-faulty human reasoning, unaided, to grasp the fugitive (albeit rational) order of things. This is the philosophical and spiritual *raison d'être* for "raillery and humor" and "the way of *chat*" (*C*, 380, emphasis in original).

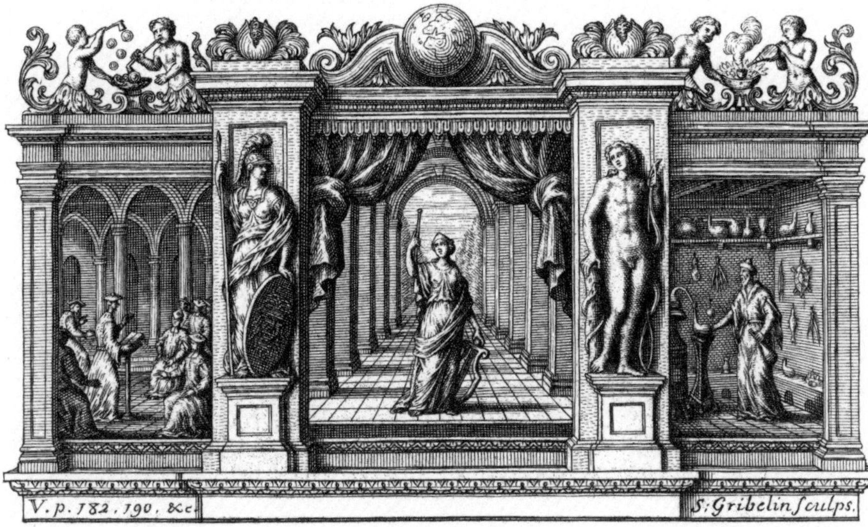

Frontispiece to volume I of Shaftesbury's
Characteristics of Men, Manners, Opinions, Times
(1727 edition)
Engraving by Simon Gribelin

Civil Raillery and Self-Fashioning

In "Sensus Communis," raillery is both an essential ingredient in the aesthetic ideal of a conversable community, and a cultural tactic. In his "Soliloquy" essay the philosophical *gravitas* of humor is expressed by according it a place in philosophy's own history. And in Shaftesbury's posthumously published philosophical notebooks a sense of humor figures as an inherent part of a regimen of spiritual re-formation.

The sunny, general definition of raillery set out in the Oxford English Dictionary—"good-humored banter or ridicule"—hardly sits well with the way characters "rail" against one another in Shakespeare's *Troilus and Cressida*:

> AJAX Do not ... my fingers itch.
> THERSITES I would thou didst itch from head to foote, and I had the scratching of thee, I would make thee the lothesomest scab in Greece.[16]

To understand the provocativeness of Shaftesbury's opening announcement in "Sensus Communis" of his intention to "speak in commendation of raillery" in philosophy and religious controversy, we need to appreciate its generally uncivil connotations before and up to Shaftesbury's time.[17] It is surely significant that Shaftesbury's first move in "Sensus Communis" is to distinguish "polite raillery" from burlesque or "scurrilous" ridicule motivated only by a lowering impulse to "raise a laugh from everything." Polite raillery is both *sociable* and aims at *truth and justice*: "seek in everything what may justly be laughed at." If truth can bear all lights, why shouldn't Christianity be exposed to, and shine through, the light of good-humored, seriously intended joshing? In this way its rational, just, beautiful, moderate kernel of truth can be pared away from enthusiastic errors and absurdities. Good-humored philosophical disagreement is both part of Shaftesbury's ideal of a civilized conversable society and a Whig cultural-political tactic directed against Tory Anglican dogmatism (*C*, 29–35, 59). "Sensus Communis" was written to defend its author against the storm of Anglican political reaction provoked by the original publication of his "Letter Concerning Enthusiasm" (the first essay in *Characteristics*).

Shaftesbury insists that he is only seeking to influence citizens of the better sort who engage in political conversation: the liberty of wit he champions is restricted to "the liberty of the club ... among gentlemen and friends" (*C*, 36). This restriction has led to the designation of his ideal political community as a lyrical "aristocracy of aesthetes."[18] So it is; yet this denigration downplays not only his concern to carve out a place at the civic table for dissent, but also the metaphysical force of the ideal that Shaftesburian raillery serves.

That ideal, of sociable/conversable community, is summed up in the term *sensus communis*. Shaftesbury pointedly reminds the reader that Horace and Juvenal originally used the expression as a counter-concept in their poetic satires on the ancient Roman courtly nobility, where it signified "a sense of the public weal ... love of humanity, obliging-ness, or that sort of civility which arises from a just sense of the common rights of mankind" (*C*, 48–50). Yet worldly Roman republicanism is not the only inspiration for Shaftesbury's "fellow-feeling." In passages articulating the affinities between artistic and natural beauty, truth, justice, and the ethical (C, 62–67) it is evident that the "just sense" part of the *sensus communis* depends on Shaftesbury's Neoplatonic aesthetic. The beauty and ugliness of actions or character is a function of whether they harmonize with those of others and enhance their well-being. He connects intuitive impressions of moral beauty or ugliness with a lack of Mandevillean self-interest, and with the spontaneity of other-regarding actions proceeding from our natural *sensus communis*. A crucial support for this ideal is the good-humored *agon* of exchanges through which we "polish" one another. But polite humor cannot be policed. In keeping with the essay's subtitle ("On the Freedom of Wit"), it is maintained that humor will refine itself, but only if we "take care not to ... bring it under constraint ... all politeness is owing to liberty" (*C*, 31).

For all the importance of aesthetic impressions and spontaneous affections in fostering ethical character informed by a *sensus communis*, the unconditional priority of liberty in the above passage reminds us that for Shaftesbury the foundation of true community is a harmony of *minds*, conceived as *intellectual centers of autonomous* agency. As affections may be pathological, their ethical value depends on rational scrutiny, the "common sense" of polite society needs philosophy to correct it. But again, philosophy's corrective power depends on its presentation. Laughing together over some "just" point of common agreement intensifies that sense of social commonality. But this is not just a good feeling: the laughter in just raillery is the soundtrack to a higher truth.

I have suggested that alongside its Roman republican roots and liberal-aristocratic "cultural politics," Shaftesbury's idea of *sensus communis* recirculates a metaphysical image of a self-governing community of minds. Yet the essay's concluding paragraph expresses a humorously non-metaphysical conception of politics. Shaftesbury acknowledges that, regarding the forces of religious zealotry that fueled the religious wars, it was "Magistrate[s]" who "took care to pare their talons." That task of social pacification owed nothing to a good-humored self-governing *sensus communis*. Like it or not, it was the accomplishment of a partly de-sacralized English civil security-state, which could afford to tolerate manifestations of religious zealotry posing no threat to civil peace. "The rage, ill-will, and fury of certain zealous gentlemen"—no laughing matter when "armed"—*today* are as anodyne and amusing as the grimaces of the grotesque figures on old buildings (*C*, 68–69). That he permits the *bête noire* of his moral philosophy—the de-sacralizing conventionalist "civil philosophy" he associates with Locke—to have the last unphilosophical word suggests that Shaftesbury is not a metaphysician through and through.

In "Soliloquy," a miniature speculative history of culture and philosophy further testifies to the salience of humor for Shaftesbury (*C*, 106–117). The comedic is located first within a cultural history of "arts," but subsequently as one of "the several geniuses of philosophy" *itself*. Epitomized by the Cynics Antisthenes and Diogenes, the comic register is located alongside three others. The first is the "sublime," interestingly epitomized by Plato, read (as common in the 18th century) as a *poetic* sage. Then there is philosophy's "methodical" genius, epitomized by Aristotle. Finally, Shaftesbury points to the "simple" model of the polite, noble "man of action" exemplified by Xenophon.

It is with this sense of the philosophically freighted family tree of the comedic in mind that we can now turn to the thematization of humor in Shaftesbury's posthumously published philosophical notebooks.[19] The notebooks differ dramatically from the more prolix rhetorical style of the *Characteristics*. In them he stages an intense imitation of the staccato manner of the ancient Stoic Epictetus: "How goes the world?—No matter; but how go I? This is … the only matter" (*N*, 102). The conflict between autonomy and sociality, a minor theme in *Characteristics,* here comes to the fore. In *Characteristics*, polite sociability is an intrinsic good, albeit in need of philosophical refinement. In the notebooks, sociability is "a concept under pressure," a source of moral rot threatening the author's integrity and autonomy.[20] A manual of philosophical self-examination exercises, the notebooks are about bracing the autonomous—rational and aesthetic—part of himself to withstand temptations to economize on truth in the name of sociability. Shaftesbury cannot shirk the public duties, appropriate demeanors, and dress expected of an aristocratic lord. But if he is to be sociable while protecting his autonomy, he needs to cultivate a *private* philosophical persona as well as a *reserved* public persona: "remember ... the involution, shadow, curtain, the same soft irony" (*N*, 192).[21]

Doubtless, the notebooks are the record of a personal crisis.[22] But their affective intensity is also an artifact of the spiritual-philosophical regimen they create. Like their Stoic precursors, many of the notebooks' spiritual exercises attempt to create a moral *aversion* to non-principled sociable behavior through the use of a lexicon of *disgusted appetite*: "May actions possibly *stink*?" (*N*, 215). Social repartee is dubbed "the scab of wit, mouth flux ... dysentery, rheum"; motives not conforming to Stoic principle are likened to "vomit" (*N*, 223–224). Some will be reminded of Jacques Derrida's argument that in Kant the aesthetic is tacitly defined by the negative pole of disgust.[23] But in Shaftesbury's notebooks, inculcation of disgust with the hypocrisies of social life is a central and conscious self-shaping technique.

As in *Characteristics*, the fulcrum of this technique is the twofold dialectical labor of soliloquizing self-division followed by balancing—especially in the notebooks' treatment of *humor*.[24] The task is to cultivate both "A mirth not out of reach of what is gravest; [and] a gravity not abhorrent to the use of that other mirth. In this balance seek a character ... manner, genius, style, voice, action ... This [is] the study, performance, and music of life ... the best practice and exercise is to *go by contraries*" (*N*, 195, emphasis added). It is a delicate but necessary balancing act. Un-dialectical earnestness—always being earnest rather than where appropriate being *in* earnest (*N*, 194)—exposes you to ridicule. Conversely, malicious or scurrilous humor prostitutes the integrity of the soul, turning you into a trifler who cares only about winning the good opinion of others by making them laugh.

Characteristics gave humor a philosophical pedigree, a way of distinguishing between just and unworthy raillery, and a tactical role in a cultural politics of religion. The notebooks prescribe a more monistic use of humor: a spiritual practice of redescribing comic manifestations so as to bring out their seriousness (and vice versa) as a prerequisite for developing the sort of autonomy that will be proof, equally, against the lures of the social and the temptations of social disengagement.

The Shaftesbury Effect

In his illness-plagued final years, Shaftesbury devoted much time and energy to supervising the specially commissioned *emblemata* embroidering the second (1714) edition of *Characteristics*. One of these, a triptych, images scholastic exercises conducted under the supervision of a master in a cloistered schoolroom (on the left). The solitary figure of a natural philosopher in a laboratory, operating some experimental equipment appears on the right. The centerpiece is a philosopher standing at the front of a perspectively receding stage, presumably addressing a wider public.[25]

Shaftesbury's resort to the emblem genre is one of several features of his thought (like its aristocratic frame) which encourage a tendency to see him, as one commentator puts it, as "a transitional figure in the history of aesthetics," encased in a Neoplatonic Renaissance view of objectivity and reason in art.[26] Yet reworkings of Neoplatonic thought, Shaftesbury's included, continue to this day to reverberate at the intersections of metaphysics, art, ethics, and political thought. In the 1930s, Ernst Cassirer attested to the powerful impact on the nature-philosophy of Goethe and Herder of Shaftesbury's reworking of the plasticity of mind-in-nature he encountered in the British Cambridge Platonists. Cassirer credits Shaftesbury with laying down the template that re-established Platonism (with all its poetical and theological connotations) as "a philosophical force" in succeeding centuries.[27]

Curiously, Cassirer's reading of Shaftesbury as a central European Enlightenment figure opens onto a remarkable example of a 20th-century "Shaftesbury effect" at the interface of popular cultural theory, the aesthetic, art, and humor. For it seems that Shaftesbury's thought, as relayed through Cassirer, exercised a significant, though largely unacknowledged, influence on Mikhail Bakhtin's theoretical representation of the emancipatory and socially unifying power of mockery and laughter.[28] Shaftesbury's aristocratically-framed model of politely restrained political uses of humor and Bakhtin's demotic celebration of carnivalesque mockery of the ruling classes seem poles apart. Yet the original connection between the two was made by Bakhtin himself; while Shaftesbury's potted history of humor as philosophy accorded a place of honor to the ancient Cynic, Diogenes, whose fiercely independent conduct, including that bearing on bodily functions, was ethically modeled on the dog.[29] In his advocacy of a "heteroglossic" and "dialogical" political imaginary, Bakhtin is a significant modern relay of Shaftesbury's ideal of a *sensus communis* insofar as this is allied to dialogical techniques for shaping autonomous personal and political conscience. Shaftesbury's *sensus communis* was to have a great future in modern theoretical idealizations of political community as a dialogue between democratic and morally reflective citizens.

There are historical studies linking these idealizations of democratic society and its centerpiece, the autonomous citizen, back to early modern political-theological conceptions of a "community of communicants"; as well as from there forward through Kant and the neo-Kantian tradition. Setting aside Shaftesbury's impact on Kant's aesthetics, many of the signature themes of the highly influential neo-Kantian aesthetic and political theorist, the philosopher and playwright Friedrich Schiller, derive from Shaftesbury: these include the limits of formal-rational thought; the unhappily divided self; the social as a conversational ideal; conversation as a means of acceding to uppermost rational truths; and, not least, the play principle as a means dialectically to mediate the rational and the affective.[30] The publicity for an exhibition of humorous art at Zurich's Migrosmuseum für Gegenwartskunst furnishes an example of the currency of this ludic aspect of Shaftesburian dialectical self-shaping in the art world: "artists do not tell the viewer how to react, but rather suspend them in limbo between amusement and discomfort, the playful and the serious, pessimism and optimism."[31]

Without downplaying the Christian lineage of Kantian and neo-Kantian metaphysics, it is evident that its modern avatars in recent theoretical discourse manifest a certain *Prometheanism*. This too can be traced back to the super-capacity for autonomous "form-making" that Shaftesbury attributed to the aesthetic self. This Promethean stripe lends support to Chytry's claim that Shaftesbury's aesthetico-ethical conceptions of the political contributed "a vital chapter in the evolution of modern radicalism" that passes through Schiller, Hölderlin, Hegel, Marx, Heidegger, and Marcuse. For instance, a Neoplatonic conception of truth combined with a theological sense of the difficulties of making oneself capable of acceding to it underpin both Shaftesbury's resort to *belles lettres*-type genres to arrive at "broken views" of the cosmos and Heidegger's resort to Hölderlin's poetry, with its invocation of the musicality of language as a means to experience Being in itself. It is no great stretch to discern the shade of Shaftesbury in the crossovers between Heidegger and "Dadasophy."[32]

Outside Aesthetics: The Ugly

I have sketched a view of Shaftesbury's intellectual program, the place of humor in it, and some aspects of its modern reception. My next question, foreshadowed by Bakhtin's presence in the inventory of "Shaftesbury effects," is how far a Shaftesburian aesthetic persists even in anti-aesthetic milieus; and whether, and if so how, artistic and architectural work might evade the control of aesthetic categories.

The fulcrum of Shaftesburian aesthetic philosophy is an ideal of spiritual wholeness and harmony and a corresponding striving to overcome "dissonance." Challenges to what Jacques Lacan termed this "pastoral" ideal have figured strongly in transactions between psychoanalysis, and art and aesthetic outlooks.[33] Mark Cousins' widely cited essay "The Ugly"—an exemplary instance of these transactions[34]—takes as its point of departure the lexicon of negatives by which the ugly is defined in classical aesthetic thought: incomplete, deficient in form, monstrous. Incapable of being incorporated into a harmonious totality, a mere foil to a disinterested experience of beauty and truth, the ugly has no interesting characteristics of its own. Yet aesthetics has traditionally acknowledged exceptions to this exclusionary rule—including the place of the ugly in ancient comedy, and later the genre of caricature—which destabilize the aesthetic ideal. Ugly elements that might defeat a lesser artist find a (sublime) place in the artwork's overall structure. The 18th- and 19th-century revolution in aesthetics and the wider culture included an intensified interest in the ugly. For Cousins this skews the aesthetic ideal of the well-proportioned whole, yet leaves it intact. Kantian and Romantic aesthetics shift the locus of this ideal onto decentered relations that reconcile—or at least balance in a self-enhancing tension—a "confronting" sublime object and the human subject, for whom the object serves as an occasion to challenge and extend itself. The significance of the ugly arises, once more, from something other than itself, from its place in the totality of the many-sided personality (*U* I, 61–62).

Against this deficit theory, Cousins argues that the ugly possesses an interest of its own, that it simply *is*. A psychoanalytic account of the ugly offers a means to comprehend how it exists *ethically* for "a subject," more precisely, for the *ego* (as partly distinct from superego and id). The ugly is ethically offensive and threatening in that by its very existence it is an obstacle to desire. The object *becomes* ugly and scary by being experienced as *there* when it ought not to be, or, like a face lacking a nose, not there when it ought to be (*U* I, 63; *U* II, 4–5). Cousins negotiates a topological disconnect between the ugly and the beautiful. While the beautiful "remains the same size as it is" the ugly object subjectively becomes too big for comfort, or gets too close, threatening to contaminate whatever it touches. It bursts or leaks out of its customary representational frame, like the invasive, drool-like substance of the "Thing" in horror movies (*U* II, 4). Normally our personal interactions rely on an "order of representation ... that is organized around the face as a vehicle of expression," and which is sustained by the fantasy of a person's "inside" engendered by repressing their head as a physical volume. Spoiling that fantasy-frame, an ugly flesh wound exposes the observer to a terrifying dose of "subcutaneous reality" (*U* II, 3-4).

Confronted with the ugly, the ego is no stoic. Its default reflex is "to scurry into the realm of the defenses" (*U* I: 64). We turn away in disgust or switch off, like children who shut their eyes to magic away a disturbing object. Thus the aesthete who eschews the ugly is being cowardly. For psychoanalysis the "true antithesis" is not between beauty and ugliness but between vivacity and "playing dead," enacting a cancellation of experience and self-suspension in a space of boredom (*U* III, 65, 68; *U* II, 6). "The ugly" offers, then, theoretical support for artistic or architectural work that bypasses aesthetic framings of the ugly in order to mobilize its vivacity and singular interest (*U* III, 68).

Without questioning the essay's central achievement one can ask how stable at its boundaries is the distinction between this way of thinking and approaches to the ugly in classical 18th- and 19th-century aesthetics (including by implication, Shaftesbury's). Cutting across this question is a concern about Cousins' insistence that only in the psychical dimension can we "accede to the problem of beauty and ugliness," and his consequent disparagement of the suggestion that ugliness might be an artifact of "cultural machineries" (*U* I, 62). I'll also touch on a problem posed by the genre of ugly humor.

The essay's topological characterization of the ugly is summed up in the image of drool. To gauge how far this redescription lies beyond the limits of classical aesthetic thought, consider a spiritual exercise recommended by the Roman Stoic philosopher Seneca for overcoming anger by instilling a sense of its *ugliness*. By examining one's face in a mirror, we are brought to see how its contortion "mars the loveliest face." Then we are to imagine how much uglier must be the countenance of the mind *within*: "Ready to break if it cannot break out ... black and mottled ... it would be, boiling twisted and swollen ... oozing out through bones."[35] Interestingly, Seneca acknowledges a problem with this mirror exercise, in that the angry person may *enjoy* the spectacle of frightfulness and savagery: "they wish to look as they are."[36]

There are striking parallels between this picturing out of the anger "inside us" and Cousins' account of the subjective reception of the ugly object. Despite very different understandings of the human soul, both appear to register a similar psychological reality. Vindicating Cousins' focus on the psychical, we may doubt that imagining the ugly as invasive slime depends on a cultural invention like the gothic horror genre. Moreover, Seneca's proviso that some will revel in images of the ugly reminds us of Cousins' mention of another face of ugliness that appears when arguments are no longer confined to relations between the ugly and the ego, but investigate its relation to unconscious desire. It is in that connection that we encounter the ugly as involving *ecstatic and unbearable enjoyment* of "all that is dirty, horrifying and disgusting" (*U* I, 64).

Considered also as a piece of "cultural machinery," however, Seneca's exercise may be seen as an exception to Cousins' general argument. The characterization of the ugly as ontological drool is all about evading aesthetic framings of the ugly. Yet Seneca's verbal picture of the inner ugliness of the angry soul is part of an historical aesthetic technique of character-formation. Reminiscent of Shaftesbury's ascetic regimen (or, rather of Shaftesbury's ancient model, Epictetus), Seneca's exercise can be characterized as deploying the rhetorical arts of moral redescription aimed at inducing a change of moral attitude in an audience. Here the aim is to foster feelings of moral disgust toward anger, by redescribing it as the antithesis of the grace or calm of *character* insofar as this forms a well-proportioned whole. In one way the need for this spiritual exhortation and discipline accords with Cousins' presentation of the ego's spontaneous, un-Stoic, response to the ugly. The problem is that for Seneca, while the ugly may be aesthetically lacking, his recommendation is not to *turn away* but to seek it out and *do battle with it*.

One way of enjoying Seneca's image of the ugly is to find it funny. If the salience of the ugly in comedy posed problems for ancient aesthetics as Cousins suggested, might it not also pose problems for his own argument? One problem might be how the treatment of the ugly in *gallows humor* puts pressure on the idea that the ego's standard response to the ugly is to *retreat* behind its defenses. For in this instance we confront hospital orderlies, doctors, pathologists, ambulance workers, who, aided by humor, are professionally attentive to and involved with the visceral "subcutaneous reality" "behind" our fantasmatic facial or bodily representations. Ego-defensiveness is surely part of the picture (witty or juvenile, it is the kind of humor that, according to Freud, tends to boost the ego's sense of freedom, grandeur, and invulnerability).[37] But neither the idea that the ego's default response to the ugly is to turn away, nor the equation of aesthetic ego-defensiveness *per se* in relation to un-Stoical cowardice, have much purchase. If anything the ego in such situations might be better described as *persevering behind its defenses*. To sustain generalization about the ego's response to the ugly in this instance would make it hard to avoid a moralizing or therapeutizing attitude toward all ugly humor.

How well does Cousins' argument for the displaced relation of the ugly to the aesthetic hold up in relation to the supposed mutation of aesthetic values exemplified by some Romantics' fascination with the ugly?[38] A simple problem is that key approbatory terms of criticism in "The Ugly"—the singularly individual, interesting, arresting, vivaciously real, disorderly, discomforting—were also much vaunted, if not invented, in Romantic thought. Friedrich Schlegel's paeon to the ugly as a window onto "the immense richness of reality at the peak of its disorder," is one example.[39] Another is the confession by a contemporary advocate of the necessity for a "return to beauty" in contemporary art to having "habitually suppressed the traditional contrariety of beauty and ugliness, pleasure and pain, in order to privilege all of these over their true contrary: the banality of neutral comfort."[40] I am not suggesting that "The Ugly" is inseparable from the Romantic mutation within aesthetics, only that locating ugly art under the sign of the interesting isn't enough to remove it from Romantic aesthetics once the latter has been redescribed as a mode of self-culture in the broadly Shaftesburian line. As I suggest below, anti-aesthetic artistic interest in the ugly as manifest in contemporary humorous artworks still has the cast of the third Earl of Shaftesbury.

Try Our Black Pudding

> Shit never stops being a fragment of God.
> —Dominique Laporte, 2000[41]

A recent exhibition by the Glasgow-based video/performance artists John Beagles and Graham Ramsay illuminates what it might mean to develop the extra-aesthetic themes of "The Ugly" with something other than transgressive abandon. In particular, their bathetically humorous preparation of black puddings made from a mixture of their own blood, resonates with Cousins' argument about the fantasmatic aspects of our facially-based sense of identity. In its early manifestations, before news media and the health authorities intervened and gave it notoriety, when the audience couldn't know whether Beagles and Ramsay would actually cook their concoction, let alone eat it, their *Black Pudding Self-Portrait* elicited real suspense and consternation: would they, in effect, commit cannibalism ... in Edinburgh's Royal Scottish Academy!? But the impact of the work does not have to hinge on that lurid eventuality. Alongside the sensationalism is a wry and sober reminder of the ugly stuff of which we are made. Because this ugly material is present in the room with the spectator it is more unsettling and affecting than the all-too-familiar simulated depravities of a horror movie. The audience witnesses the blood donations being poured into a pot and blended with barley, suet, and onions, notionally to be transformed into "something to eat." But all the while this sanguinary self-portrait signifies—if that's the right word—through its increasingly pervasive *stench*—its olfactory "drool." The impact of disgusting smells, as Dominique Laporte suggests, is related to their relative resistance to formally articulated meaning.[42] So *Black Pudding Self-Portrait* somewhat contests the fantasy that as persons we form a meaningful whole; but does so without a Hannibal Lecter-like aesthetic frisson of taboo-breaking, or some childish display of egoistic self-assertion. The "self" they display is a common food product, a feature that I think also tells against reading its allusions to the host and religious transubstantiation as more than parodic.[43] If there is an ethical pedagogy at work here it is not animated by an impulse to preserve a self-purifying transcendence of the mundane, for the holy-sublime, as in Stuart Brisley's *And For Today ... Nothing* (1972) in which the artist is filmed lying in a cold bath containing rotting meat. Nor is it inviting us to wallow in the realm of the disgusting.[44] By comparison, Beagles and Ramsay stage a highly contained form of confrontation which retains footings in common life.

The formidable Dadaist Baroness Elsa von Freytag-Loringhoven furnishes an example of art as perverse variation of Christian ascetic flight from the exigencies of worldly existence. In her revisionist history of New York Dada, Amelia Jones argues that the Baroness incarnates the movement's subversive truth. The American Dada establishment (Man Ray, Marcel Duchamp, and Francis Picabia) generally limited their outrages to what could be shown in a gallery, and sold. They lived off Dada—and exploited the Baroness' body-image as a tool of publicity (as is apparent from the illustration of her accompanying Man Ray's "merdelamer ... de l'amerique" letter cited above. The Baroness poetically incarnated the screamingly offensive Dadasophical refusal of capitalist-patriarchal modernity, living out Dadaist rhetoric, not only in (formerly neglected) artworks and writing, but even more so in her wildly, hilariously inventive dress, aggressive sexual stances, and indifference to the demands of making a comfortable living. Jones' description of her way of life is at times reminiscent of the ugly-effect outlined by Cousins, though here understood as a support for a purely transgressive ethic:

> The Baroness literally makes use of her own excrement [depositing it in the window box of her apartment] ... [W]ith her leaky, smelly body and flamboyant costumes cobbled together from urban detritus and stolen commodities, [she] performed an irrational, anti-masculinist, and radically queer subjectivity against the grain of New York's abstracting spaces and phallic skyline.[45]

What is it to take the shit of Dada seriously? Tristan Tzara: "Dada remains within the framework of European weakness, it's still shit, but from now on we want to shit in different colors."[46] While this can be understood metaphorically, must we take seriously someone who literally acts out Tzara's prescription—as in the case of British punk rock performer G.G. Allin, who expelled and then ate a stream of blue-dyed diarrhea on stage, purportedly as a commentary on the shitty condition of society? Of course not; but there's reason to be to be wary of representations of the artistic vocation which take the form of a ladder ascending to extremes, in which "to go too far," to seek revolutionary or personal transcendence, becomes obligatory.

Naturally there are artists who do not feel constrained to conceive their work or self-image in this way, though one could mention Dubuffet's Art Brut or ugly art, especially his polite raillery against Picasso's melodramatically macho bulls in the form of his series of cow paintings. For my final example of polite raillery, however, I want to return, perhaps surprisingly, to Manzoni's *Merda d'artista*. For all its anti-aesthetic performance of incivility and its context in the angry activism of the 1960s art scene, Manzoni's work can still be seen more in terms of its engagement in polite persiflage regarding the art institution than as a savage attack. Its shit is contained, odorless, and quite possibly not even present in the cans at all. Moreover, by dint of its allusion to gold, the work is not just a commentary on the art institution, but a distillation of the tangled history (attended to by Laporte) that associates shit with wealth, productivity, and beauty-treatment.

Taking Shaftesbury's attempt to clearly demarcate polite and just from uncivil raillery as a point of reference, Manzoni's work might be seen to demonstrate, to the contrary, the way in which rudeness is not simply the negation of civility, any more than ugliness is the negation of beauty, and (now agreeing with Shaftesbury) that humor is not simply the negation of seriousness. In this last account, where, we might ask, is the artist or curator with a commitment to the art of revolution, or to the radical mission of art, who dares to practice raillery in respect of those ideals, as Shaftesbury did with Christianity? And as to rudeness, we often allow for areas of tolerated or licensed incivility inside certain civil bounds or spaces (such as art spaces). (The opposite is often true too.) In ugly humorous art that does not abhor its footing in civil society, these three pairs of opposites typically circle around each other, woven together by threads of irony and social and political history. To be sure, we need not fashion ourselves ethically around such oppositions. For there surely exists an art of seriousness and unmitigated ugliness that brooks no ironization—perhaps we can find this in Henry Tonks' pastel portraits made during World War I for use in surgery, and, more recently, in Paddy Hartley's *Project Façade* (2004–ongoing) which also uses treatments of facial disfigurement and surgical reconstruction during the Great War. But in the case of rudeness and civility, if we heed Freud on the moral costs and psychical pressures of civilized existence, we can speak of a psychical need or demand, maybe both, for what the historical sociologist Norbert Elias termed a *span* of civility and incivility. Without prejudice to possible roles for art in creating climates of sensibility favorable to making life better, it should be no derogation of humorous ugly artworks like *Merda d'artista* or *Blood Pudding Self-Portrait* if their amalgams of rudeness and civility were thought of as *lightening up* social existence as opposed to bringing it radical enlightenment.

NOTES

1
I'd like to thank Lesley Stern, Ian Hunter, and especially John C. Welchman for their comments and criticism.

2
Man Ray, letter to Tristan Tzara (1921), reproduced in Amelia Jones, *Irrational Modernism: A Neurasthenic History of American Dada*, MIT Press, Cambridge, Massachusetts 2004, p. 4.

3
Clement Greenberg, cited in Peter Wollen, "The Triumph of American Painting," *Raiding the Icebox: Reflections on Twentieth-Century Culture*, Verso, London 2008, p. 72.

4
In support of this generalization, see Umberto Eco, *On Ugliness*, Harvill Secker, London 2007.

5
Anthony Ashley Cooper, third Earl of Shaftesbury, *Characteristics of Men, Manners, Opinions, Times*, ed. Lawrence Klein, Cambridge University Press, Cambridge 1999, p. 433; henceforth referred to in-text as *C*.

6
Ibid.

7
Letter to Michael Ainsworth, June 3, 1709, in B. Rand ed., *The Life, Unpublished Letters and Philosophical Regimen of Anthony, Earl of Shaftesbury*, Macmillan, New York 1900, p. 403.

8
Ernst Cassirer, *Philosophy of the Enlightenment*, trans. Fritz Koelln and James Pettegrove, Beacon Press, Boston 1932, 1951; Robert Norton, *The Beautiful Soul: Aesthetic Morality in the 18th Century*, Cornell University Press, Ithaca 1995; Joseph Chytry, *The Aesthetic State: A Quest in Modern German Thought*, University of California Press, Berkeley 1989; Stephen Darwall, *The British Moralists and the Internal "Ought," 1640–1740*, Cambridge University Press, Cambridge 1995.

9
Stephen Darwall, *British Moralists*, p. 21; and Lawrence E. Klein, *Shaftesbury and the Culture of Politeness: Moral Discourse and Cultural Politics in Early Eighteenth-Century England*, Cambridge University Press, Cambridge 1994.

10
Chytry, *Aesthetic State,* lxix-lxx.

11
Ian Hunter, *Rival Enlightenments: Civil and Metaphysical Philosophy in Early Modern Germany*, Cambridge University Press, Cambridge 2001.

12
See, for example the excellent political and cultural background sections of Klein, *Shaftesbury and the Culture of Politeness*.

13
J.G.A. Pocock, "Enthusiasm: The Anti-Self of Enlightenment," in Lawrence E. Klein and Anthony J. La Vopa (eds.), *Enthusiasm and Enlightenment in Europe, 1650–1850*, Huntington Library, San Marino, California 1998, p. 15; Klein, "Solitude, Sociability, and Enthusiasm," in Klein and La Vopa (eds.), *Enthusiasm and Enlightenment*, p. 153–179; Michael Heyd, *"Be Sober and Reasonable": The Critique of Enthusiasm in the 17th and Early 18th Centuries*, E.J. Brill, Leiden 1995, p. 211–240.

14
Klein, *Shaftesbury and the Culture Of Politeness,* p. 178ff.

15
Shaftesbury, "Soliloquy," p. 93.

16
William Shakespeare, *Troilus and Cressida*, Act II, Scene 1.

17
An 18th-century doyen of English polite culture offers testimony to the *uncivil* associations of raillery: "There is a shocking familiarity both in his railleries and civilities." Joseph Addison, *The Works of Joseph Addison*, J.B. Lippicott, London 1854, p. 589.

18
John Dunn, *The Political Thought of John Locke*, Cambridge University Press, Cambridge 1969, p. 255.

19
See Rand, *Life, Letters and Regimen*; henceforth the notebooks will be referred to as *N*.

20
Klein, *Shaftesbury and the Culture of Politeness*, p. 72–80.

21
This unpublishable self is a "creation" requiring management, according to Laurent Jaffro, "Shaftesbury on the Natural Secretion and Philosophical Personae," *Intellectual History Review*, vol. 18, no. 3, 2008, p. 337–348.

22
Klein, *Shaftesbury and the Culture of Politeness*, p. 71–73.

23
On Derrida's argument, see John Macarthur, *The Picturesque: Architecture, Disgust, and Other Irregularities*, Routledge, London 2007, p. 71–72.

24
See *N,* p. 192–206, under the heading of "Character"; and *N*, p. 225–228, under the sub-headings of "Laughter" in a section entitled "Maxims."

25
Shaftesbury, *Characteristics*, 2nd edition (1714), vol. II, p. 181.

26
Peter Kivy, *The Seventh Sense: Frances Hutcheson and Eighteenth-Century British Aesthetics*, Clarendon, Oxford 2003, 2nd edition, p. 20–23.

27
The canonical German Romantic Herder praised Shaftesbury as "the Plato of Europe"; Norton, *Beautiful Soul*, p. 106.

28
On Bakhtin's evident but excusable plagiarism of Cassirer and the Bakhtin-Shaftesbury connections, see Michael Billig, *The Hidden Roots of Critical Psychology: Understanding the Impact of Locke, Shaftesbury and Reid*, Sage, London 2008.

29
Michel Onfray, *Cynismes*, Grasset, Paris 2007, p. 28–34.

30
See especially Ian Hunter, *Rival Enlightenments*, "The History of Theory," *Critical Inquiry*, 33 (2006), p. 78–112. On Schiller's philosophy as a technique of self-formation and its role in the formation of literary studies, see Ian Hunter, *Culture and Government: The Emergence of Literary Education*, Macmillan, London 1988.

31
Reproduced in the blurb for an anthology of essays and artworks based on the exhibition, Felicity Lunn and Heike Munder (eds.), *When Humour Becomes Painful*, JRP|Ringer, Zurich 2005.

32
Peter Sloterdik, *Critique of Cynical Reason*, trans. Michael Eldred, University of Minnesota Press, Minneapolis 1982, p. 195–210.

33
Jacques Lacan, *The Ethics of Psychoanalysis (Seminar VII, 1959–60)*, trans. D. Porter, Routledge, London 1992. An example of this interface is the role of Surrealism in the dissemination of Lacanian psychoanalysis in France.

34
Mark Cousins, "The Ugly," *AA Files* (Architectural Association), vol. 28, Autumn 1994, p. 61–64; vol. 29, Summer 1995, p. 3–6; and vol. 30, Autumn 1995, p. 65–68. Henceforth abbreviated to *U* I, *U* II, and *U* III.

35
Seneca, "On Anger" (*De Ire), Moral and Political Essays,* ed. John Cooper and J.F. Procopé, trans. John Cooper, Cambridge University Press, Cambridge 1995, p. 73–74.

36
Ibid., p. 74.

37
Sigmund Freud, "Humour" (1927), *Standard Edition of the Complete Psychological Works of Sigmund Freud, Vol. XXI* (1927–1931), Hogarth Press, London 1961; in this volume, p. 25–33.

38
I leave aside the moment in which "The Ugly" seems to make its closest approach to Romanticism: its analysis of Victor Hugo's tale of the symbiotic relationship between Quasimodo and Notre Dame cathedral as a paradigm case of the ugly (*U* III, p. 65–67).

39
Cited in Eco, *On Ugliness*, p. 273.

40
Dave Hickey, *The Invisible Dragon: Four Essays on Beauty*, Art Issues Press, Los Angeles 1996, p. 6.

41
Dominique Laporte, *History of Shit*, trans. Nadia Benabid and Rodolph El-Koury, MIT Press, Cambridge, Massachusetts 2000, p. 111.

42
Ibid., p. 76–89.

43
See Mark Hutchison, "Sanguis gratia artis" (2005), http://www.beaglesramsay.co.uk/press/markhutchinsonessay.html. I am indebted to his commentary, which relates *Black Pudding Self-Portrait* to Cousins' work on the ugly.

44
See Slavoj Žižek, *The Fragile Absolute – Or, Why is the Christian Legacy Worth Fighting For?* Verso, London 2000, p. 25–27; Suzanna Biernoff, "The corporeal sublime," *Australian and New Zealand Journal of Art*, vol. 2, no. 2, 2001, p. 61–75.

45
Amelia Jones, *Irrational Modernism: A Neurasthenic History of New York Dada*, MIT Press, Cambridge, Massachusetts 2004, p. 222.

46
Tristan Tzara, *Dada Manifesto*, 23 March 1918, http://www.391.org/manifestos/19180323tristantzara_dadamanifesto.htm.

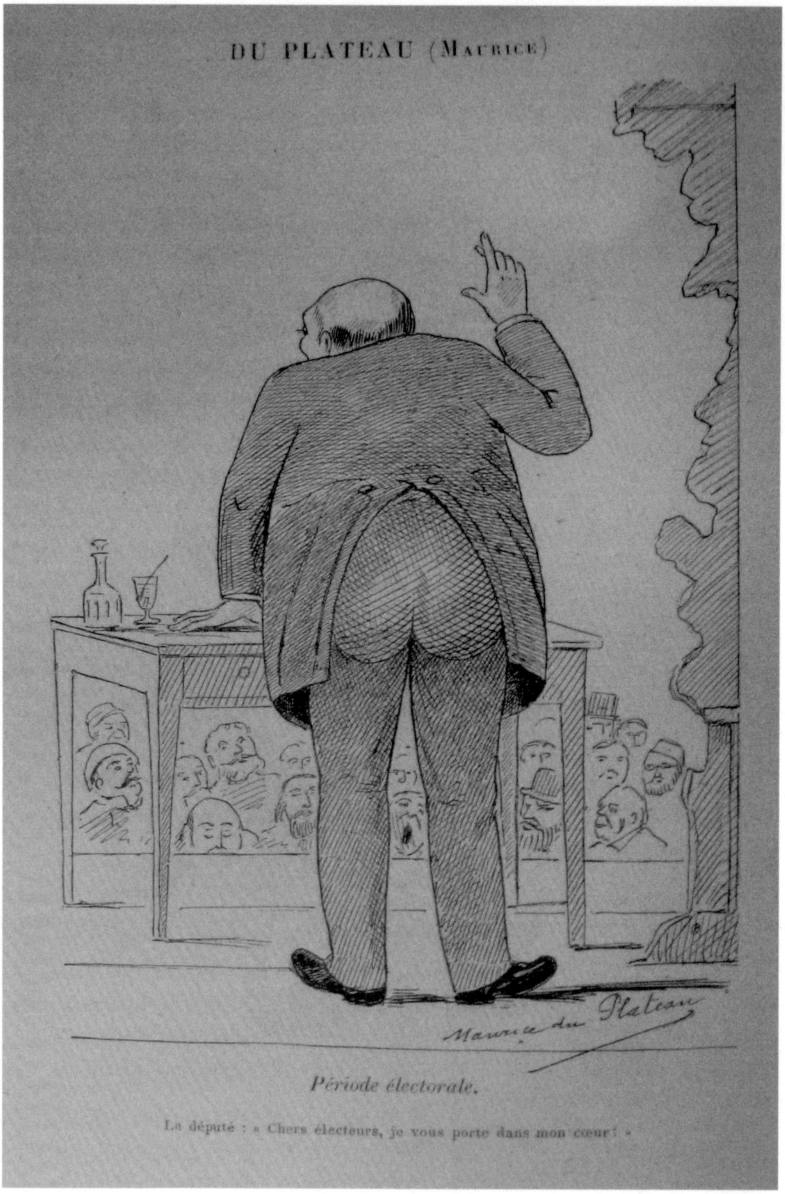

Maurice du Plateau
***Période électorale*, 1884**
Catalogue illustré de l'exposition des Arts Incohérents
(E. Bernard et Cie, Imprimeurs-Editeurs, 71 rue Lacondamine, Paris 1884)

Janet Whitmore

IRREVERENT, ILLICIT, INCOHERENT: BELLE EPOQUE COMEDY

Belle Epoque Paris. The phrase conjures up images of the Moulin Rouge, fashionable shops along the Champs-Elysées, and the explosion of modernist art at the independent exhibitions of the Impressionists. It was a period when France was emerging from the combined crises of the Franco-Prussian War, the Commune, and the loss of Alsace-Lorraine to the Germans, as well as a crippling war indemnity of five billion francs. By 1880, Paris was in the mood to enjoy its self-proclaimed leadership position as the cultural capital of Europe, and to celebrate its reinvigorated economy.

Contributing to the general air of insouciance was a loosely organized group of artists known collectively as Les Incohérents (The Incoherents), who satirized society—sometimes gently and sometimes sharply—using visual images (sketches, doodles, drawings, and prints) and objects, as well as writing and performance. Part of the fast-growing avant-garde art community that emerged in late 19th-century Paris, they played out their satirical social commentaries using what came to be known as *fumiste* techniques of wise-cracking humor and irreverence. The term *fumisme* derives from the French verb *fumer* ("to smoke"). However, French artists also used the word to signify someone who was a joker, or even a crackpot. For the artists who called themselves *fumistes*, the term carried an additional meaning: it inferred that those associated with it would "blow smoke" in the form of humor and innuendo, so that straightforward political or social critique would be obfuscated. Perhaps the most recognizable *fumiste* image is Eugène Bataille's *Mona Lisa with a Pipe* published in *Le Rire* in 1887. Here the iconically enigmatic Florentine (appropriated as a *fumiste* herself perhaps?) is, quite literally, wreathed in wafts of smoke that "mocked the halos of Art and Genius."[1] No subject was exempt from *fumiste* humor, least of all the history of Western art.

The long tradition of social satire in France has several points of origin, including the related, but rather differently focused, writings of the late medieval poet, François Villon (1431–1463), and François Rabelais (1494–1553), author, in the succeeding generation, of *Gargantua and Pantagruel*. As with the most convincing works of their 19th-century admirers, both authors offered an unflinching perspective on contemporary social conditions, mocking the solutions proferred by the church and the hypocrisy of the bourgeoisie. Villon's humor tended to be dark and sardonic, while Rabelais' was based on wildly improbable exaggerations that force readers to reconsider their own assumptions. Both made abundant use of lewd jokes, scatological comedy, and grotesque overstatement. When the *fumistes* arrived on the scene in the 1870s, they built on these long-established foundations as well as on the extraordinary work of their immediate predecessors in the earlier decades of the century.

The generation of artists who matured in the 1830s inherited both the idealism and the despair embedded in the experience of the French Revolution of 1789. They were also heir to the benefits of technological improvements in lithographic printing brought about by industrialization. With the expanded resources now available to the image-publishing industry, the newspapers of Paris were flooded with new graphic styles and genres of cartoon. The so-called Citizen King, Louis-Philippe, was an especially tempting target. His legendary corruption attracted the biting pen of the most prominent of the new political artists, Honoré Daumier, who was imprisoned for his 1831 lithograph entitled *Gargantua*, in which the oversized king is shown sitting on a "throne" that is, in fact, a toilet. Published in *La Caricature,* Charles Philipon's weekly journal, this image pays tribute to its Rabelaisian model in its use of exaggeration, scatological humor, and stinging criticism of government bureaucracy and favoritism run amok.

It was not only Daumier who turned to scatological satire during the July Monarchy of the 1830s and 40s; many of the visual artists working for Philipon produced similarly harsh criticism. The convergence of grotesque humor and grim commentary is evident, for example, in Charles-Joseph Traviès de Villers' lithograph, *Le juste milieu se crotte* [Self-Important Centrists Dirty Themselves] published in *La Caricature* in 1832. In this work, two *vidangeurs*, the men who collected and transported human fecal matter to a central collection site every night, are shown in the *commedia dell'arte* costumes of Pierrot and Harlequin. Between them, they carry a waste container shaped like a pear with Louis-Philippe's facial features. As Gabriel P. Weisberg has noted, "The way in which they transport their burden on a pole, as if it were so much dead weight, and the fact that they are ankle-deep in what appears to be the effluent from an open sewer are a sufficient comment both on the king and his policies and on the ministers appointed to carry them out."[2] Despite frequent censorship and the occasional imprisonment of artists and writers, such acerbic commentary continued to flourish in the French press until the fall of the July Monarchy in 1848.

In the spring of 1863, humor in the visual arts took an unexpected turn when the Parisian art world was rocked by vociferous protest against the annual Salon jury's rejection of more than 4,000 paintings. Emperor Napoleon III resolved the issue by proclaiming that the artists whose work was refused could exhibit their paintings in a separate section of the Palace of Industry, and the public could judge for itself whether or not the jury had chosen wisely. The now famous Salon des refusés was a *succès de scandale;* and the most scandalous painting on display was Edouard Manet's *Déjeuner sur l'herbe* [*Luncheon on the Grass*], widely viewed as a practical joke perpetrated by a young artist.[3] A year later, when Manet exhibited the equally controversial *Olympia*, both the public and the critics were convinced that he was mocking them. Art critic Jules Claretie unwittingly stated the case for satire in the May 15 issue of *L'Artiste*.

> Once upon a time there was a young man called Manet who, one fine day, bravely exhibited among the rejected paintings a nude woman lunching with some young men dressed in sack suits and capped with Spanish sombreros. Many cried shame, some smiled, other applauded, all noted the name of the audacious fellow who already had something and who promised much more. We find him again this year with two dreadful canvases, challenges hurled at the public, mockeries or parodies,

> how can one tell? Yes, mockeries. What is this Odalisque with a yellow stomach, a base model picked up I know not where, who represents Olympia? What Olympia? A courtesan no doubt.[4]

Indeed, *Olympia* did appear to be a well-paid Parisian courtesan, and that was part of the reason her presence was so disturbing to bourgeois gentlemen accompanying their wives to the Salon. Both *Déjeuner sur l'herbe* and *Olympia* challenged accepted stylistic assumptions about contemporary painting, but they also introduced an innovative satirical element to the realm of the official Salon. In a sense, the very formation and definition of the Parisian avant-garde was underwritten by a new kind of representation deeply, yet inscrutably, imbued with parodic or ironic undertones, as humor struck up a crucial new alliance with formal innovation and everyday subject matter.

Manet's use of ambiguous imagery that *implied* satire rather than overtly proclaiming it was very much in keeping with the philosophy of "*fumisme*." The composer and *fumiste* Georges Fragerolle explained that, "in order to be considered a wit, sometimes you need only to be an ass in a lion's skin; to be a good *fumiste*, it is often absolutely necessary to be a lion in the skin of an ass. In the former case, the effect is direct; in the latter, it is once, twice, often ten times removed."[5] It is this closely calibrated but finally indirect skewering of social issues that makes *fumisme* so subversive—the initial effect may often be overtly comic, even sentimental, but the underlying barbs are very thorny.

The apparently silly story of St Nicholas' encounter with the devil, published in the *Les Contes du Chat Noir*, illustrates the sophistication of the *fumiste* approach.[6] Superficially, this is an amusing, cautionary tale about how even the most beloved of saints can be fooled by the wily devil, especially when he's disguised as a *fumiste*; though naturally, a mystical host of angels appear to save the drunken St Nicholas from himself at the last moment. Beneath the droll puns and wordplay, however, are several layers of more caustic commentary on the hypocrisy of the Church, the prevalence of alcoholism—with its attendant social violence—and the utter lack of moral judgment that characterized the French bourgeoisie.[7] Written by Rodolphe Salis, *fumiste extraordinaire* and owner of the Chat Noir cabaret, this piece does exactly what Fragerolle suggested in his definition—the effect is "once, twice, often ten times removed."

It is not surprising then that Salis' Chat Noir cabaret became the headquarters for many like-minded artists, including Les Incohérents. The Chat Noir opened in December 1881 at 84 boulevard Rochechouart in Montmartre, and immediately attracted the crowd associated with the Hydropathes, some 80% of whom would later become Incohérents as well.[8] Founded in the fall of 1878 by the poet Emile Goudeau, they published a bi-monthly journal, *L'Hydropathe*, hosted a variety of performances and exhibitions and, ultimately, became what might be termed "artists-in-residence" at the Chat Noir. All were devoted *fumistes*, eager to engage in whatever performance, parade, or prank was sounded out across the cabaret's raucous tables.

The first event dubbed Arts Incohérents was organized by Hydropathe member Jules Lévy, who was asked to arrange an exhibition to support a charity benefit for the victims of a gas explosion in the first arrondissement of Paris in August 1881. Lévy recognized an opportunity for promotion and willingly agreed to gather some of his fellow Hydropathes for a rollicking display of satirical images. The resulting show took on a particularly incongruous appearance when the front of the roof of the boathouse where the exhibition was installed collapsed, cutting off convenient access as well as electricity. In typical Incohérent fashion, the group turned this calamity into art, providing candles to each visitor so that the exhibition could be viewed in the ruins of the building. As Catherine Charpin put it in her study of the Incohérent decade, *Les Arts Incohérents (1882–1893)*: "One couldn't dream of a more picturesque and incoherent beginning."[9]

The positive public reception of the boathouse exhibition encouraged the group to consider developing another independent display of work. Thus, on a Sunday afternoon (October 1, 1882), Lévy hosted an exhibition in his apartment at 4 rue Antoine Dubois. The invitation, designed by Henri Boutet, depicted a young woman, with brush and palette in hand, painting the words "Arts Incohérents" as she balances precariously on a ladder that seems to be leaning against a wall without any means of support—a sure sign of more "incoherence" to come. Although no visual record of the works on display was produced, the list of attendees suggests that this exhibition attracted a remarkable cross-section of Parisian society; as might be expected, other independent artists such as Manet, Pierre-Auguste Renoir, and Camille Pissarro showed up, but so too did the German composer Richard Wagner, and King Ludwig III of Bavaria. The event was carefully choreographed so that visitors entered the building amid an array of theatrical displays on the mezzanine, and then proceeded to Lévy's apartment where visual puns and satirical drawings formed the nucleus of the exhibition. Reportedly, two thousand people attended over the course of the afternoon—an unprecedented success for this casually organized group of visual artists, performers, and musicians.[10] Their reputation for knowing how to have fun undoubtedly contributed to the popularity of the event, but the satirical quality of the work also seems to have attracted the political and aesthetic avant-garde, thus mingling several disparate factions of Parisian society.

The second Incohérent exhibition took place a year later at the Galerie Vivienne, a commercial gallery on the right bank in the ninth arrondissement just south of Montmartre; again, it was a charitable benefit for the poor of Paris. This time, the organization of the group was more polished: they produced a poster, invitations, and special tickets for each day of the week. Henri Gray's poster showed a bare-breasted muse—sporting a jester's cap—with a collection of classical busts at her feet, who had apparently fallen under the spell of "les arts incohérents." Similarly, Luigi Loir's ticket design for the special Friday viewings featured "L'Arc de Triomphe de l'Avenir" [The Future Arch of Triumph], a reference to the location of the Galerie Vivienne on the right bank. More importantly, his proposed design for the arch took the form of a folded paper *cocotte*, a popular image that referenced young, easily misled girls who were viewed as disposable sexual playthings.[11] As in most Incohérent images, there is a delayed sting here; at first glance, the ticket design is a visual joke showing visitors marching under the exaggerated, folded paper "arch," suggesting, perhaps, that they are being naively lured into the dangerously disrespectful humor of Les Arts Incohérents. Beneath that comic veneer, however, is an unpalatable—but undeniable—reminder that many adolescent girls were prostituted daily on the streets of Paris, even on fashionable boulevards like the Champs-Elysées where "proper" bourgeois businessmen looked for their pleasures.

The 1883 exhibition, with 284 works on display and a reported attendance of 20,000 people, was considered a success.[12] In 1884, Lévy organized another show, which opened on October 15 at the Galerie Vivienne. For this exhibition, two versions of the catalogue were printed, a large one with images (approximately 7 x 12 inches) and a smaller one with only a printed list of artworks (approximately 5 x 9 inches). Like many other publications that were printed in different versions, these catalogues allowed the visitor to purchase the more elaborate and expensive edition, if desired, and thus to augment the coffers of the organizing artists; while the smaller one, without images, was usually cheap, or free. The fortunate survival of these ephemeral pieces allows us access to the rich texture of satirical visual humor typical of Les Incohérents. Almost irresistible is Maurice Du Plateau's drawing entitled *Période électorale* [*Election Time*]. Here, a member of the French parliament stands with his back to the viewer as he proclaims sincerely to a crowd of voters: "Dear Voters, I carry you in my heart" [Le Député: "Chers électeurs, je vous porte dans mon coeur"]. What the observer sees, however, is the rear view of Monsieur le Député, with the tails of his fashionable topcoat revealing his heart-shaped derrière. Then, as now, politicians seem perennially bereft of integrity, presenting themselves as honest brokers of the public interest while subverting those objectives through misrepresentation and outright deception.

Another work exhibited in 1884 was *Le Vieux et Le Neuf* [*The Old and the Young*] by Paul Baron. This is the kind of image that no doubt provoked groans from viewers because of its indulgence in an obvious visual pun. While the title suggests some sort of counterpoint between age and youth, the image actually depicts an old man with a long beard, wire-rimmed spectacles, and a pipe (le vieux) carrying a very large number nine (le neuf) under his arm. The word "neuf" in French means both "young" and "nine," thus giving rise to an absurd visual joke. Visual puns of this nature run rampant in almost all of the Incohérent work, foreshadowing the visual/verbal interplay of later generations, but especially the Dada and Surrealist artists of the 1910s and 20s.[13]

The social pretensions of Parisians from all walks of life provided ample material for *fumiste* barbs. In *Mars et Vénus*, a drawing by O. Loys of a young man and woman flirting with each other on a park bench, we encounter a working-class couple with clear delusions of grandeur. Unlike their classical predecessors, this mustachioed Mars is dressed in ragtag armor with a broom sticking out of the top of his "helmet" and a plumber's wrench rather than a sword dangling between his legs—a very impressive "tool" on view for Venus' delectation one presumes. Loys' modern Parisian Venus is equally ridiculous in her provocatively short dress, elbow-length gloves, and stylish *japoniste* parasol, behind which she coyly smiles at

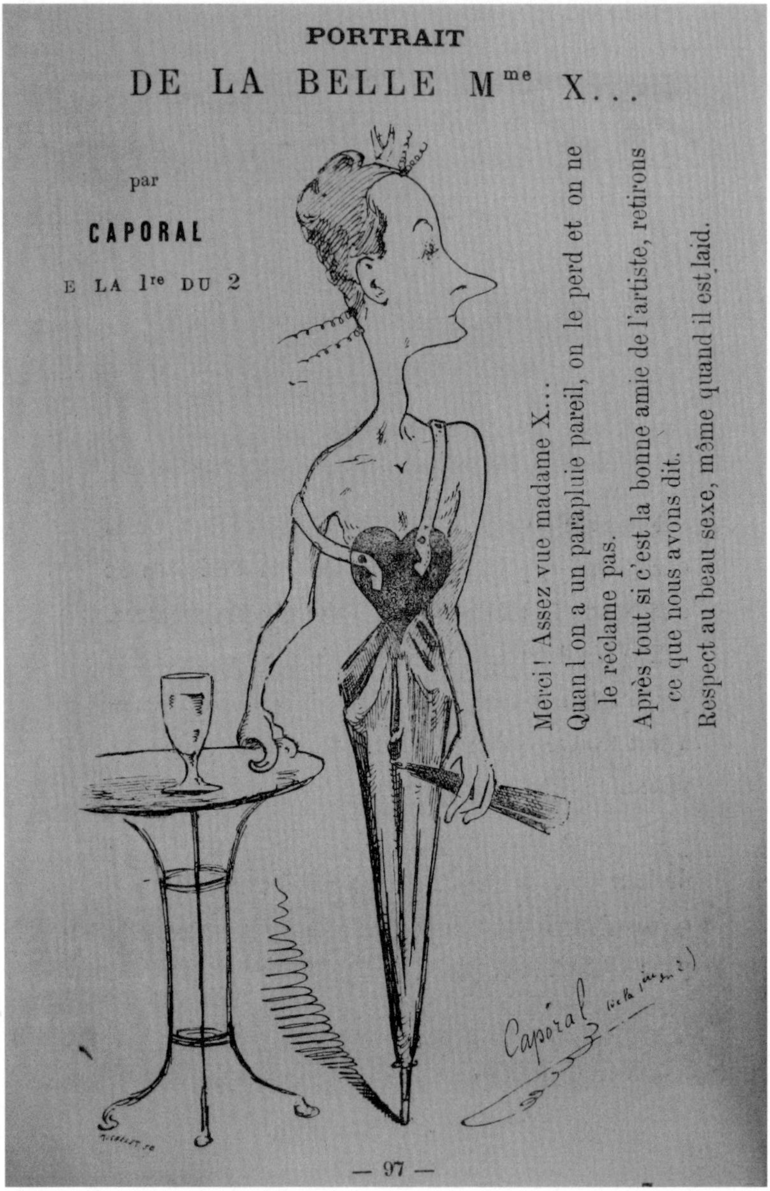

Caporal
***Portrait de la belle Mme X ...*, 1884**
Catalogue illustré de l'exposition des Arts Incohérents
(E. Bernard et Cie, Imprimeurs-Editeurs, 71 rue Lacondamine, Paris 1884)

her over-eager suitor. On her back is a quiver of arrows, and across her pelvis she cradles a bow as if to invite young Mars to direct his attention to the obvious charms she offers. To complete the picture, Mars' mongrel dog—hardly the sleek hound of a Roman god—lifts his leg beside the park bench. Undeniably mocking and more than a little contemptuous, Loys' perspective on this obviously affected couple could be understood as an instance of class snobbery; or it might be a comment on the sheer folly of everyday folk who swallow popular pap without knowing—or questioning—its origins.

The upper class fares no better. In *Portrait de la belle Mme X ...* , the artist Caporal used the Rabelaisian technique of grotesque exaggeration to spotlight the excessive attention that fashionable women devoted to their appearance. The "beautiful Mme X ... " in question has slimmed herself into the shape of an umbrella, with almost no hips, a very flat chest, and a scrawny neck. She steadies herself against a nearby table as she poses—with her nose in the air—so that others may see her elegant profile. To the right of this portrait of vanity is a typeset caption running at a 90° angle, forcing the viewer to turn the page in order to read it. The caption reads: "Thank you! Enough of Madame X ... When one has an umbrella such as this, one loses it and does not reclaim it" [Merci! Assez vue madame X ... Quand l'on a un parapluie pareil, on le perd et on ne le réclame pas]. The amusing parody of fashionable excess, just as fundamentally pretentious and transparent as Loys' working-class Mars and Venus, is underscored by the solicitation of a certain sympathy for Madame X, who becomes both undesirable and an object of mockery because of her own ultimately pathetic pursuit of style. Even in Paris, the most fashionable of capitals, it seems that style has its limits.

From an aesthetic perspective, the positioning of the type at a right angle to the image in the *Portrait de la belle Mme X ...* presents an intriguing anticipation of later developments in poetry and the visual arts. The Incohérent exhibition in Nantes three years later, in 1887, included a similar typographic rearrangement, as letters were organized in an apparently arbitrary pattern on the page.[14] Here the deliberate disconnection of letters from each other, and from the word of which they are part objects, creates a visual puzzle for readers to solve.

Les
ARTS
  IN
    CO
      HE
        RE
          NT
            S

Little is known about the direct influence of this visual play with letters and words. But the Symbolist poet Stéphane Mallarmé, for example, wrote his graphically innovative late poem, *Un coup de dés jamais n'abolira le hasard* [*A Throw of the Dice Will Never Abolish Chance*] during the 1890s, and may well have encountered these precedents during his frequent visits to the Chat Noir; he was a personal friend of many visual artists, and an occasional art critic. It seems probable that he would have seen the Incohérent exhibitions; although whether or not he was inspired by their example remains a matter of speculation.[15] By the early 20th century, with the development of Analytic Cubism after 1909, the use of stenciled letters and word fragments had emerged as a leading indicator of avant-gardist experiment. Paintings, and later collages, by Pablo Picasso and Georges Braque, and soon after works by Juan Gris and Fernand Léger, all made recourse to the inscription of words and letters as part of their compositions. And with Filippo Tommaso Marinetti's *parole in libertà* [words in freedom][16] and the wild textual and sonic experiments of the Dadaists, the annexation and rerouting of fragmented text became a signature device that would be caught up in another round of dialogue and dispute by the Lettrist and Fluxus movements in the second half of the century. It seems reasonable to claim that some element, at least, of the widespread cultivation of contradictions and chance encounters created by the arbitrary juxtaposition of incongruous words or objects, letters, and meanings, can be attributed to the innovative protagonists who came together in comedic crucible of the Incohérents and the Chat Noir.

The Incohérents were also fascinated by the comic potential of incorporating incompatible or absurd elements in the framework of an implausible story. The catalogue for the 1886 exhibition, held at the Eden-Théâtre for two months from October 17 to December 19, introduced each participant

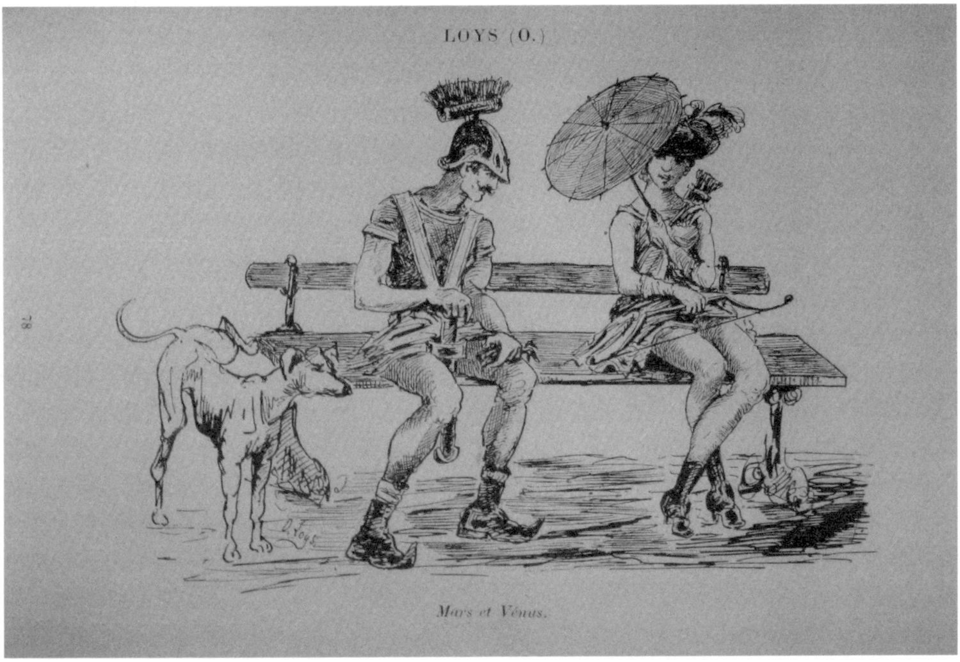

O. Loys
Mars et Vénus, 1884
Catalogue illustré de l'exposition des Arts Incohérents
(E. Bernard et Cie, Imprimeurs-Editeurs, 71 rue Lacondamine, Paris 1884)

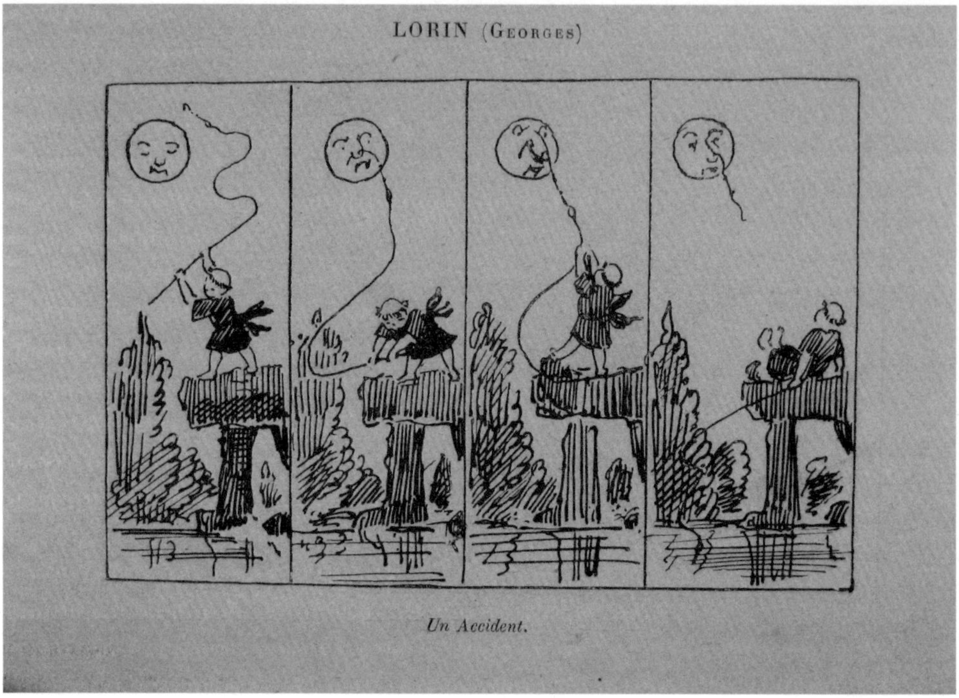

Georges Lorin
Un Accident, 1886
Catalogue de l'exposition des Arts Incohérents au profit des œuvres de protection de l'enfance à l'Eden-Théâtre (Printed by Georges Chamerot, 19 rue des Saints-Pères, Paris 1886)

with a short fictional biography and a caricature. While most of these artists are unknown today, the *fumiste* spirit of their descriptions offers a playful sense of who they might have been—although readers would not be expected to gain any credible information about the facts of their lives. The description of Biblo-Pingo suggests that he lived beneath the fourth arch under the Pont des Arts; Bezodis' biography claims that he lived a "demure and chaste life in town."[17] Yet again, the cohorts of the Incohérents are "blowing smoke," this time at each other, for the sheer amusement of one and all. The same tone governs Georges Lorin's droll visual narrative entitled *Un Accident*. In a series of four panels, Lorin depicts a young boy trying to fish at the end of a pier on a sunny day. As he casts his line, it goes astray, catching the nose on the face of the sun. In the second panel, the boy begins to realize that his fishing line isn't responding; in the third, he looks up at the now frowning sun and pulls on the line to free it. The fourth panel shows the final outcome: the line has broken leaving the boy sitting dejectedly on the pier and the woeful sun with a piece of fishing line hanging from his nose. This is a kind of sophomoric humor, but suggestive of the unexpected and unintended consequences that can arise when humans become entangled with forces beyond their control. Jokes such as this one are purely visual, dependent on the ability of the artist to suggest improbable connections between objects (such as the sun and the boy's fishing line) that cannot exist in the everyday world. Such imagery provokes a smile at the inexplicable nature of life as well as a rueful acknowledgment of our inability to control it in any meaningful way.

A more sophisticated and subtle work is Théophile Steinlen's *Lézards-Cohérents*, a disarming image of two lizards embracing—or "cohering." The pun is both visual and aural; when the phrase "lézards-cohérents" is spoken, it sounds like "les arts cohérents," or "coherent arts," as well as "cohering lizards." The joke is part self-parody, partly a suggestive pun, for beneath its homonymic surface there is, perhaps, a more pointed implication: that all the "coherent" arts are essentially reptilian—the product of earlier evolutionary times. In fact, Jean-Léon Gérôme—one of most ardent advocates of the "coherent arts" practiced at the conservative École des Beaux-Arts—was reported to have admitted only to a "mediocre laugh" at the 1883 exhibition.[18] Gérôme's attendance at the event was occasioned, no doubt, because of its charitable purpose,

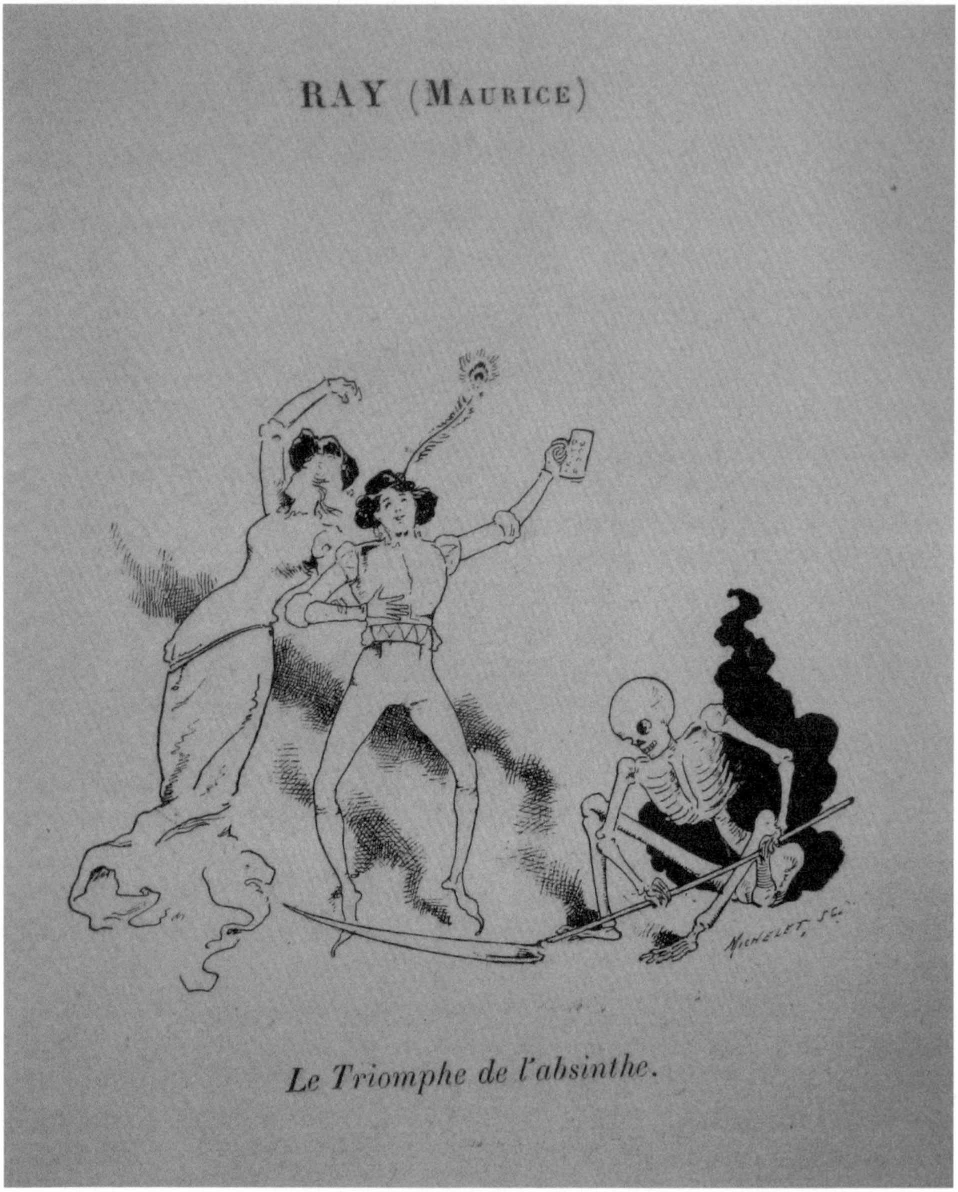

Maurice Ray
Le Triomphe de l'absinthe, 1886
Catalogue de l'exposition des Arts Incohérents au profit des œuvres de protection de l'enfance à l'Eden-Théâtre (Printed by Georges Chamerot, 19 rue des Saints-Pères, Paris 1886)

since he publicly proclaimed his antipathy to any form of non-academic art on numerous occasions. Steinlen's sly laughter at the expense of advocates of the "coherent arts" would have underscored the position of the Incohérents as outsiders, and invited the public to join in with the joke.

Other images from the 1886 exhibition are informed by political satire similar to those in the 1884 show, but there is an increased focus on more sardonic humor related to the profound social depredations of the time. Maurice Ray's *Le Triomphe de l'absinthe* [*The Triumph of Absinthe*], departs from the *fumiste* model in that it does not attempt to create the teasing humor of works such as *Période électorale*. It offers, instead, a grisly *danse macabre* as a drunken couple skips obliviously into a scythe positioned in their path by a skeleton. Ray is especially effective in placing the razor-sharp scythe blade directly in the center of the composition so that the viewer sees it even before realizing that the thoroughly inebriated couple are about to stumble over it. The skeleton seems particularly sinister, silhouetted against a black flame, concentrating resolutely on tripping the absinthe-sodden drinkers, and nicely emblematizing the dual entrapments of fate and delinquency.

During the Third Republic, the issue of alcoholism—especially the abuse of the exceptionally toxic, green mixture known as absinthe—was the subject of profound concern at almost every level of society. Significantly, it was the artists of Montmartre, where the brutish effects of drunkenness were so clearly visible, who contributed some of the most affecting—and effective—images of the public consequences of overindulgence. André Gill, Hydropathe, Incohérent, and lifelong *fumiste*, engraved the excruciatingly realistic *Drunken Man* in 1880 for *Le Journal illustré;* as his wife and children cower behind the door, terrified of his temper and irrationality, the filthy, bloodied drunk falls flat on the floor. Likewise, Steinlen's etchings, such as *The Big Sister*, illustrated the weighty, long-term effects of alcoholism on children abandoned to poverty, who were forced to fend for themselves and their siblings, in the poorest, most dangerous neighborhoods of Paris.[19] *Le Triomphe de l'absinthe* sums up the problem succinctly—alcoholism is not only pervasive and life-threatening, but willfully ignored by the majority of citizens. The comic element in this drawing is fleeting, giving way almost immediately to gallows humor unredeemed by any indication of hope. The seriousness of this image also serves as a reminder that the Incohérents exhibitions were always held as benefits for the Parisian poor and disenfranchised, with a substantial percentage of profits gifted to local charities.

Beginning in March 1885, the Incohérents also sponsored occasional costume balls, at which all of the participants arrived in the most outrageous outfits they could devise. Henri de Sta illustrated a selection of costumes and characters from the first ball in *Le Courrier français*: they included a chef with a menu on his back; two soldiers dressed in tutus and helmets; a haloed hermit holding a lily in front of himself as if it were a cross [perhaps Oscar Wilde was in attendance?]; and an assortment of sexually suggestive musical instruments with extra long pipes, tubes, and mouthpieces.[20] These celebrations were equal parts theater, public art, and *fumiste* entertainment—and clearly one of the most sought after invitations in Paris. As the 1880s drew to a close, both the balls and the art exhibitions began to dwindle. Jules Lévy had already hosted an Incohérent funeral in 1887, and despite several subsequent balls and exhibitions, the tenor of the times had changed. Lévy ran into numerous challenges with the 1889 exhibition, not least of which was finding a suitable location while the monumental Exposition Universelle was in progress. Press coverage was devoted, overwhelmingly, to the startling new Eiffel Tower and the events at the fair; even the highest jinks of the Incohérents couldn't compete. At the end of 1893 the group held its final Exposition des Arts Incohérents, having devoted a decade to creating humorous, insightful, and satirical imagery and performances that signaled the birth of a modern comic sensibility.

Les Incohérents provided a model for satirical humor in 20th-century modernist movements, introducing many of the characteristic elements later associated with Dadaism and Surrealism. Like many other largely unknown and unstudied artists in the multifaceted jumble of late 19th-century Paris, the Incohérents' contribution is easy to overlook. Their work was ephemeral, often topical, and not always comprehensible in translation. Nonetheless, they built a strong foundation on the French comic tradition of skewering the hypocrisy of society, and added a *fumiste* sensibility that juxtaposed dissimilar concepts in order to provoke laughter as well as thought—often as Fragerolle noted, "once, twice, or ten times removed."

A closing image of "incoherence" might be the Monty Python-esque drawing by Jules Michelet entitled *Les effets de l'art incohérent* [*The Effects of Incoherent Art*] from the 1886 exhibition. On the right side of the composition stands a fashionably dressed man holding his head (complete with top hat) in his hand; on the left is a jester with his head facing backward; and in the center is a bewhiskered businessman turned upside down with his now-detached arms creating a graceful dance in-between the two upright figures. Michelet's signature is also positioned upside down at the top of the page. Clearly, the effects of incoherent art disrupt not only one's physical well-being, but also permanently alter one's perception of the world. Ultimately, it was the Incohérents' ability to challenge social and artistic conventions that gave their brief movement its most lasting "effet" in the already tumultuous concoction of *fin-de-siècle* Paris. Like all successful guerrilla strategists, they made their points and moved on.

NOTES

I would like to thank the staff of the McCormick Library of Special Collections, Northwestern University Library for unfailing and insightful assistance with this project.

1
Phillip Dennis Cate and Mary Shaw (eds.), *The Spirit of Montmartre: Cabarets, Humor, and the Avant-Garde, 1875–1905*, Jane Voorhies Zimmerli Art Museum, New Brunswick, New Jersey 1996, p. 104–105.

2
Gabriel P. Weisberg, "In Deep Shit: The Coded Images of Traviés in the July Monarchy," *Art Journal*, Fall 1993, p. 36–40.

3
George Heard Hamilton, *Manet and His Critics*, Yale University Press, New Haven and London 1986, p. 45.

4
Cited in Hamilton, p. 73.

5
Cited in Cate and Shaw (eds.), *The Spirit of Montmartre*, p. 23.

6
Rodolphe Salis, *Les Contes du Chat Noir*, Libraire Dentu, Paris 1888.

7
For a fuller discussion of this story, see Janet Whitmore, "Absurdist Humor in Bohemia," in *Montmartre and the Making of Mass Culture*, ed. Gabriel P. Weisberg, Rutgers University Press, New Brunswick, New Jersey 2001, p. 205–222.

8
For more information about the Hydropathes, and their origins in the Bon Bock dinners hosted by Emile Goudeau in the 1870s, see Cate and Shaw (eds.), *The Spirit of Montmartre* p. 18–22. For a discussion of the origins and meanings of the name "Hydropathes," see Armond Fields, *Le Chat Noir: A Montmartre Cabaret and Its Artists in Turn-of-the-Century Paris*, Santa Barbara Museum of Art, Santa Barbara, California 1993, p. 10–11. For a first-hand account of the creation of the Hydropathes and their development, including the splinter group, Les Hirsutes, see Jules Lévy, *Les Hydropathes prose et vers*, André Delpeuch, Paris 1928, p. 5–16.

9
Catherine Charpin, *Les Arts Incohérents (1882–1893)*, Éditions Syros Alternatives, Paris 1990, p. 14. [On ne pouvait rêver inauguration plus pittoresque et incohérente.]

10
Ibid., p. 16.

11
Elizabeth Menon, *Evil by Design: The Creation and Marketing of the Femme Fatal*e, Univeristy of Illinois Press, Chicago 2006, p. 121–122. Menon explains the origin of the folded paper *cocotte* [little bird], a Spanish children's toy, designed to represent a baby chick that became very popular in France. As she notes: "Meant to resemble a chicken, the abstract form facilitated a complicated punning relationship dependent on the French use of double and triple entendres. The *cocotte* was a disposable toy, a 'chick,' and easy prey for the French male on the make."

12
Cate and Shaw (eds.), *The Spirit of Montmartre*, p. 40.

13
For a discussion of the humorous interplay between words and images in the Dada and Surrealist movements, see Judi Freeman and John Welchman, *The Dada & Surrealist Word-Image*, exh. cat., Los Angeles County Museum of Art and MIT Press, Cambridge, Massachusetts 1989.

14
Les Arts Incohérents, Première exposition à Nantes, Imprimerie du commerce, Nantes 1887, title page.

15
See Stéphane Mallarmé, *The Poems* (bilingual edition translated by Keith Bosley), Penguin Books, New York 1977, p. 253–297.

16
See F.T. Marinetti, "Distruzione della sintassi-Immaginazione senza fili-Parole in libertà," in *Lacerba* (Florence), June 15, 1913, reprinted in English as "Destruction of Syntax-Imagination without Strings-Words in Freedom," in F.T. Marinetti, *Critical Writings*, ed. Günther Berghaus, trans. Doug Thompson, Farrar, Straus and Giroux, New York 2006; and Johanna Drucker, *The Visible Word: Experimental Typography and Modern Art, 1909–1923*, University of Chicago Press, Chicago 1997.

17
Catalogue de l'exposition des Arts Incohérents au profit des œuvres de protection de l'enfance à l'Eden-Théâtre, Georges Chamerot, Paris 1886, entries no. 31, no. 33, n.p.

18
Catherine Charpin, *Les Arts Incohérents*, Éditions Syros Alternatives, Paris 1990, p. 20.

19
For a discussion of the effect of alcoholism on children, see Jill Miller, "Les enfants des ivrognes," in *Montmartre and the Making of Mass Culture*, ed. Gabriel P. Weisberg, Rutgers University Press, New Brunswick, New Jersey 2001, p. 72–93.

20
Henri de Sta, "Quelques types et costumes du bal des Incohérents du 11 mars 1885," *Le Courrier francais*, March 22, 1885, p. 4.

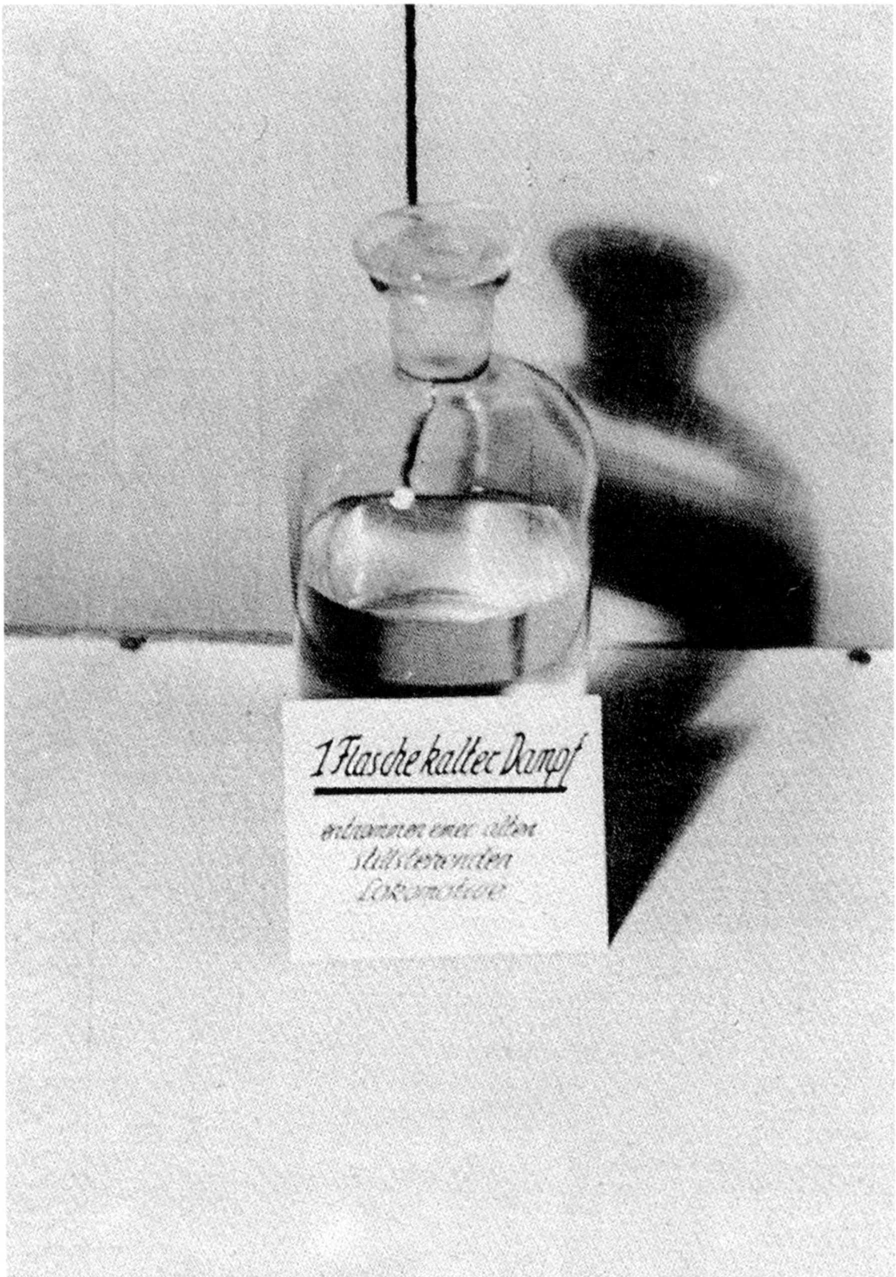

Karl Valentin
Cold Steam of An Express Train Locomotive

David Robbins

CONCRETE COMEDY

In comedy, there is, most assuredly, a mainstream, and it's sustained by specific conventions.

There are three. Mainstream comedy is verbal, narrative, and illusionistic. It is comedy that a) is communicated principally through speech (funny lines); b) tells a story (however tiny or fragmentary); and c) involves pretending (make-believe people—characters—encountering make-believe situations). Mainstream comedy is, in short, everything that's likely to occur to you when you think of professionally manufactured comedy. The experts contribute to this take by penning histories of comedy that showcase only verbal, narrative, illusionistic examples culled from stage or screen or broadcast media—funny plays, funny movies, funny TV or radio programs, funny stand-up. *Film Comedy from 1915 to Today*; *Sitcoms, Sitcoms, Sitcoms*; *Didja Hear the One About ... ?: A Comprehensive Guide to Stand-Up*—although their range may seem broad, such histories assume a narrow definition of comedy and of comic performance that altogether ignores an alternative sensibility that surfaced in Europe around 1915 and gradually took hold on the modern imagination. This alternative, which I call "concrete comedy," is a comedy of doing rather than saying, communicated through objects and gestures rather than sitcoms and stand-up: it is a comedy of things and of things done. Since its emergence, concrete comedy has been practiced on occasion by visual artists, by entertainers, by fashion designers, by architects, by advertisers, by housewives and traveling salesmen ... and it shows no signs of abating.

Though I coined the term "concrete comedy" I didn't invent the idea. Concrete comedy has two fathers. The primary father is Karl Valentin, the most popular and ambitious comedian at work in Germany in the first half of the 20th century. During the roughly 40 years of his performing life, Valentin recorded dozens of 78s, starred in nearly 40 films, and trod the boards in literally hundreds of stage works. In the American context, his sheer adaptability was matched only by Jack Benny, Bob Hope, Burns and Allen, and Fanny Brice, all of whom fluidly moved between the stage, radio, film, and (with the exception of Brice) television. But Valentin did something they didn't do. He expanded our idea of what comedy could be. For in addition to his considerable abilities in the performing arts, Valentin also created objects and installations of a certain, highly specific, ambition.

"Cold Steam of an Express Train Locomotive," like Valentin's other objects, does not reward us visually in the way that art objects do. It doesn't luxuriate in its materiality. It is carefully presented but not aesthetically minded. We are not invited to lose ourselves in the contemplation of some profound animalistic gesture open to as many interpretations as there are interpreters. To the contrary: "Cold Steam of an Express Train Locomotive" starts specific and it stays specific: "this water in this flask is intended to be interpreted so." The specific interpretation we are to make of the water in the flask is even provided to us, written on a little card placed before it. The words express Valentin's attitude toward the object. "Cold Steam" represents the typical Valentinian transaction: we have the real thing, slightly altered (if at all)—here, some water in a flask—and we have the attitude toward the thing—here expressed in words on a card.

Is that all? Yes. But that's plenty. When all is said and done—and, for that matter, whether it is said or done—comedy is nothing but attitude, really. Comedy is the little card placed before, and directing our perception of, the real.

If life really were theater, if life and theater were one and the same, we'd be justified in categorizing such classic Valentinian creations as "Cold Steam of An Express Train Locomotive" as nothing more than a prop. And, in the next breath, we'd be able to dismiss that prop as being beneath serious consideration, since everyone knows that, as measured on the scale of the existential, a prop is inferior because 1) it's fake, 2) it only looks real, and 3) it only exists for the purpose of propping up a narrative. A theatrical prop hasn't any ambitions of its own. It lives to serve a story, it doesn't create a story.

Thing is, though, "Cold Steam of An Express Train Locomotive" isn't a prop. Or if it is, it's a life-prop, not a theater-prop—a far more complex notion. "Cold Steam" is physically real, first of all, and not merely made to look real. Secondly, where's the play? Where's the narrative? Other than the story that the object itself supplies, there is none. Valentin has consciously placed "Cold Steam" outside the magic force-field of proscenium-arch illusionism.

Life is not theater. Life is life, and theater is a subset of it, a single reading of it, a perspective on it; theater is a metaphor for life, not the other way around. For that quite excellent reason, when we consider Valentin's theatricalizing objects, we can't resort to our usually dismissive attitude toward props. The not-so-simple fact is that a theatricalizing object which is introduced into the raw actuality that is life isn't a true prop. It exists instead in a condition more aptly described as prop-like—which makes all the difference in the world. The prop-like will have a more richly dimensioned relation to reality than a mere prop. What, after all, is a prop-like object, exactly?

I don't know. And neither do you.

Nor did Valentin, I expect. He did understand, though, that to consign this Something Else, this theater, preserved, this cross between an art object and a theatrical prop, to venues normally reserved for the display of self-conscious imaginative objects—the art gallery or art museum—would be a bad idea. A very bad idea: for doing so would cause them to be interpreted as art, squelching the special vibe that gave an object like "Cold Steam" its purr. Valentin intuited that for their distinctive hum to be audible, his objects required another context. He must have, for in the early 1930s, in Munich, he undertook to establish that context.

The site that Valentin chose for his experiment was the cellar of the Hotel Wagner, where he adapted an exhibition model—the Panoptikum—that was common throughout Europe during the 19th century. The traditional Panoptikum presented theatrical tableaux that featured

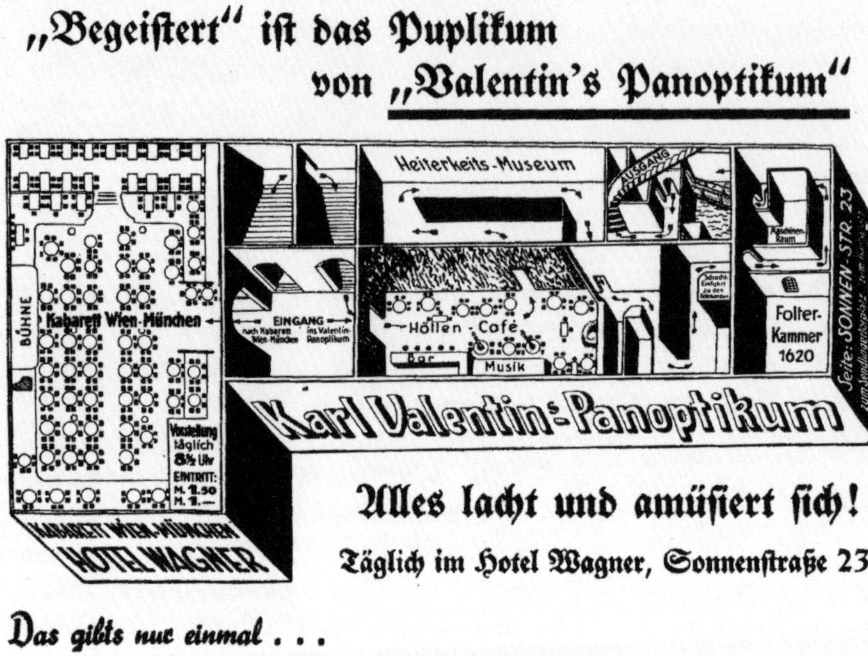

Floor plan of Karl Valentin Museum in Hotel Wagner, Munich

reproductions, usually in wax, of some of the more sensational aspects of humankind's cruel and wacky existence. Adjusting the Panoptikum's earnest tenor to the skeptical 20th-century mind, Valentin tweaks its customary categories—science, recreations of historical scenes (including the common occurrence—for some reason—of scenes involving physical torture), aberrations of nature, sundry wonders trivial or grand—according to his own skewed comic vision.

Dozens of comic objects and installations feature in Valentin's Panoptikum. There are sly comedies, blunt comedies, vulgar comedies, refined comedies. There is banal stuff that, with the addition of a simple label, has been elevated to the status of historical objects: "The Apple, From Which Adam Took The Bite," "The Jacket That Janitor Josef Maria Meier Was Wearing When He Met His Wife." Other displays betray, in varying degrees, more intervention: the "Cold Steam of an Express Train Locomotive"; an empty bird's nest designated the "Nest with Unlaid Eggs"; a wax boy demonstrating the "Electric Nose Picking Apparatus for Kids." Here are roses that smell of gasoline and a gasoline can that smells like roses. A hotplate is labeled "Chamber Oven for the Production of Heat, or Oven Not an Exhibit, It's Just Here." Two umbrellas, one smaller than the other become "Father and Son." A portrait of a child is now "Portrait of An Eighty-year-old Geezer At One Year Old." Standing here and there are wax figures representing such figures as "Mr Empfenzeder, the Inventor of the Sponge Bath." A collection of natural history specimens is now "Karl Valentin's Zoological Garden." Included in this section is the "Tragic Mistake of Nature, or Camping Site for Turtles," a (taxidermied) turtle climbing toward a birdhouse that's lodged in branches near the ceiling.

Valentin widened comedy's possibility set. With his prop-like creations, Valentin, who was not an artist but a popular comedian intent on making comedy, establishes a category of production—the comic object—that is not lodged between life and art, but, rather, between life and theater. By itself this invention of the comic object as a separate and valid category of production is enough to establish Valentin's place in the history of the imagination. His subsequent creation of a context for these objects only reinforces his importance.

Karl Valentin invented a context and signed his name to it. His invention isn't limited to those objects that he personally created. The Valentinian context expands to include similarly configured objects made by others, not only other comedians, but visual artists, fashion designers, architects, and traveling salesmen.

The art world places a great deal of stock in intentionality. But intentionality is always conditioned by an awareness of possibilities. Were Valentin's achievement recognized earlier and more widely, it is not only possible but likely that a great many objects heretofore considered art objects might have been more properly assigned by their makers to another category. Ruthlessly applied, this happy revisionism modifies our view of the history of 20th-century art. More significantly, since it recognizes a kind of comedy that adopted a materialist approach to humor, it calls for a readjustment of the accepted history of the 20th-century imagination. Emphasizing actions over words, preferring the actual to make-believe, this concrete comedy pops up in many different facets of the imaginative life over the course of the century.

Because concrete comedy is pre-eminently a theatrical expression not a pictorial one, many differences arise between a comic object and an art object. The core difference is that the comic object, theatrical and prop-like, focuses our attention in a way that is distinct from art's iconic focus. Insofar as the comic object does successfully signal 1) the fact of the gesture of its making and 2) the theatricalizing perspective, we perhaps go too far when we characterize the comic object as non-iconic, but we must still recognize that such iconicity as does exist in the comic object is beside the point. (A good joke, this: iconicity being beside the point.) Rather than concentrate focus on an iconic payoff in the manner of art, the object in concrete comedy disperses focus onto qualities other than the visual or physical, namely the literary, the theatrical, the attitudinal. Unlike the art object, the comic object is not separable from the theatricalized moment which produced it and which it necessarily reflects.

It is for this reason, perhaps, that the comic object cannot sustain too much aestheticization. Too much art, too much aesthetic inventiveness, obscures the comic gesture, and the comedy disappears. When significant technical effort or material invention is engaged in order to create a comic object, it is usually done in order to establish the finished product's referent to its origin in the real. The real is a necessary presence in the comic object, as it is in all comedy. Remove reality and comedy has nothing to make fun of.

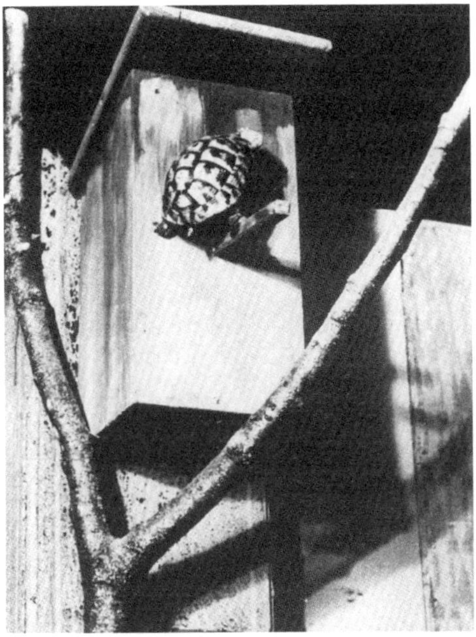

Karl Valentin
Tragic Mistake of Nature or Camping Site for Turtles

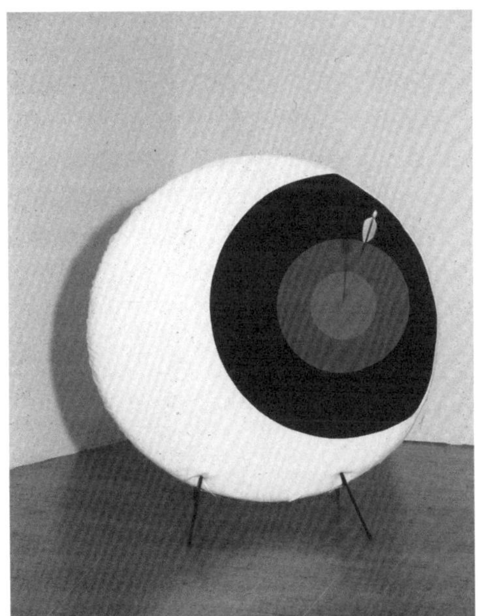

David Robbins
The Off-Target, 1994

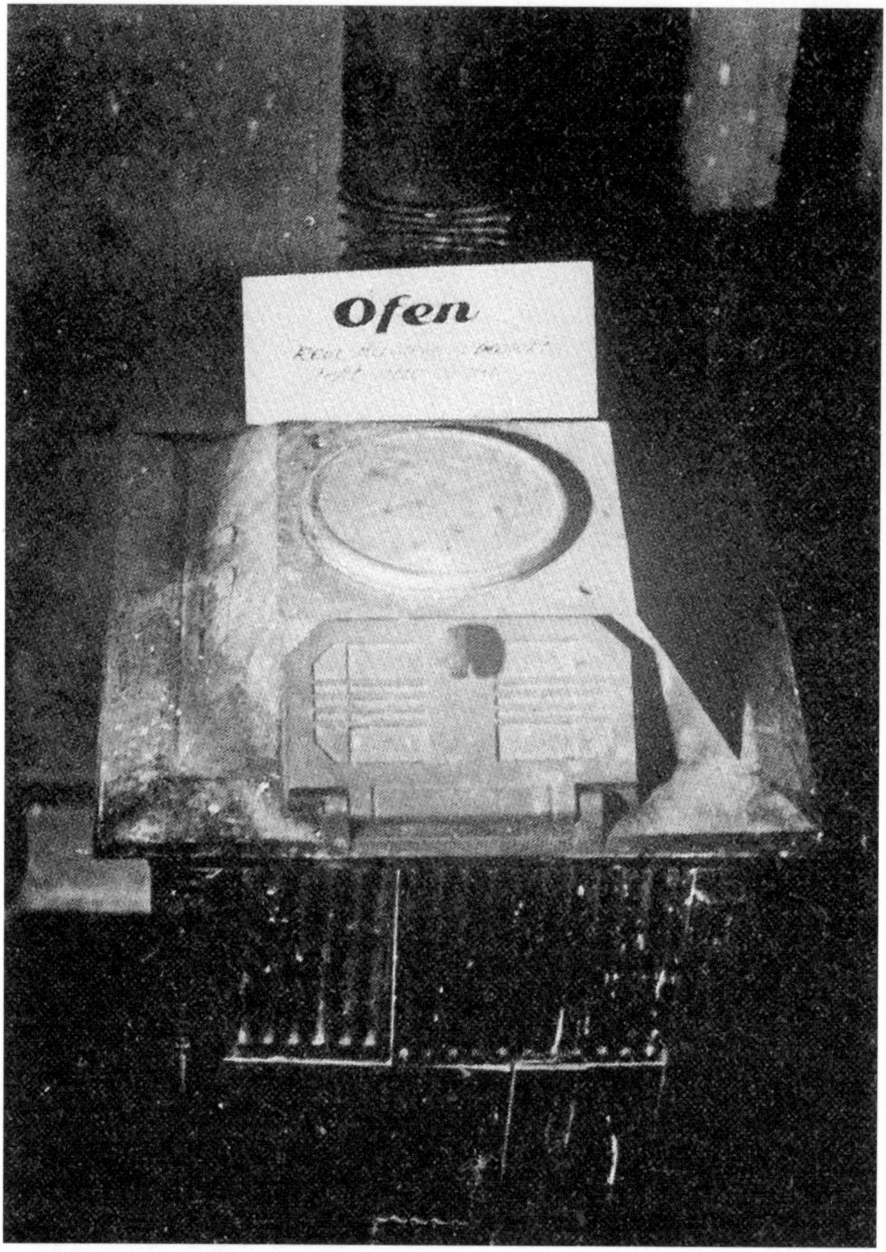

Karl Valentin
A Chamber Oven for the Production of Heat or Oven Not An Exhibit Object, It's Just Here

Another Comedian of the Actual

"Making fun of things": here is disrespect, in some measure, and belligerence as well. However much we dress it up or disguise it, comedy is aggressive. It may be just cream in that pie, but that pie is a missile. Indeed, comedy is so violently contrarian in essence that, were it possible, its trajectory would carry it free of the gravity of reality entirely. Comedy in its purest condition would secede from reality. Secession is impossible, though. Gravity—call it reality, call it the Actual—exists. Comedy is and always will be a subset of reality. The two are forever yoked. Tension is the result. A constant tension—pronounced or muted, savage or sublime—runs through comedy. Comedy expresses this tension. But comedy represents this tension too.

Although the tension is constant, the degree of its intensity does vary. It can be modulated. Conventional stage and screen comedies relax the tension. They dilute comedy's attack on reality through the addition of illusionism and make-believe. Concrete comedy, by contrast, comprises those strategies that intensify the tension between reality and comedy's argument with reality. Done for real, in real space, by people who are not make-believe characters in make-believe scenarios but instead and only themselves, concrete comedy consciously exploits the unsentimental power of the actual.

Among the imagination industries, the context of visual art has always been the official context of the actual. It is the site designated for self-conscious meditation upon our experience of the real. Michelangelo's *David* (1501–1504), seven feet of alabaster marble originally located on a pedestal outside the Palazzo Vecchio in Florence, and since 1873 removed to the Accademia Gallery, is as ineluctably real as you or me. The Accademia is not a movie set. The *David* wasn't created by an actor pretending to be a sculptor in a movie or a play about a sculptor but, rather, by a real 16th-century sculptor working with real marble in real space over a course of real time. Michelangelo enacted his brilliant behavior not for the sake of cameras or some make-believe scenario but for its own sake. The power of visual art is, and always has been, the power of real actions, inscribed, for their own sake, in the real. It is this power that the art context values, celebrates, reinforces, and protects.

No artist exploited the power of the actual in a more straightforward, unadulterated manner than Marcel Duchamp, the second father of concrete comedy.

The galvanized iron rack for drying wine bottles that makes up Duchamp's *Bottle Dryer* (1914) was purchased by the artist at a Paris department store in 1914, and was then signed by him. The term "readymade" would not be coined until after his move to New York in 1915, when more readymades appeared—pre-manufactured, intact objects to which, save for the addition of a signature or a title to lend "verbal color," nothing is done. There's no conversion of matter, only a conversion of energy. In 1915, Duchamp elevated a snow shovel to readymade status with the title *In Advance of the Broken Arm*, and, later that same year an unpainted tin chimney-ventilator becomes *Pulled at Four Pins* (1915). Sometime during January 1916 Duchamp considered designating as a readymade the Woolworth Building on lower Broadway in Manhattan. The readymades of 1917 include a wooden hat rack and the notorious *Fountain*, a porcelain urinal.

The readymade strips the two poles that define the comedic proposition—The Actual, And What Is Said About The Actual—of all stylistic decoration, then thrusts them forward into the heightened, magnified, amplified actual that defines the art context. There is the bottle dryer, and there is Duchamp's activation of an attitude toward the bottle dryer; actuality and perception are goaded into a stare-down. It's the latter that blinks, because, of course, only perception can blink. The object's hold on reality doesn't budge—it won't, it can't, it's too proudly, stubbornly real; so what shifts instead is our perception of it—our, yes, attitude toward it. The readymade is thus essentially performative, a prop on which perceptual change turns. Duchamp's is a theatricalizing gesture. The readymade reveals the art context as the Theater of the Actual.

Concrete comedy springs, then, from two sources. Concrete comedian Valentin contributed the idea that an object might be made with comic rather than aesthetic intent, and, furthermore, that a separate context for this new class of object might be established. Concrete comedian Duchamp contributed the idea that the context of heightened, magnified actuality we call the art context might itself be designated as theater. Even the art context, which is generally regarded (and most certainly regards itself) as the last word in imagination—might be treated as, annexed to, or absorbed into an amusement, a comedy. Out of this discovery will eventually grow the sophisticated comedies of Marcel Broodthaers, Maurizio Cattelan, and others.

That comedy might even be spoken about in this way; that some of us would prefer not to dilute comedy's power, its potential, its most radical promise by resorting to illusionism; that some among us might pursue, by the purest possible means, the challenge to reality which is intrinsic to all comedy—all this is, without question, a modern phenomenon. It is the sensibility of our time, not another. Yes, the Trojan Horse was a witty object. Yes, it's interesting to consider the mechanical amusements that Count Robert of Artois devised in the 14th century for his chateau of Hesdin, where "[s]tatues in his garden squirted water on visitors when they walked past or squawked words at them like parrots; a trapdoor dropped the passerby onto a featherbed below; a room, on the opening of the door, produced rain or snow or thunder" and "conduits under certain pressures 'wet the ladies from below.'"[1] Site-specific concrete comedy, in the 14th century! Remarkable! Count Robert is a predecessor to Herr Valentin. But the Count's gags were one-offs, the passing fancy of a rich man. A few centuries more will have to pass before anyone perceives a comedy of the real, for real, in real space and real time, to be a valid line of work. That doesn't come about until 1) an oddball Munich comedian demonstrates its validity, and 2) an audience concurs.

When it occurs it's an enormous change; from the strictly illusionist approach that dominated comedy to the Valentinian comedy of real things is quite a leap. There's no official date for the transformation, no recognized manifesto, no public declaration: "Once we were that, now we are this." We have only the evidence, strewn across the century just concluded, that something sparked and, then, having sparked, accelerated an expansion of our idea of what comedy could be. Initially manifested in the work of a handful of people, over the course of the century the anti-illusionistic impulse gathers steam, seeming to more and more comedic imaginations an appropriate stance, becoming a consistent strategy with strong appeal to a certain sensibility that, while uncommon, is not an iota less comic than those who chose to work the verbal, narrative, illusionistic side of the business.

The reasons for the change matter far less, of course, than the particulars of the comedy that have resulted from it. But since an evolutionary advance such as the concretist approach to comedy doesn't just happen, all by itself and out of nowhere, the curious mind naturally seeks to identify origins. Should we be searching for some catalyzing trauma, or did the change come about more positively, perhaps through some innovation in materials? Did it occur as a result of some trajectory within comedy itself or was it a response to outside forces? Had the idea of a concrete comedy lurked in the imagination through the centuries until something made it snap into focus and seem—just like that—attractively, irresistibly true?

We can't know. Because the concept of concrete comedy is an invention, and lacking a literature to help guide our inquiry, we can only speculate on its origins. And yet the speculative mist is not altogether formless. It is contained. It has a shape. Clues to the origin of the phenomenon do exist.

First of all, recall that we're discussing here a comedy of objects, a gestural, physical comedy, so we'd do well to concentrate our search on identifying historical events that affected our conception of objects, object-making, and, broadly, the man-made environment.

Another clue: concrete comedy emerged as a consistent approach to comedy only a decade or two into the beginning of the 20th century. With comedy such a fundamental response to existence, we can expect that anything substantially reconfiguring its nature will be sizeable, seismic, even cataclysmic. Nor does change on this scale and of this depth occur overnight; whatever brought about the transformation of our imagination of the comic from a near absolute reliance on the verbal and illusionistic to an increasingly full recognition of the value and the singularities of wit manifested physically and in real space, it got started well before its manifestation in the output of a lanky Bavarian comedian. It's a glacier we're looking for, not an avalanche.

Combine these scant yet substantive clues, and a strong candidate does eventually emerge: the Industrial Revolution. Beginning late in the 18th-century in England with a wave of steam, grease, and iron, spreading tsunami-like through the 19th century, and later gathering renewed momentum with innovations in electricity and chemistry, in each place where it took hold the Industrial Revolution destroyed a social order that had been in place for centuries and established a new one, countless aspects of which we still contend with today.

The Industrial Revolution forces abstraction onto the lives of everyone that it touches. Machines insinuate a wedge between the individual and the centuries-old handicrafts that had sustained existence and organized quotidian reality. "Nothing is now done directly, or by hand; all is rule and calculated contrivance," observed Thomas Carlyle in "Signs of the Times: the 'Mechanical Age,'" first published in 1829 in the midst of the upheaval. "For the simplest operation, some helps and accompaniments, some cunning abbreviating process is in readiness. Our old modes of exertion are all discredited, and thrown aside ... There is no end to machinery."[2] As the juggernaut of the revolution rolls over them, craft traditions suffer a trauma from which they never recover. Thousands of people are thrown out of work, their services replaced, disproportionately, by a small number of huge, tireless contraptions.

It is a kind of psychic violence. The machines disconnect people from a continuous, integrated sense of the relation between an action and the impact of that action on their environment. The sense of efficacy is diminished. The average person's knowledge of how the world worked gets abstracted away from them, and it stays abstracted. Self-reliance is cast adrift. Here's Carlyle, again:

> Not the external and physical alone is now managed by machinery, but the internal and spiritual also. Here too nothing follows its spontaneous course, nothing is left to be accomplished by old natural methods. Everything has its cunningly devised implements, its pre-established apparatus; it is not done by hand, but by machinery. Thus we have machines for Education: Lancastrian machines; Hamiltonian machines; monitors, maps, and emblems. Instruction, that mysterious communing of Wisdom with Ignorance, is no longer an indefinable tentative process, requiring a study of individual aptitudes, and a perpetual variation of means and methods, to attain the same end; but a secure, universal, straightforward business, to be conducted in the gross, by proper mechanism, with such intellect as comes to hand.[3]

Increasingly, finished products now just arrived, as if by magic, and the knowledge of how they're made becomes common to fewer and fewer people—to specialists. For most people, what had once, certainly, derived from hands-on experience, gradually grows blurrier and more infirm, until, eventually, the question of how the world gets put together takes on the condition of mystery.

And all of this is, it turns out, is only Phase One of abstraction's rule! Phase Two involves the conversion of all those people who previously had been self-reliant producers. They now have to be trained to consume, since someone has to absorb the machines' production!

With a flow of finished goods directed unceasingly at them, people get sophisticated about consuming. They learn quickly. Their attitudes toward the qualities of the inanimate grow ever baroque and abstract. The inanimate has been introduced into a web, and it can never again be considered apart from its place in that web: there is the thing, yes, but there is also what you say about the thing. What is said about the thing, it is soon discovered, can make people want the thing; thus, toward the end of the 19th-century, are born the modern advertising industry, the modern fashion industry, and the art market—culture emergent as industry. For the average person, life after the Industrial Revolution is an increasingly synthetic affair.

X-raying the effects of all this, Carlyle noted with dismay that:

> These things ... indicate a mighty change in the whole manner of existence. For the same habit regulates not our modes of action alone, but our modes of thought and feeling. Men are grown mechanical in head and in heart, as well as in hand. They have lost faith in individual endeavor, and in natural force, of any kind. Not for internal perfection, but for external combinations and arrangements, for institutions, constitutions—for Mechanism of one sort or other, do they hope and struggle. Their whole efforts, attachments, opinions, turn on mechanism, and are of a mechanical character.[4]

Is the broad psychological change that will eventually yield, among other phenomena, the attitude toward objects that we're terming "concrete comedy" manifested immediately, in the very generation that has had machine-bred abstraction brutally interjected between hand and production? It is not. It can't show up there because, for that generation, the change is trauma. A way of life ... gone! Shock and trauma attend its disappearance. Where is the comedy in that? What is there to have fun with in a mass of psychic wounds? Years must pass—will 50 be enough, will 70?—for the trauma to subside sufficiently that a subsequent generation might have the option of making sport with the abstraction. How many years must pass before a generation might regard the abstraction as a given, and find some comedy in it?

To speculate on the origins of a category of production that one has oneself invented is as audacious as it is amusing. Nevertheless, I believe that the successive generational responses to the effects wrought by the Industrial Revolution come closest to explaining the emergence of a concretist attitude toward comedy. Two generations after that first traumatized generation—after the traumatized parents, after the children of the traumatized parents, themselves shaped by contending with the parents' trauma—a fresh, young kind of mind steps forward, one that enjoys a different, more relaxed, natural, and even (gasp!) disrespectful relationship to the abstraction that now suffuses the man-made environment. For these fresh young minds of the early 20th century, the disconnect between hand and product is no longer the catastrophe it had been for their parents and grandparents. The disconnect is a done deal. The new kids dwelled in the done deal of the abstraction that the machine had introduced into their grandparent's lives. To the kids, this abstraction had acquired the neutrality of a fact. They were free to be philosophical about it. They were free to be amusing. They were free to take the disconnect and warm it up.

Not every kid, mind you. Particular kids. The kind of kids who, in any generation, are inclined to detect and/or contemplate and/or marry action to such invisible matters as these. Every generation turns up a few. (Valentin was one of them, Duchamp was another.) A few is usually all it takes, if they're the right few and the cards fall for them.

NOTES

1
Barbara W. Tuchman, *A Distant Mirror: The Calamitous 14th Century*, Alfred A. Knopf, New York 1978, p. 235.

2
Thomas Carlyle, "Signs of the Times: The 'Mechanical Age'" [first published in the *Edinburgh Review*, no. 98, 1829]; *The Collected Works of Thomas Carlyle*, vol. 3, Chapman and Hall, London 1858, p. 97–118. Available on-line at: http://www.victorianweb.org/authors/carlyle/signs1.html.

3
Carlyle, "Signs of the Times."

4
Ibid.

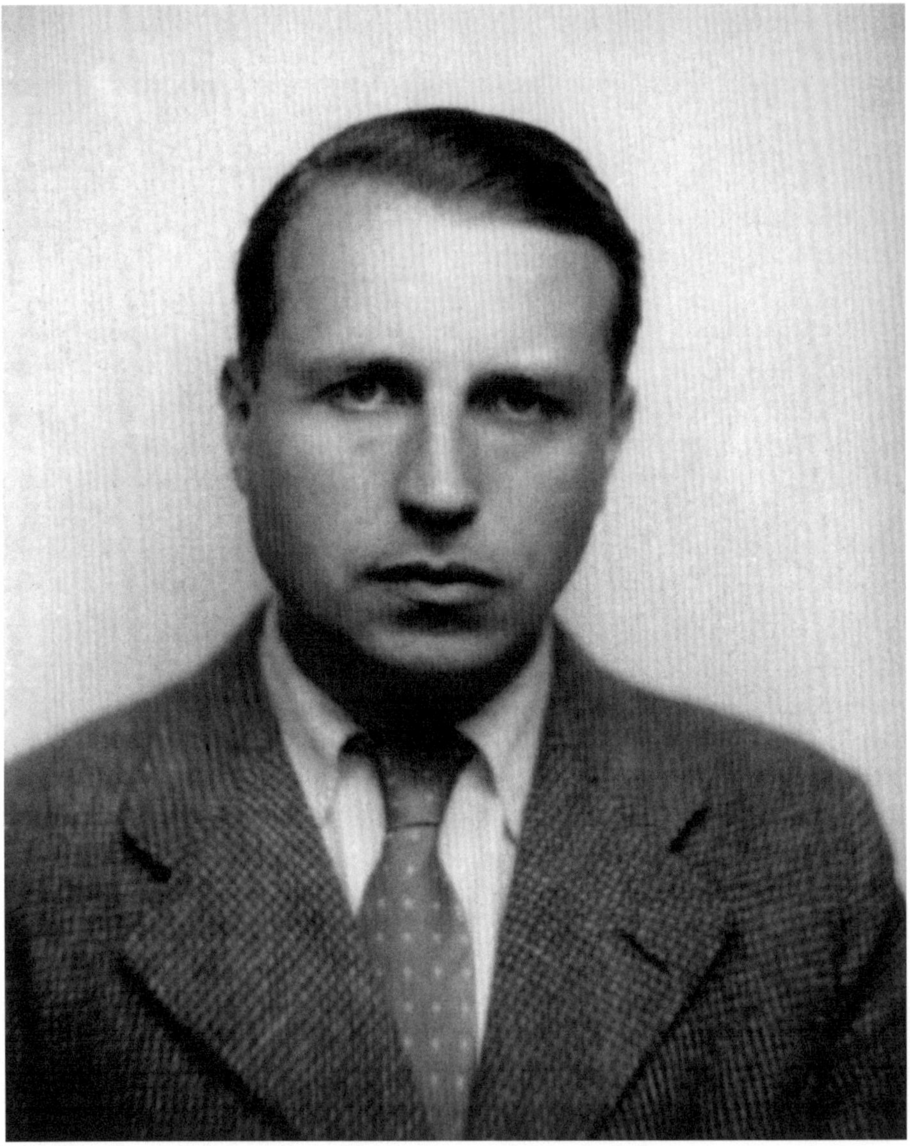

Portrait of Georges Bataille around 1933
Published in *Encyclopedia Acephalica (Atlas Arkhive Three: Documents of the Avant-Garde)*, ed. Robert Lebel and Isabelle Waldberg, Atlas Press, London 1995, p. 8

Louis Kaplan

BATAILLE'S LAUGHTER

> I told myself that if I happened to know what laughter was, I would know everything, I would have resolved the problem of philosophies. It seemed that to resolve the problem of laughter and to resolve the philosophical problem were evidently the same thing.
> —Georges Bataille, "Nonknowledge, Laughter, and Tears"[1]

Introduction: *Formless* Laughter

In *Formless: A User's Guide*, Rosalind Krauss and Yve-Alain Bois look at the story of modern art through the lens of Georges Bataille, focusing specifically on the force of the formless (*informe*) in all its valences as a means by which to understand a range of Euro-American avant-garde artistic practices from the suspended sculptures of Alberto Giacometti in the late 1920s to the horizontal canvases of Jackson Pollock in the 1950s, and beyond.[2] Organized as an artistic dictionary of operations and strategies that foreground Bataille's excessive and formless demand that the "universe resembles nothing" and "is something like a spider or spit,"[3] the project delivers a new mapping of artistic modernism that cuts across old debates between formalist, thematic, and historical accounts of the period. Staged as an exhibition at the Pompidou Center in the summer of 1996, *Formless* did much to elevate the writings of Bataille as a key resource for understanding "the originality of the avant-garde."[4]

Given the practical desires guiding Bois and Krauss' exercise, it is appropriate that one of the sections of *A User's Guide* cites Bataille's important essay "The Use Value of D.A.F. Sade" composed as a response to the shortcomings of André Breton's *Second Manifesto of Surrealism* (1930). In "Base Materialism," Bois reviews Bataille's anti-idealist and transgressive stance exemplified in his definition of heterology as the "science of what is totally other" and its alignment with agiology (sexual activity diverted from its useful functions) and scatology (the study of excrement).[5] What is surprising about this close reading is that it never alludes to the important role that laughter plays in what Bataille called a "heterological theory of knowledge." Bataille, in fact, makes this turn just a few pages later in the same essay when he insists that laughter marks the limit of philosophical speculation and that it is the necessary result (or end product) of "the practice of intellectual scatology" that overflows with waste products that cannot be assimilated by the philosophical system and its rational mode of thinking. Bataille writes: "As soon as the effort at rational comprehension ends in contradiction, the practice of intellectual scatology requires the excretion of unassimilable elements, which is another way of stating vulgarly that a burst of laughter is the only imaginable and definitively terminal result—and not the means—of philosophical speculation."[6] In heterological terms, Bataille's terminal laughter illustrates the transformation of the mouth from an organ of consumption to excretion. Heterology thus "leads to the complete reversal of the philosophical process which ceases to be the instrument of appropriation and now serves excretion."[7]

Unfortunately, Bois' analysis of heterology in "Base Materialism" avoids soiling itself as a practice of intellectual scatology and it thereby misses an encounter with this burst of Bataillean laughter. More broadly, *Formless* never discusses the paradoxical "use value" of Georges Bataille as an excremental or scatological humorist. It never considers what Bataille's heterological "philosophy of laughter" can bring to an investigation of the force of the formless. After all, Bataille put laughter (rather than the formless) at the center of both his philosophy and the problems that occupied him throughout his life. For the philosophy of laughter "is a philosophy that doesn't concern itself with problems other than those that have been given to me in this precise experience."[8] Perhaps there is something about the excessive aspects of Bataille's heterological thinking—whether scatological humor or the cuts of black comedy—that are too explosive or fragmentary to reduce, formalize, and comprehend, and that problematize the foundations of any cataloging project. The same oversight also arises in Hal Foster's discussion of Bataille in *Compulsive Beauty* in the context of a reading of Hans Bellmer's subversively sexualized *Dolls*. Foster recalls a Bataillean wing of Surrealism that recognized "the uncanny power of desublimation" and "its imbrication with the death drive."[9] But while he reviews Breton's critique of Bataille in the *Second Manifesto* as "an excrement philosopher,"[10] Foster also represses Bataille's own laugh track leading one to wonder what an analysis of Bellmer's *Dolls* would look like if processed through the lens of scatological or black humor.

I want to redress this shortcoming by reviewing a number of Bataille's texts that take up the question of laughter, particularly the pivotal lecture "Nonknowledge, Laughter, and Tears" (1953). In contrast to Bois, Krauss, and Foster, my goal is to address the ways in which the bursts of laughter that inform Bataille's reflections on death and nonknowledge as a crucial nexus of heterological forces can help us to think about the role of the comedic in modern art. As part of his "unfinished system of nonknowledge," Bataille's laughter mocks the instrumentalist desire of the academic treatise to codify knowledge of modern art in terms of a user's guide. A major section of this essay takes up a later text by Bataille in which he frames the exceptional cosmography of Max Ernst—completely absent from *Formless*—in terms of hilarity. But before attending to Bataille's reading of Ernst, I want to examine the contexts for and arguments of "Nonknowledge, Laughter, and Tears"—in particular how it engages with two major philosophical precedents on the question of laughter (in the work of Friedrich Nietzsche and Henri Bergson).

Unpacking "Nonknowledge"

On February 9, 1953, Georges Bataille gave a lecture on "Nonknowledge, Laughter, and Tears" [*"Non-savoir, rire et larmes"*] as the last of seven talks at the Collège Philosophique in Paris delivered over a six-year period. Bataille noted that this lecture resonated with the themes of the other three previous ones—"Consequences of Nonknowledge" (January 12, 1951); "The Teaching of Death" (May 8–9, 1952); and "Nonknowledge and Rebellion" (November 24, 1952)—to form a "coherent series of lectures."[11] It was for this reason that he published them together in *Tel Quel* in the summer of 1962 as "Lectures on Nonknowledge" ("*Conférences sur le non-savoir*") in one of his last publications. Nevertheless, Bataille thought that the final resting place for this series should be with *Theory of Religion* in an unpublished volume that was to bear the title *To Die Laughing, To Laugh Dying* (*Mourir de rire et rire de mourir*). The atheological thinker saw this book as a "general work on the effects of nonknowledge," and accordingly wrote a few notes toward a "Preface de *Mourir de rire*" at the end of 1952.[12] Bataille's projected title points to the fabled figure of fatal hilarity, to the reality or fantasy of a lethal joke that inflicts death by laughter on the one who hears or reads it. Whether leading to cardiac arrest or asphyxiation, the history of fatal hilarity goes back to the third century BC and the ridiculous demise of the Greek Stoic philosopher Chrypsippus, who supposedly died of laughter after giving his donkey wine and watching it trying to feed on figs.[13] It has been articulated more recently in a sketch from the first episode of the British TV comedy series, *Monty Python's Flying Circus* as "The Funniest Joke in the World."[14] The Python's review of joke warfare by the British against the Germans in World War II features the attempt to produce a joke so funny that it triggers death by laughter. Interestingly, Bataille contemplated the possibility of death by laughter while he was writing *Guilty*, begun five days after the German invasion of Poland in September 1939. Moreover, "The Divinity of Laughter" sections were written in 1943 against the backdrop of Nazi-occupied Vichy France and the Holocaust as a work in progress. Denis Hollier notes that "no other book has given me such an impression of being impregnated with war atmosphere, the weather of wartime."[15] In this way, Bataille's anguished and culpable laughter plays itself out in close proximity to the catastrophes of World War II.

Bataille wrestles with these contingencies by questioning the oddness of the conjunction of death and laughter. In the section "I'm Trembling, Laughing," Bataille speculates on this bizarre image: "Can someone really laugh to death? (The image is bizarre, but I don't have another.)"[16] A little earlier in "The Need For Laughter," he directs the fantasy of fatal hilarity at himself, exclaiming: "Oh, if I could *die* from this laughing!"[17] The second part of the projected book title ("To Laugh Dying") goes to the heart of Bataille's vision of laughter as intimately bound up with our relationship to death—laughing in the face of death and on account of death. Bataille locates a nervous and ambivalent laughter brought on by the fear of death as well as his attempts to overcome it in *Guilty*. "I react to the fear of death with laughter—it stimulates me!—while I struggle against it (against fear, against death)."[18]

While Bataille's intimate confessions and speculations on laughter are present in *Guilty* and numerous other texts, "Nonknowledge, Laughter, and Tears" was one of the few public addresses he made about this favorite topic; and it afforded him the opportunity to make a sustained and sophisticated reflection in the context of an intellectual forum. The lecture text gives the reader access to Bataille's liminal approach to laughter and its relationship to the impossible. Bataille's theory of laughter (if we can so describe it) can be summarized in these five words: "*the unknown makes us laugh*" (NLT, p. 135). For Bataille, "the unknown character of the laughable would not be accidental, but essential" (NLT, p. 135). Nevertheless, "the unknown makes us laugh" should not be read as a direct causal explanation. For how could one ever properly account for or comprehend the experience of laughter when one is exposed to what is "unknown" through it? In other words, Bataille's theorem is framed by an aporetic structure that takes us to the point where thinking can no longer venture and where a burst of laughter exceeds or ruptures it. This is why nonknowledge remains the unforeseeable and mysterious "cause" of our laughter. Bataille's insistence on the intimate connection between laughter and nonknowledge at the limit of philosophy reflects his ongoing discontent with the restricted economy of Hegelian dialectics and its quest for absolute knowledge. For Bataille, Hegel's thinking constitutes a refusal to acknowledge laughter as an expenditure without reserves that cannot be contained by the system. The staking out of this wasteful position for laughter that exceeds or ruptures any totalizing claims put Bataille at odds with Breton's more Hegelian approach to humor and his belief in its philosophical apprehension. In his *Anthology of Black Humor* (at the very point, in fact, where he inserts the metaphor of the black sphinx), Breton takes up Hegel's concept of objective humor, praising it as an idea that permits "humor [to] take a giant step forward in the domain of knowledge."[19]

In Bataille's text we can distinguish two registers that organize his discussion of nonknowledge and the laughter that it brings in its wake. On the one hand, there is a restricted economy that conserves and reserves knowledge even as it unleashes what Bataille calls a "minor laughter" (NLT, p. 144). In this register, nonknowledge leads to laughter on account of the suspension or bracketing of knowledge. Here, the one who laughs does not "know nothing by the fact" of his laughter, nor belongs automatically to a know-nothing party. Instead, laughter bursts forth when something unexpected happens in contradiction to what we know: "If laughter is the effect of nonknowledge, in principle, laughter does not have the fact of not knowing as its object, we don't accept the idea that we know nothing by the fact that we laugh. Something unexpected is produced, something contrary, something in contradiction to the knowledge that we have" (NLT, p. 144). To develop his notion of "minor laughter," Bataille turns to an essay by Charles Eubé on "The Tragic Foundation of Laughter."[20] For Eubé, laughter functions as a type of Nietzschean "active forgetting" because it implies "the refusal to *accept* that which most profoundly within us, we *know*" (NLT, p. 144). Laughter thus functions in the realm of an "as if" and in terms of a willing suspension of knowledge and belief. Bataille continues: "In fact, someone who laughs, in principle, does not abandon his science, but he refuses to accept it for a while, a limited time, he lets himself pass beyond it through the movement of laughter, so that what he knows is destroyed, but in his depths he preserves the conviction that, just the same it isn't destroyed" (NLT, p. 144).

With its emphasis on the preservation of beliefs and convictions and its refusal to abandon what science knows, "minor laughter" remains trapped in a restricted economy. It is steeped in a mode of calculation rather than inscribed in a general economy of "meaningless play."[21] Bataille was quite aware of the limits of Eubé's position and he therefore spoke of the need to place a "major laughter beside a minor laughter" (NLT, p. 144). This second register, of major laughter, affirms nonknowledge in a more ecstatic way. It is more absolute in its inflection as it engages the experience of laughter as a consequence of "knowing nothing" and sets itself in relationship with the impossible.[22] In the following passage, Bataille articulates this vision of nonknowledge as *nothing*, using italics to stress the difficulty of speaking silence in the language of philosophy, even a philosophy of laughter. This register of nonknowledge appears almost

Buddhist in tone: "When I speak of nonknowledge now, I mean essentially that I know nothing, and that if I am still talking, it is essentially insofar as I have a knowledge that brings me to *nothing*. This is particularly true in the kind of knowledge that I am developing before you, since it is in order to succeed in placing myself before this *nothing* about which I am speaking, to put myself and my interlocutors, if it is possible, before this *nothing*" (NLT, p. 140–141). Bataille's discourse on nothing can be read as a mission statement for the laughing philosopher, exposing the comic paradoxes in which he is necessarily embroiled. He seeks to coax his interlocutors into a sovereign experience or a direct confrontation with nothing, while at the same time he knows (and laughs about the fact) that the sovereign operation demands life. Speaking (of) silence, he wants to bring language to the limits of language and to the point where laughter breaks out. Derrida has written beautifully of the double binds of the laughing philosopher who seeks to affirm Bataille's major laughter as "absolute risk," or better, as the simulation of absolute risk. "Laughter, which constitutes sovereignty in its relation to death, is not a negativity as has been said. And it laughs at itself, a 'major' laughter laughs at a 'minor' laughter, for the sovereign operation also needs life—the life that welds the two lives together—in order to be in relation to itself in the pleasurable consumption of itself. Thus, it must simulate, after a fashion, the absolute risk, and it must laugh at this simulacrum."[23]

Laughing Divinely with Nietzsche

"Nonknowledge, Laughter, and Tears" also gives Bataille the opportunity to express his indebtedness and "fundamental connection" (NLT, p. 142) to Friedrich Nietzsche and the *fröhliche Wissenschaft* [gay science]. Insisting on the experience of laughter as that which marks the limits of philosophical appropriation, Bataille suggests that his rapport with Nietzsche is not only reducible to their shared thinking about the meaning of laughter. He also points to their shared experience of laughter as divine, as an effect of nonknowledge that stops thinking in its tracks. Bataille writes: "I think Nietzsche's thought makes this experience very clear. It is given in particular, naturally, in the importance that Nietzsche attributed to laughter, and this in a very large number of passages, but especially in a rather late text in the posthumous work: 'To see tragic characters founder and to be able to laugh ... this is divine.' I don't think that what I am representing in general when I talk about nonknowledge and about the experience [of] its effects [can] be disassociated from an expression like this one" (NLT, p. 143). Bataille omits here part of the original text from Nietzsche's posthumous *Will to Power* and so the above citation differs from Bataille's full quotation of the same passage in his essay "Nietzsche's Laughter" (1942).[24] This elision has an impact on his thinking about "the divinity of laughter" and its meaning. In "Nonknowledge, Laughter, and Tears," laughter puts the one who laughs in a dominant position over and against the one who is laughed at (i.e., the tragic character who founders). As Bataille interprets Nietzsche's text, "In order to laugh, for example, it is necessary that one not risk losing one's dominant position" (NLT, p. 143). Even if this laughter takes place within the ensemble of effects that he connects with nonknowledge, Bataille sketches a fundamental power relationship that offers a corollary to the Hegelian master and slave dialectic. Simply put, this particular vision of laughter allows the one who laughs to occupy the space of mastery (*Herrschaft*). As Bataille phrases it, this is "laughter that becomes divine insofar as it can be the laughter that one has in seeing a tragic character founder" (NLT, p. 143). Bataille's position corresponds to the visions of aggressive or tendentious humor articulated by Henri Bergson, Sigmund Freud [see, "Humour," in this volume] and others in which the one who laughs feels superior.[25]

Nevertheless, if we were to stop the laugh track at this point, we would only have access to half the story of Bataille's laughter. That is why it is necessary to stress the difference between "minor laughter" and "major laughter." For only major laughter raises the comic stakes of sovereignty and takes laughter from a logic of domination to the level of the impossible. The only way to make this leap involves a paradoxical identification and sympathy with the tragic character who founders in a gesture that explodes the very notion of the subject and contaminates the distinction between the agents of laughter and their objects. In this way, Bataille links "the divinity of laughter" to the affirmation of death and the impossible, to the contagious affirmation of the demise of the one who laughs. In his perceptive essay on "The Laughter of Being," Mikkel Borch-Jacobsen puts it this way: "We do not laugh, in other words, because we are not dead. We laugh, very much to the contrary, because we are dead, because we are, laughing, ourselves the dead man."[26] In other words, major laughter shifts the locus of divinity from a position of dominance to an affirmation of death. Nietzsche's communication of sympathy, emotion, and profound understanding prevents any attempt at distancing his laughter from his mortal end (what Bataille marks as Nietzsche's inability to forget himself). Such sympathy is figured by Bataille as impersonal because the impossibility of the subject (always other than itself) has been exposed in a becoming that laughs at being. In "Nietzsche's Laughter," Bataille recites the same posthumous text without elision: "He said no to life while it was easy: but yes when it took the form of the impossible. He could not forget himself, noting these few words around the time of Zarathrustra: 'To see tragic characters founder and to be able to laugh, despite the profound understanding, emotion, and sympathy that we feel, this is divine.' In principle, laughing is the reaction the impossible offers when sympathy isn't personally at stake."[27]

The "divinity of laughter" as the lesson of Zarathrustra is intimately linked to the "putting to death of God."[28] Bataille affirms the experience of laughter in "Nonknowledge, Laughter, and Tears" as atheological: "I will willfully give this experience, and the reflection that accompanies it, the name *atheology*, formed with the privitive prefix *a*, and the word *theology*" (NLT, p. 146). And he asks rhetorically in "Nietzsche's Laughter": "But what does the divine attained in laughter mean, if not the absence of God?"[29] By making laughter the sacred cornerstone of his atheology, Bataille points to another outcome of positing nonknowedge and embracing *amor fati* in place of the theological solemnities of divine will and providence. Naked in the night of nonknowledge and laughing in the face of death, the one who laughs takes up the subject position of a god who affirms his/her own demise and loss of subjectivity and with the (sovereign) will to make such a claim.[30] This is a vision of laughter grounded in tragedy but one that does not allow itself the comforts of Aristotlean catharsis and its flight from the impossible. In contrast, "Nietzsche's Laughter" is a divine gesture that holds "life, without elusion, to the standard of the impossible."[31] It transmutes tragedy into the divinity of laughter by means of an affirmation of becoming and in a sovereign letting go of being and its essence. It offers a comic posture that laughs at being (revealing it as always other than itself) and at the death of being. Bataille substitutes the laughing god

Zarathrustra for the tragic philosopher Aristotle. "Laughing at the impossible as it overcomes me, laughing knowing I am sinking, I am a god who mocks the possible that he is. I no longer hold life to the standard of the impossible in order to escape it, as nature does in tragedy, in Aristotle's theory of catharsis. Zarathrustra made laughter *sacred*."[32]

The Disappointment of Bergson's *Laughter*

> My only contact with accepted philosophy around this time (in 1920) was meeting Henri Bergson in London. Forewarned, I read *Laughter*, which, like the philosopher in person, disappointed me (as early as this period I had an extreme mind). But the problem of laughter appeared indisputably foundational.
> —Georges Bataille, "Aphorisms for the 'System'"[33]

While Nietzsche is a positive role model for Bataille on the question of laughter, this is not the case for Henri Bergson, who gets mixed reviews in "Nonknowledge, Laughter, and Tears" and elsewhere. Bataille recalls a primal scene in his philosophical life when he met Bergson in 1920. This was an encounter that Bataille had a compulsion to repeat, and the retellings mark the anxiety-fraught influence exerted by the authorial voice of *Laughter* over a young Bataille as he sought to surpass a philosophical father figure with his own ideas about laughing matters. At the age of 23 the bibliophilic Bataille traveled to London to research at the British Museum where he was "received into a home where Bergson was also received" (NLT, p. 139). In order to make a good impression, the aspiring intellectual boned-up on the work of the famous thinker in preparation for the meeting. Bataille confessed that he did some remedial reading at the museum and that the book of—rather overdetermined—choice was Bergson's *Laughter* (1899). Bataille's description of his preparations to overcome his Bergsonian lack points to what becomes crucial for his own reflections on and experiences of why it is that we laugh—the nonknowledge that brings one to the limit of philosophy in general. "But I had the very common reaction that one might have to the idea that one is going to meet a great philosopher; one is embarrassed to know nothing, or nearly nothing, about his philosophy.

Then … I went to the British Museum, and I read *Laughter* by Bergson" (NLT, p. 139).

Bergson begins his book with a fundamental question: "What does laughter mean?"[34] He responds to the enigma of laughter and its meaning by providing a mechanized account in tune with the move toward assembly-line processes and thereby prefiguring the formalization of slapstick comedy that would dominate silent film in the first decades of the 20th century. Bergson postulates a comic theory based on the advent of mechanical personhood, legislating thus for laughter: "Let us at once state the law which seems to govern all the phenomena of this kind. It may indeed be deduced without any difficulty from the considerations stated above. *The attitudes, gestures, and movements of the human body are laughable in exact proportion as that body reminds us of a mere machine.*"[35] Bataille never doubted that this was an important theory ("one of the most profound theories that anyone has developed" [NLT, p. 139]) and he even defended it against unjustified criticism (Bergson's "very well known … theory"—"that of the mechanism applied to the living being"—"is sometimes the object of a hardly justified discredit" [NLT, p. 134]). But what did warrant criticism in Bataille's estimation was that Bergson's theory did not actually solve the enigma of laughter: it provided only a delimited theory of the comic.[36] Nevertheless, the most important thing that Bataille took away from Bergson was that laughter was a worthy philosophical subject that demanded his rigorous reflection. But Bataille would part ways with Bergson by contending that laughter was not just some "little problem."[37] On the contrary, Bataille conceived of it as the most important philosophical problem to think about and live with: "I told myself that if I happened to know what laughter was, I would know everything, I would have resolved the problem of philosophies" (NLT, p. 140). In contrast to Bergson, Bataille believed that solving the riddle of the Sphinx of laughter demanded that we take philosophy to its limit.

In his unpublished autobiographical notes, "Aphorisms for the 'System'" (1952), Bataille was more candid in his philosophical criticism of Bergson's *Laughter*, and his personal disappointment with it given his own "extreme mind" (AFS, p. 153). This self-description also resonates with Bataille's attitude toward laughter as an experience at the limits of thinking. "Aphorisms for the 'System'" is an impassioned, even intoxicated, text that reads like the confession of a lapsed Catholic forced to leave the sober fold while doubled over in laughter and riding high on its atheological revelations. In it, Bataille moves quickly from a would-be, self-abnegating, Catholic monk to an aspiring, stand-up comic philosopher who espouses the "divinity of laughter" and for whom laughter "was tantamount to God on the level of lived experience" (AFS, p. 153). By joining this heretical and subversive cult of laughter (mixed with some equally transgressive "pleasant sensuality"), Bataille confesses that his "entire thought resolved itself in this immense hilarity" (AFS, p. 154). This telling statement takes the comic philosopher to the limits of telling in a movement that signals the explosion of thought into laughter. But because Bataille's religious beliefs cannot withstand "the flood of laughter that I underwent [that] made a game of these beliefs" (NLT, p. 140), he situates the problem of laughter as "indisputably foundational" rather than "reduced to this insignificance that is commonly accorded to it, and which Bergson described very poorly" (AFS, p. 153). For Bataille, such a reduction was the result of a one-sided consideration of "laughter without thought" (AFS, p. 153).

Bataille's invocation of laughter as "indisputably foundational" affords a comic aporia or impasse for thinking in that it offers as ground something which subverts or mocks the very possibility of foundations. Bataille refuses to see laughter like Bergson as a "little problem" or "seedy comedy" (AFS, p. 153) housed within the confines of philosophical thought. Meanwhile, Bataille also argues that "thought without laughter seemed mutilated" (AFS, p. 153). This is a fascinating figure in that it points to the castration of thinking if and when it disavows or suppresses the will to laughter. Mired in the restricted economy of instrumental use and function, such mutilated thinking does not risk itself. It cuts off and cuts itself off as a mode of thinking that forecloses the possibility of laughter rather than openly celebrating those comic cuts that affirm our finitude. In a radical reversal, the philosopher of play gives laughter precedence situating it as both "antecedent to my thought" and something that can "carry me further than thought" (AFS, p. 153). All in all (or nothing in nothing), Bataille inscribes laughter, then, as an effect of nonknowledge set in relation with death and the impossible.

Max Ernst: The Imprudence of Hilarity

During a difficult period for Bataille's health (he was in the advanced stages of cerebral arteriosclerosis),[38] just two years before his death, Bataille published "Max Ernst, Philosopher!" (1960).[39] In this short homage to Ernst, Bataille refuses to follow art historical conventions that would frame or classify him as an exemplary Surrealist artist—in fact, he never uses the word "Surrealism" at all. Instead, Bataille brings Ernst into relationship with philosophical discourse noting the autobiographical detail that "as a young man Max Ernst would have liked to become a philosopher, to study philosophy" (MEP, p. 134). Bataille frames Ernst as a philosopher but with a difference that is registered by means of inflection or intoxication, by raising the stakes of philosophy's normally sober and restrained tones. One is immediately struck by the exclamation point in the title of the article that emphatically marks the excess of philosophy whether in its declarative or interrogative mode. By invoking the apposition in the form of an exclamatory utterance, Bataille announces that Max Ernst is a philosopher with something more—or that philosophy has gained some pith or punch from its association with this artist, who is envisioned, in turn, as a philosopher of exclamation. From the perspective of an inquiry into the role of the comedic in modern art, one suspects that for Bataille the "surplus value" that accrues to Ernst's practice on account of this exclamation mark is already linked to a burst of laughter, to those "explosive noises from the larynx" (NLT, p. 134).

A marked contrast opens up between the philosophical stances of Ernst and Bergson with a clear preference given to the playful antics of Dadamax. While Bergson is mocked in a derogatory fashion as "this prudent little man, this *philosopher*,"[40] Ernst and his exclamatory philosophy are celebrated for acquiring what Bataille calls the "imprudence of hilarity." Hilarity is imprudent because it does not hold back or reserve itself, allowing laughter to burst forth. Bataille delivers this message in a rhetorical flourish that puts Ernst face to face with a new type of philosophy comparable in its mission to Nietzsche's gay science: "If one day philosophy acquired the imprudence of hilarity, could we still say that Max Ernst, creating the universe from his canvases, would turn his back on it?" (MEP, p. 135). While Bergson confines the problem of laughter to a restricted economy in his little book, the playful Ernst risks philosophical prudence and the loss of meaning in cosmographical creations and hallucinatory visions that are more than willing to imagine what is disorderly, hilarious, and ridiculously absurd. Ernst's work entertains an economy without reserves that confronts its own worklessness. Inscribing meaning as a function of play, Ernst is the visionary artist in the guise of the laughing philosopher who "recognizes the powerlessness of work, [and] on the contrary, is dazzled and fascinated by the *play* which serves no purpose" (MEP, p. 135). By imagining Ernst's artistic practice as if "one day philosophy acquired the imprudence of hilarity," Bataille returns to the same figure that he used in writing about his own comic conversion experience when his "thought resolved itself in this immense hilarity" (AFS, p. 154). In both cases, philosophy comes up against its limit and gives way to the explosion of laughter contained within it. It is interesting to point out that in another one of Bataille's essays on contemporary art he frames his friend André Masson in terms of the painter's desire for liberation from any purposeful and restricted economy driven by work. The artist must break away from the servility that would confine him to a single function. As Bataille writes, "At this moment, his passion ceases to be painting, and becomes liberty."[41] For Bataille, this is how Masson's art "carries us to breaking point" and "from that moment, we can only remain in the impossible."[42] As we know from other texts, such tarrying with the impossible signals the opening onto laughter.

In *Cut with the Kitchen Knife: The Weimar Photomontages of Hannah Höch*, Maud Lavin reviews the career of the most famous female artist associated with the practice of photomontage in its formative period and whose work reflected on the mass media image of the New Woman in Weimar Germany. Lavin insists that Höch's photomontages are two-pronged attacks where "strategies of pleasure are coupled with the representation of anger to generate ideas of liberating, transformative utopias."[43] She also emphasizes the role that ironic humor plays in these utopian imaginings that put the pleasure principle into the service of critique. "The intriguing tension between the anger and pleasure of her works, often manifested through an ironic humor, also raises questions about the interaction of critiques of present-day and utopian desires for the future in representation."[44] While such anger implies that a degree of violence is exercised through Höch's kitchen knife collage cuts in their slashing against domestication, Ernst's "imprudence of hilarity" moves well beyond ironic humor. In Bataille's reading of Ernst's abysmal laughter, the pleasure principle confronts the death drive or, as Denis Hollier puts it, the carnival acknowledges the slaughterhouse.[45]

From a Bataillean perspective, the cosmological game played by Ernst is far from frivolous. Ernst's humor (like his proper name) is deadly serious: it laughs in the face of the abyss and answers to the fear of being swallowed up in the collapse of the real.[46] The playful Ernst also becomes a stand-in for Bataille in a clear-cut case of artistic cross-identification. Whether using paper or canvas, these two brothers in arms sound the death knell of philosophy and "throw the possibility of work into disorder" (MEP, p. 135). Bataille looks to Ernst's corpus of paintings and collages as a type of body double in which the disorderly forces of the formless are inscribed visually. "Next to this friend he accepts being swallowed up in this collapse of the real, in which death, half-glimpsed, compellingly represents the decisive move [*le jeu décisif*], in which the world, as it ceases to exist, falls apart; where thought is only the measureless applause given to the death of thought" (MEP, p. 135). It is significant that these speculations about the powerful impact of Ernst's artistry end in "the death of thought" as another figure for nonknowledge. The "measureless applause given to the death of thought" (like the Zen master's sound of one hand clapping) is a response to the hilarious laughter provoked by Ernst's collaged staging of the collapse of the real where the cosmos goes slapstick, where it ceases to exist and falls apart.

In *Max Ernst und die Romantik*, Ursula Lindau interprets Ernst's project in relation to the German Romantic tradition that began with Friedrich Schlegel and his keen interest in the power of wit and irony as literary devices. Lindau argues that Ernst's artistic innovations of collage and frottage exemplify the principle of wit that underlies his entire work. As she puts it, "For Max Ernst, wit is in this comprehensive sense a founding principle of his work which realizes itself first as collage and later also as frottage technique."[47] Lindau stresses in particular how Ernst portrays the discovery of both collage and frottage as "shocking experiences, in which 'the unexpected and the sudden' entered" (MER, p. 26), and one notices how such language parallels the eruption of laughter itself. Lindau's book offers close readings of numerous examples that demonstrate Ernst's coupling of wit and collage in works that breed a "systematic confusion" (MER, p. 28). In contrast, what is most peculiar about Bataille's "Max Ernst, Philosopher!" arises from the fact that there is no direct reference to a painting or collage by the profilic Ernst to illustrate what Bataille says about his "turbulent and violent world" (MEP, p. 135) and apocalyptic wit. This leads us to the ironically entitled *Quiétude* and other pieces in Ernst's stunning collage novel *The Hundred Headless Woman/La femme 100 têtes* (1929).[48] But before discussing these images, I want to invoke some of the compelling connections between Ernst's monstrous figure (which plays and puns between the hydra-headed and the headless woman) and Bataille's Acephalic man, for they make a lovely post-humanist couple. The decapitated figures of the Acephalic man and the hundred headless woman point both to Bataille's and Ernst's critiques of rationality and to their fascination with the violent cuts upon which collage depends. Ernst acknowledged that he composed his first collage novel "with systematic violence"[49] and reflected on his own complex character and the difficulty of reconciling "the gentleness and moderation of his expressions with the calm violence which is the essence of his thought."[50] Whether decapitating or multiplying, the violence exercised in the collaged universe of *The Hundred Headless Woman* provokes playful reshufflings, bizarre displacements, and absurd incongruities. Furthermore, by its very exemplification of Ernst's collage practice, *The Hundred Headless Woman* insists on the affirmation of the irrational. As Ernst remarked, "What is the noblest conquest of collage? The irrational. It is the magistral eruption of the irrational in all fields of art, poetry, science, fashion, the private life of individuals, the private life of nations. He who says collage, says the irrational."[51]

Illustrated by André Masson for the first issue of the journal *Acéphale* in June 1936, the headless man underscores Bataille's anarchic vision of the cosmos emblematized by a society that cuts off the head and refuses its governance of the human organism. In a displacement that foregrounds Bataille's fascination with the connection between eroticism and death, Acephalic man has the image of a death's head or skull in the place of the male genitals. The figure also brandishes a knife in one hand (the better to cut things up) and a blazing heart (of the excessive god Dionysius) in the other. Posed simultaneously as a critique of cerebral rationality and an affirmation of the belly laugh, this is an unsettling and monstrous vision of atheological abandon where "man has escaped from his head like the condemned man from his prison."[52] Bataille explicates Masson's illustration in "The Sacred Conspiracy": "Beyond what I am, I meet a being who makes

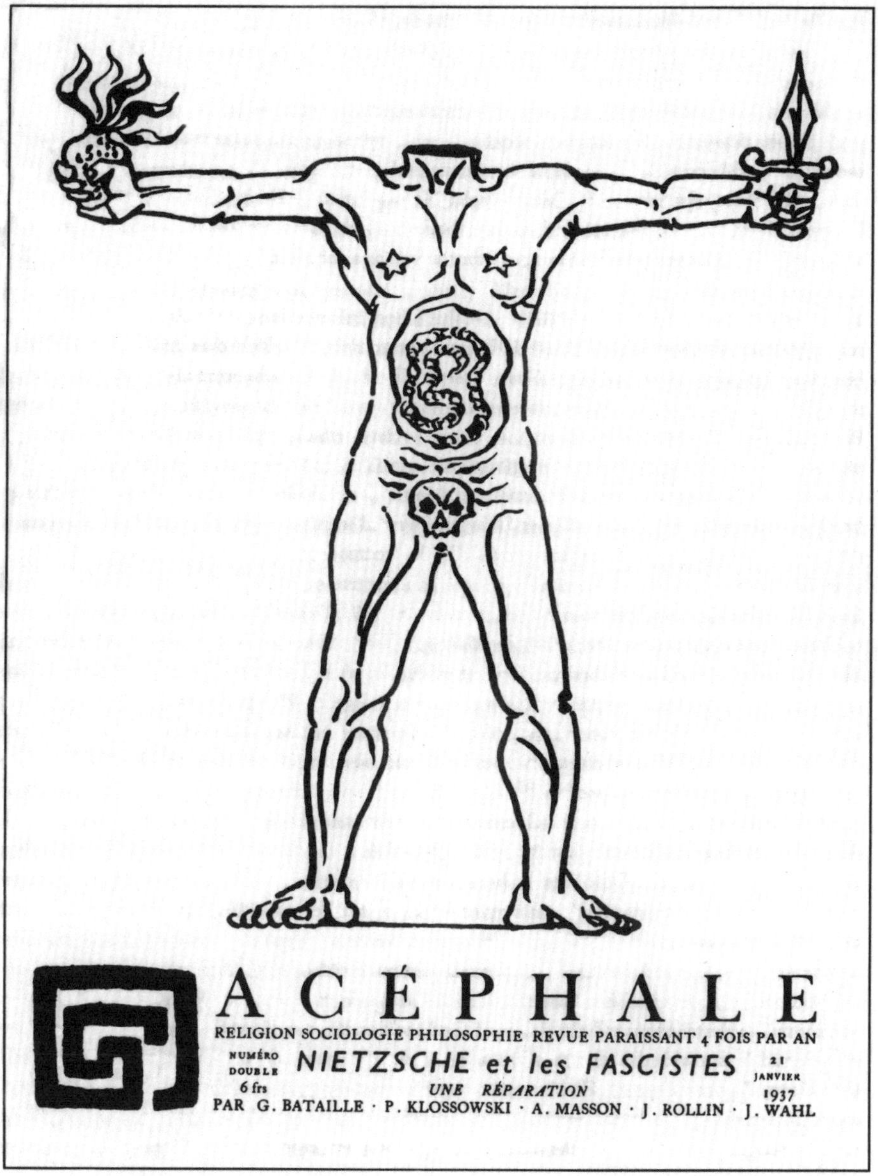

Cover of the first issue of *Acéphale* (June 1936) with a drawing by André Masson
Published in *Encyclopedia Acephalica (Atlas Arkhive Three: Documents of the Avant-Garde)*, ed. Robert Lebel and Isabelle Waldberg, Atlas Press, London 1995, p. 13

me laugh because he is headless, who fills me with anguish because he is made of innocence and crime." Bataille's dialectical conjunction of criminality and innocence alludes to the ways in which anarchic Dionysian laughter trumps any rule-bound sense of morality that seeks to distinguish between good and evil. Instead, Acephalic laughter is aligned to the affirmation of "the ridiculous absurdity that would be *undifferentiated being*" which Bataille locates in Ernst's collage visions (MEP, p. 134).

Quiétude exemplifies "the *playful* and *violent* way" (MEP, p. 134) in which Ernst responded to philosophy and its totalizing claims by making mocking use of collage. It is a staging of the unknown and disastrous forces that make us laugh. The collage features a man adrift at sea dressed in the uniform of business reclining on a comfortable chair, with his eyes shut as if asleep. Unbeknownst to him, a wild and turbulent storm in the order of a tsunami rages around him threatening to sink his armchair/ship. A detached arm swimming next to him may belong to someone who has already been drowned in the deluge. Meanwhile, a geyser of water jets sky high, engulfing a lighthouse that is no match for the impending forces of the formless. The collage shows us how the formless is often a source of gallows humor, for *Quiétude* offers a perfect demonstration of "being swallowed up in this collapse of the real." It illuminates the limits of instrumental logic and rational thinking because "philosophy cannot escape the perspective of the instant when the ground will slip away, of this instant in which nothing more will remain which does not slip away" (MEP, p. 135). In this way, *Quiétude*'s laughter rests on unraveling any false sense of security or tranquility. Such laughter in the face of the abyss affirming the slipping away and the dissolution of the subject pervades *Quiétude*, "Sea of Serenity," and a number of Ernst's collages stitched together from disparate images culled from 19th-century illustrated novels.

Bataille's blinding insights into the violence of these practices confront how "cut up" engages both collage and comedy. In "Beyond Seriousness," Bataille praises the sacrificial and sacred space of the slaughterhouse "where nothing remains that is not cut to pieces."[53] While Bataille does not address collage directly in "Max Ernst, Philosopher!" he clearly sees something of the *abattoir* in both Ernst's collage practice and the cutups of comedy.[54] Indeed, in a short passage where its operations are implicated, Bataille first imagines a "universal vanishing" where "nothing remains" (MEP, p. 134), then quickly backtracks from this vision in the face

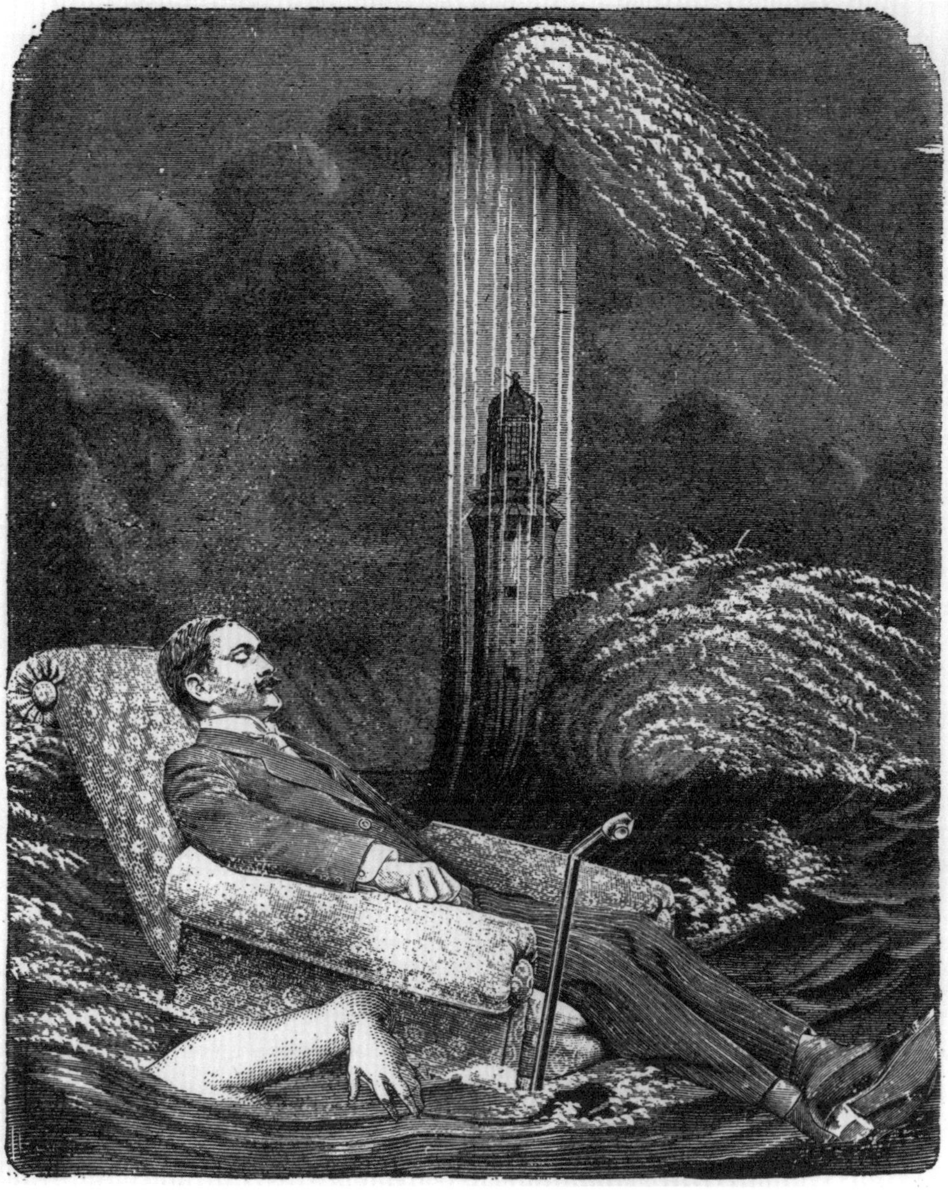

Max Ernst
Quiétude
plate 100 in *La femme 100 têtes*,
Paris, 1929

of something excessive that cannot be reduced to total disappearance, in which "the universe of Max Ernst would remain" (MEP, p. 134). Bataille's style at this point becomes elliptical and distended: "But nevertheless ... A *chink* would remain ... "[55] What is this remainder or *restance* that allows for the universe of Max Ernst? The English translation, "*chink*" does not catch the multiple meanings of the French "*défaut*"—a fault, flaw, or defect. The *défaut* of collage ruptures the desire for totality on which systematic philosophy depends. Thus, the collage practice of Max Ernst relies on remainders and defects to cut and paste its alternative universe, with a fantastic and exceptional cosmography that relies on "the cultivation of the effects of a systematic displacement."[56]

According to Bataille, laughter also depends on locating these chinks in the armor of reason and logic, and bringing them into communication with nonknowledge. In *Inner Experience*, Bataille likened laughter to a kind of rupture that opens up and unto the abyss: "Laughter intuits the truth which the rupture at the summit lays bare: that our will to arrest being is damned ... [I]ts rupture opens the abyss."[57] Applied to the collage universe of Max Ernst and explosive works such as "Drum-roll among the stones" or "Dilapidation, dawn, and excessively meticulous phantom," in *The Hundred Headless Woman* we witness collapsing buildings turning into ruins and scattering debris while a businessman happily consumes his meal.[58] Such images of rupture reinforce Bataille's understanding of Ernst's collages "in which the world, as it ceases to exist, falls apart" (MEP, p. 135) such that we encounter hilarity and experience laughter in dissolution. Indeed, such comic images underline Bataille's view of laughter as "The Practice of Joy before Death." This final Bataillean formula envisions how an explosion of laughter responds to a world of ticking time bombs ready to detonate bodies and to disperse them into collage fragments: "There are explosives everywhere that perhaps will soon blind me. I laugh when I think that my eyes persist in demanding objects that do not destroy them."[59]

Postscript: Rethinking Modern Art, Laughing

This analysis of Bataille's "Max Ernst, Philosopher!" focusing on laughter, nonknowledge, and the "imprudence of hilarity" suggests a reconsideration

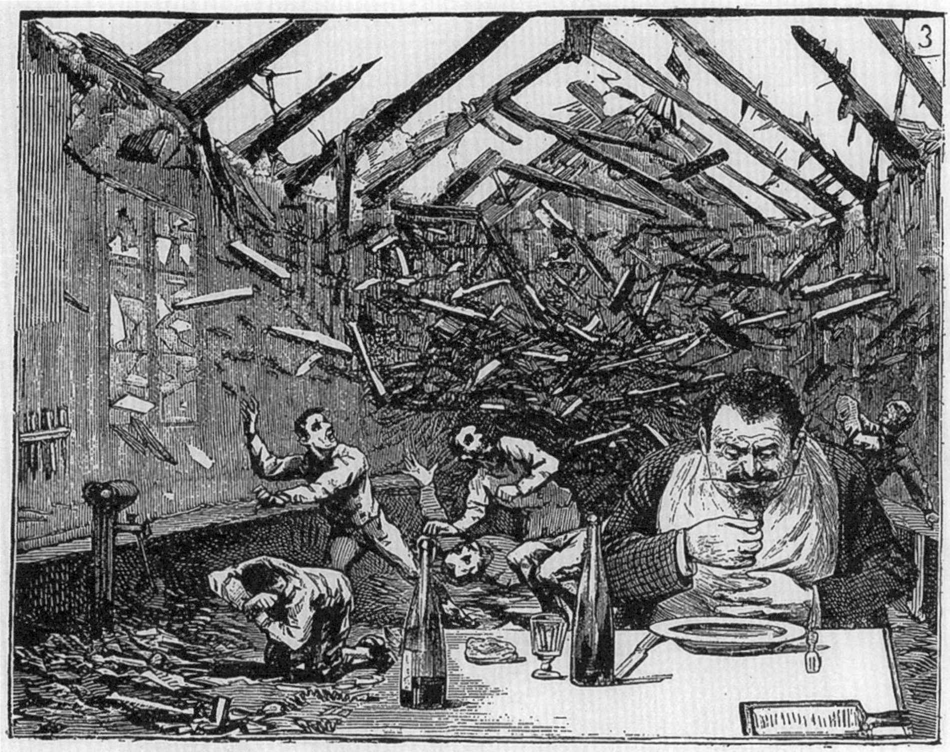

Max Ernst
Dilapidation dawn and excessively meticulous phantom,
plate 89 in *La femme 100 têtes*, Paris, 1929

of other key figures in the history of modern art along similar lines. Seeking to unpack the comedic in modern art from Bataille's perspective, we would do well to return to his engagements with such figures as André Masson, Salvador Dalí ("The 'Lugubrious Game'"), and Vincent van Gogh ("Sacrificial Mutilation and the Severed Ear of Vincent van Gogh") in terms of a practice of intellectual scatalogy in order to (dis)articulate and (dis)locate their heterological effects and to experience their laughter. In contrast to Bois and Krauss' *Formless*, such an investigation would lead to an art historical remapping of the terrain of modern art in terms of Bataille's laughter.

NOTES

1
Georges Bataille, "Nonknowledge, Laughter, and Tears," in Stuart Kendall (ed.) *The Unfinished System of Nonknowledge*, University of Minnesota Press, Minneapolis 2001, p. 140. (All future references to this essay are in parenthesis in the text as NLT.)

2
Yve-Alain Bois and Rosalind E. Krauss, *Formless: A User's Guide*, Zone Books, New York 1997.

3
Georges Bataille, "Formless," *Visions of Excess: Selected Writings, 1927–1939*, trans. Allan Stoekl, with Carl R. Lovitt and Donald M. Leslie, Jr., University of Minnesota Press, Minneapolis 1985, p. 31.

4
I am alluding of course to the well-known essay that titles Krauss' *The Originality of the Avant-Garde and Other Modernist Myths*, MIT Press, Cambridge, Massachusetts 1985, p. 151–170.

5
Bois and Krauss, *Formless*, p. 52. Bois quotes the second footnote of "The Use of Value of D.A.F. Sade" in which Bataille defines heterology. See *Visions of Excess*, p. 102.

6
Bataille, *Visions of Excess*, p. 99. For the original, see Georges Bataille, *Œuvres Complètes*, Gallimard, Paris 1970, vol. II, p. 64. (Hereafter, *OC*) For an excellent discussion of this passage that points to Bataille's laughter as "pure elimination and waste," "a mode of nonknowledge," a "rupture with thought, within ideality," and "a moment in which rationality is exceeded by a gratuitous affirmation of life, of contingency, of the body," see Allen S. Weiss, "Impossible Sovereignty: Between *The Will to Power* and *The Will to Chance*," *October* 36 (Spring 1986), p. 140. The essay was published when Krauss served as one of the co-editors of *October*.

7
Bataille, *Visions of Excess*, p. 97.

8
This passage begins, "In fact, I can say that, insofar as I am doing philosophical work, my philosophy is a philosophy of laughter. It is a philosophy founded on the experience of laughter, and it does not even claim to go further." See Georges Bataille, "Nonknowledge, Laughter, and Tears," p. 138. This important text (translated by Annette Michelson) also was included in the special issue of *October* entitled *Georges Bataille: Writings on Laughter, Sacrifice, Nietzsche, Un-Knowing* (Spring 1986). This makes the absence of Bataille's laughter from the *Formless* project even more glaring.

9
Hal Foster, *Compulsive Beauty*, MIT Press, Cambridge, Massachusetts 1993, p. 110. Interestingly, Bois and Krauss frame their analysis of Bellmer's *Dolls* in terms of the Freudian uncanny in *Formless* (p. 193–196).

10
Foster, *Compulsive Beauty*, p. 112.

11
OC, vol. 6, p. 362.

12
This "Preface" is found in Bataille's notes (*Boite* 18, A, p. 22–23) reproduced in *OC* vol. 8, p. 581–582.

13
For a lively discussion of fatal hilarity, see the Wikipedia entry at http://en.wikipedia.org/wiki/Fatal_hilarity [accessed May 26, 2008].

14
"The Funniest Joke in the World" sketch appeared in the first episode of the television show *Monty Python's Flying Circus*, "Whither Canada," which aired on October 5, 1969. The sketch was later remade in a shorter version for the film *And Now For Something Completely Different* (Dir., Ian MacNaughton, 1971).

15
Denis Hollier, "A Tale of Unsatisfied Desire," in Georges Bataille, *Guilty*, Lapis Press, Venice, California 1988, p. xiii.

16
Bataille, *Guilty*, p. 101.

17
Ibid., p. 90

18
Ibid., p. 118.

19
André Breton, "Lightning Rod," *Anthology of Black Humor*, City Lights Books, San Francisco 1979, p. xvi.

20
Charles Eubé, "Le Fond tragique du rire," *Critique* 68 (January 1953), p. 33–47.

21
Derrida insists that the reframing of meaning within play no longer binds it to the regime of knowledge but rather to the force of inscription. In contrast to Hegelian dialectics, Bataille's nonknowledge is open "to the fact that play *includes* the work of meaning or the meaning of work, and includes them not in terms of *knowledge*, but in terms of *inscription*; meaning is a *function* of play, is inscribed in a certain place in the configuration of a meaningless play." See Jacques Derrida, "From Restricted to General Economy: A Hegelianism Without Reserve," in *Writing and Difference*, trans. Alan Bass, University of Chicago Press, Chicago 1978, p. 260.

22
Simon Critchley writes about this distinction using the terms "Laughter I and II" in *On Humor*, Routledge, New York 2002. He affiliates Nietzsche's and Bataille's tragic laughter in the face of death as follows: "But there is laughter *and* laughter. On the one hand, there is the laughter of what Nietzsche calls 'eternal return,' the golden laughter of tragic affirmation, that so influenced Georges Bataille and his epigones. This is the heroic laughter that rails in the face of the firing squad—'Go ahead, shoot me, I don't care'" (p. 105).

23
Derrida, "From Restricted to General Economy," p. 256. Because the "sovereign operation also needs life," Derrida reminds us that Bataille once wrote in *Inner Experience* that "in a sense, *comic operation* would be less deceptive"; Derrida, "From Restricted to General Economy," p. 274.

24
Georges Bataille, "Nietzsche's Laughter," in *The Unfinished System of Knowledge*, p. 22. This subtle but important difference will be discussed below.

25
As Bergson put it, "[Laughter's] function is to intimidate by humiliating." See Henri Bergson, "Laughter" (1899), in Wylie Sypher (ed.), *Comedy*, Doubleday Anchor Books, New York 1956, p. 188.

26
Mikkel Borch-Jacobsen, "The Laughter of Being," *MLN* vol. 102, no. 4 (September 1987), p. 759. I have gained many insights from this astute reading of the divinity of laughter.

27
Bataille, "Nietzsche's Laughter," p. 22. The original quotation is from Friedrich Nietzsche, *The Will to Power*, vol. II, §585.

28
Georges Bataille, *Inner Experience*, trans. Leslie Anne Boldt, SUNY Press, Albany, New York 1988, p. 203.

29
Bataille, "Nietzsche's Laughter," p. 23.

30
For an excellent discussion of the divine laughter that compares Nietzche's "gay science" and Bataille's "nonknowledge," see François Warin, "De Dieu: Baubô et le rire de Déméter. Du gai savoir, au non-savoir," chapter 3 of *Nietzsche et Bataille: La Parodie à l'infini*, Presses Universitaires de France, Paris 1994. Warin affirms "this major laughter of which Bataille speaks, this exterminating laughter which absolutely swallows up the subject and sense," [*ce rire majeur dont parle Bataille, ce rire exterminateur qui engloutit absolument le sujet et le sens*], p. 96.

31
Bataille, "Nietzsche's Laughter," p. 23.

32
Ibid.

33
Bataille, "Aphorisms for the 'System'" (1952), p. 153. (All future references to this essay are in parenthesis in the text as AFS.)

34
Bergson, *Laughter*, p. 61.

35
Ibid., p. 79.

36
As Bataille put it: "It is no less true that Bergson's hypothesis is, from his own point of view, far from being able to be given as the solution of the enigma for which he himself offered it as explanation, not of the laughable in general, but of a particular aspect of the laughable that he names the comic" (NLT, p. 134).

37
Bergson, *Laughter*, p. 61.

38
Max Ernst along with Joan Miró, Pablo Picasso, and others organized an auction of their paintings at the Hotel Drouot in Paris on March 17, 1961, to help Bataille out financially.

39
Georges Bataille, "Max Ernst, Philosopher!" in *The Absence of Myth: Writings on Surrealism*, trans. Michael Richardson, Verso, London 1994, p. 134–135. The text was originally published in *Avant-propos de Bataille*, Gonthier-Seghers, Paris 1960. (All further references are in parenthesis with the abbreviation, MEP.)

40
Georges Bataille, "Antecedents to the Torment (or the Comedy)," in *Inner Experience*, 66 (*OC* vol. 5, p. 80). To fill in Bataille's disparaging remarks, "While at the British Museum I asked for *Laughter* (the shortest of his books); reading it irritated me—the theory seemed to me to fall short (for this reason, the public figure disappointed me; this prudent little man, this *philosopher*) but the question—the meaning of laughter which remained hidden—was from then on in my eyes the key question."

41
Georges Bataille, "André Masson," in *The Absence of Myth*, p. 180. This essay was originally published shortly after World War II in *Labyrinthe*, no. 19 (1 May 1946).

42
Ibld., p. 181.

43
Maud Lavin, *Cut With the Kitchen Knife: The Weimar Photomontages of Hannah Höch*, Yale University Press, New Haven, Connecticut 1993, p. 12.

44
Ibid.

45
"Otherness, in other words, is not only a matter of pleasure and enjoyment. There is no carnival without loss. No Luna Park without a slaughterhouse." See Denis Hollier, "Introduction," in *Against Architecture: The Writings of Georges Bataille*, trans. Betsy Wing, MIT Press, Cambridge, Massachusetts 1989, p. xxiii.

46
The base materialism embodying Bataille's thinking situates Ernst's project in terms of the collapse of the real in contrast to Breton's Surrealism and an idealism that seeks to rise above the real.

47
Of course, the German word *Witz* translates into English as both wit and joke. The original reads: "*Ist für Max Ernst der Witz in diesem umfassenden Sinne ein Grundprinzip seines Werks, das sich als Collage- und später auch als Frottageverfahren verwiklicht.*" See Ursula Lindau, *Max Ernst un die Romantik: Unendliches Spiel mit Witz und Ironie*, Wienand Verlag, Cologne 1997, p. 25. (All future references to this book are in parenthesis in the text as MER.) In contrast to this "endless play with wit and irony," Werner Spies does not come to terms with Ernst's laughter in the massive catalogue, *Max Ernst Collages: The Invention of the Surrealist Universe*, Abrams, New York 1988.

48
Max Ernst, *The Hundred Headless Woman*, Braziller, New York 1981. The original was published as *La femme 100 têtes* in Paris with André Breton's preface by Éditions du Carrefour in 1929.

49
Max Ernst, "Beyond Painting," in Lucy R. Lippard, ed., *Surrealists on Art*, Prentice-Hall, Englewood Cliffs, New Jersey 1970, p. 123. This was originally published in French as "Au-delà de la peinture," *Cahiers d'Art* (Paris, 1937), p. 13–46.

50
Ibid., p. 133.

51
Ibid., p. 131. Ernst continues in the same paragraph indexing his three collage novels. "By placing one collage after another, at random, we were surprised by the clarity of the irrational action that resulted: 'The 100 Headless Woman,' 'Dream of a Little Girl Who Wanted to Become a Carmelite,' 'One Week of Kindness.'"

52
Bataille, "The Sacred Conspiracy," *Visions of Excess*, p. 181. Originally published in *Acéphale*, vol. 1 (June 24, 1936), p. 2–4.

53
See Michael Surya, *Georges Bataille: An Intellectual Biography*, trans. Krzysztof Fijalkowski and Michael Richardson, Verso, London 2002, p. 457. It was originally published in Bataille's "L'au-delà du sérieux," *OC*, vol. 12, p. 315.

54
In another register of Bataille's extreme thinking, one recalls his fascination with the gruesome photographs of the Chinese "Death by A Thousand Cuts" (*Lingchi*) which offers the victim's body as bloody sacrifice. The image of a butchered body where nothing remains that is not cut to pieces poses again the Nietzschean question of anguished gaiety, of the possibility of a major laughter in the face of death and the impossible. Bataille discussed these extreme images in *The Tears of Eros*, trans. Peter Connor, City Lights Books, San Franscisco 1989, p. 206–207.

55
The elliptical text reads in French: "*Mais pourtant ... Un défaut pourrait subsister ...*" See "Max Ernst, Philosoph!," *OC* vol. 12, p. 518.

56
Ernst, "Beyond Painting," p. 126.

57
Bataille, *Inner Experience*, p. 91.

58
Ernst, *The Hundred Headless Woman*, p. 197 (plate 88) and p. 199 (plate 89).

59
Bataille "The Practice of Joy Before Death," *Visions of Excess*, p. 239; originally published in *Acéphale* V (June 1939), p. 1–8. Bataille makes a similar point in "Nonknowledge, Laughter, and Tears," where he writes: "The strangest mystery to be found in laughter is attached to the fact that we rejoice in something that puts the equilibrium of life in danger. We even rejoice in the strongest way" (p. 144).

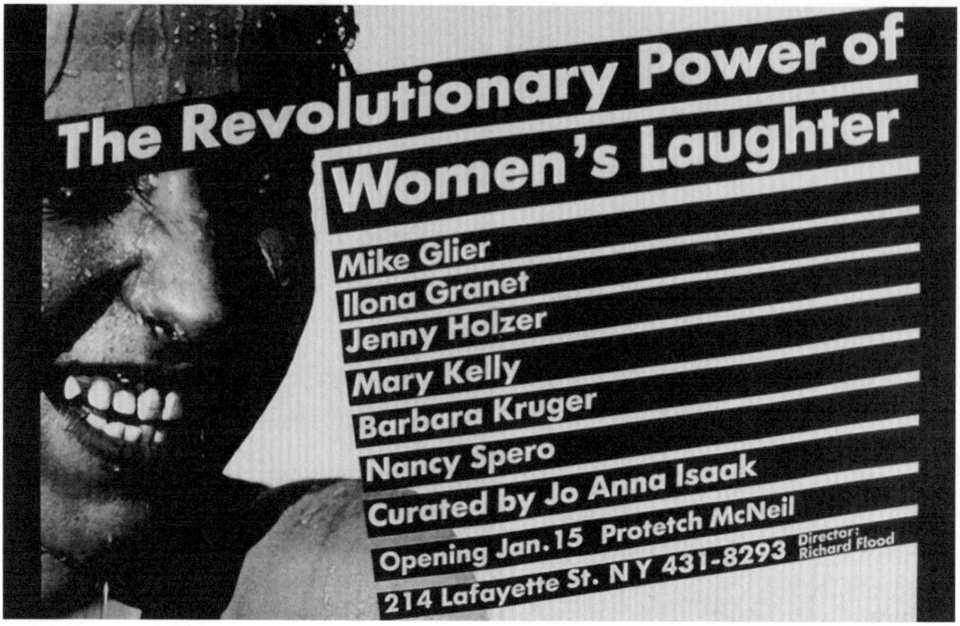

Jo Anna Isaak
Poster for *The Revolutionary Power of Women's Laughter*
Exhibition opened in New York City in January 1983 and traveled in the US and Canada

Jo Anna Isaak

WHOEVER WANTS TO UNDERSTAND IS INVITED TO PLAY

One of the happy consequences of having written a book and organized art exhibitions about women and laughter is that I have been invited to participate in numerous discussions about humor and women and their connections with various topics—art, representation, revolution, resistance, revolt, refusal, even refuse. Over the past ten years there have been numerous symposia in Europe and America.[1] In addition, there have been a prodigious number of recent publications on the relationship between women and humor. All this activity attests to the current interest in the topic.

This has not always been the case. Historically there has been an assumption that women and humor are almost unrelated; in fact, it was generally thought that another thing women lacked was a sense of humor. When I began my search for material on the connection between women and humor, I found surprisingly little. Even during the Surrealist era which opened up the arena of humor for a wide spectrum of artists and writers, there was little recognition of the role women could play in the comedic revolution. The search for the comedic and the erotic that lay at the heart of what the Surrealists called "convulsive beauty" led them to celebrate the hysterics of the Salpêtrière Hospital in Paris. As André Breton and Louis Aragon put it in *La Révolution Surréaliste* in 1928: "We Surrealists are anxious to celebrate here the quinquagenary of hysteria, the greatest poetic discovery of the end of the 19th century." Hysteria, they claim, is the subversion of the "relations which are established between the subject and the moral world." But while the Surrealists may have thought of themselves as artists "at the service of the revolution," the only revolution they thought the women of the Salpêtrière would service was the sexual one. Consider, for instance, Breton and Aragon's account of what was revolutionary about the hysterics of the Salpêtrière: "Does Freud, who owes so much to Charcot, remember the time—confirmed by the survivors—when the interns at Salpêtrière confused their professional duties and their taste for love, after nightfall, when the patients met them outside or received them in their beds? Afterwards those women patiently recounted, for the good of the medical cause which does not defend itself, their (supposedly pathological) mental attitudes under the influence of passion, which were so precious to them and are still precious to us as human beings."[2] While Surrealism invested its faith in the revolutionary potential of repressed (male) desire, the role for women was that of sexually liberal muse, not fellow revolutionary. Breton and Aragon's conception of the role women were to play in revolution was exactly the same as Stokely Carmichael's—as evidenced by his response to a question about what position he thought women should have in the Black Liberation movement. His answer: "Prone!"[3]

It is Sigmund Freud, of course, who sets out the theoretical basis for the Surrealists' explorations of both sexuality and humor. But when I turned to his writings for insights into the relation between women and humor, oddly, I found very little. In his 1914 essay "On Narcissism," Freud links women with humorists in a rather bizarre sequence that also includes great criminals, children, cats, and large beasts of prey: all seem to him to have maintained an original, primary narcissism that the adult male has renounced. Women who love only themselves are, in Freud's account, "the type of female most frequently met with, which is the purest and truest one," and he declares these characteristics in women are the greatest source of fascination for men. "It is as if we envied them for maintaining a blissful state of mind—an unassailable libidinal position which we ourselves have since abandoned."[4] Freud does not indicate what advantage women might derive from their retention of primary narcissism; in fact, he offers motherhood as a way for the narcissistic woman to overcome this condition and learn to love according to the masculine model. It is not until his essay

"Humour," written in 1927, that we begin to see the potential of narcissism for women. Rather than merely being a vehicle to elicit the admiration or envy of men, narcissism has now become a laudable quality in its own right. What Freud calls the "triumph of narcissism" occurs as a result of the "grandeur" of humor: "Humour has something liberating about it; but it also has something of grandeur and elevation ... The grandeur in it clearly lies in the triumph of narcissism, the victorious assertion of the ego's invulnerability. The ego refuses to be distressed by the provocations of reality, to let itself be compelled to suffer. It insists that it cannot be affected by the traumas of the external world; it shows, in fact, that such traumas are no more than the occasions for it to gain pleasure."[5]

We recall that the human beings who are able to maintain this primary narcissism into adulthood include women, criminals, and humorists. The importance of this grouping becomes clearer when, to illustrate the dynamics of the humorous gesture, Freud cites the example of a criminal about to be hanged on a Monday. On the way to the gallows the criminal remarks, "Well, this week is beginning nicely." A certain rationale for narcissism now becomes apparent. The criminal, like the narcissistic woman, is outside the law; both are attempting to evade its effects, if only briefly, through humor or pleasure. In the essay on narcissism, Freud assured us that the theory was not developed out of "any tendentious desire on my part to depreciate women."[6] In fact, Freud is not discussing biological imperatives but rather social structures, the constraints they impose upon the individual, and the psychic mechanisms the individual develops to evade these constraints. Indeed, he comes very close to delineating a political strategy for those without access to power: "Humour is not resigned; it is rebellious. It signifies not only the triumph of the ego but also of the pleasure principle, which is able here to assert itself against the unkindness of the real circumstance."[7]

This aspect of Freud's theory of humor—its rebelliousness, its connection to the pleasure principle, its assertion of the power to evade political and social constraints, is related to a much older and more overtly political theory of laughter: Rabelais' theory of the carnivalesque. Here we encounter the laughter of misrule, laughter with the potential to disrupt the authority of church and state. This is not the private, arcane, black humor of the Surrealist movement explored by Breton, but what Rabelais describes as the red humor of the masses, in which the explosive politics

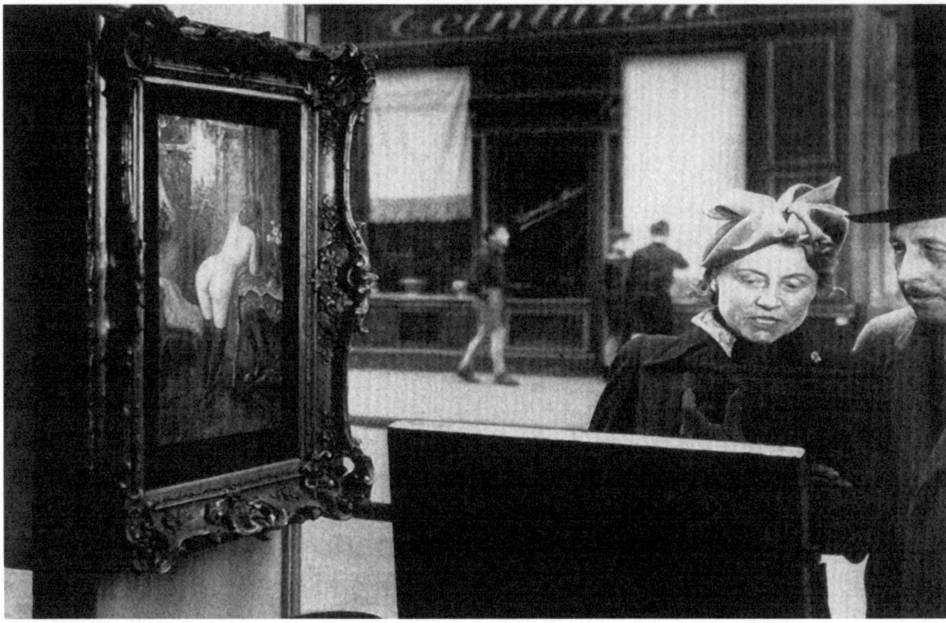

Robert Doisneau
Un regard oblique, 1948
The Metropolitan Museum of Art

of the body, of the erotic, and the licentious, are pitted against all forms of authoritarianism. Mikhail Bakhtin's monumental study *Rabelais and His World* reveals that women have historically been aligned with the popular comic tradition of misrule and that they have a political stake in this site of insurrection. Because it existed unofficially, outside the church, the carnivalesque was marked by exceptional radicalism, freedom, and ruthlessness: "carnival celebrates temporary liberation from the prevailing truth of the established order; it marks the suspension of all hierarchical rank, privileges, norms, and prohibitions."[8] Although the carnivalesque was eventually suppressed, Bakhtin suggests that at certain historical moments or in certain cultures, the carnivalesque as a form of social revolt would reemerge. Bakhtin finds remnants of this transgressive laughter in all-female gatherings such as the celebrations at the bedsides of women recovering from childbirth, and this humor is recorded in what were called caquets, or cackles.

These disparate theories were the thin thread onto which I started beading my notions of humor, women, art, power, and subversion. I was not working alone, however. A feeling of solidarity was developing in the early 1980s as women working in various fields were looking for "liberation from the prevailing truth of the established order." As more and more women artists and writers started to analyze the systems of representation into which they as artists were hoping to enter, they came to understand their position within these systems. The use made of images of women was a huge obstacle to their participation as artists. Images of women have long been used as part of the continuous barrage of exhortation and entrapment that, as Susan Sontag put it in *On Photography*, a capitalist society needs "to stimulate buying and anesthetize the injuries of class, race, and sex."[9]

But more perniciously, images of women were often deployed like tendentious jokes to keep women out of the field of representation. Mary Ann Doane finds the mechanism of the tendentious joke perfectly encapsulated in Robert Doisneau's photograph *Un regard oblique* (1948). A middle-aged couple is looking in a shop window. The woman is speaking and gesturing to something in front of her that we as viewers do not see. She, on the other hand, does not see what her male companion is looking at ... but we do. He is looking at a painting of a nude woman posed provocatively to display her naked bottom. Freud noted that the operation of the dirty joke is linked to scopophilia and the exposure of the female body. In peasant cultures, the smut starts when the woman enters; in more highly educated and thus more repressed societies it starts when she leaves. In either case, the woman, who is the object of the hostile or sexually aggressive joke, is a necessary conduit for this form of exchange between men. The tendentious joke functions as a bond between teller and listener. The listener responds to the joke by laughing and is thereby won over into pseudo-identification with the teller by "the effortless satisfaction of his own libido."[10] In the case of Doisneau's photograph, the joke enables the male viewer, the man in the photograph, and the photographer to bond in the effortless satisfaction of their libido, while the woman in the photograph, the female viewer, and even the image of woman in the painting whose buttocks are so prominently displayed, are the butt of the joke. Doane ends by pointing out that behind the painting of the nude woman there is another barely visible woman "imaged differently, in darkness—out of sight for the male, blocked by his fetish." Yet she admits that for her to have discovered this image only reveals her own perpetual desire to find a not-seen that might break the hold of representation. Or, as she put it, "to laugh last."[11]

By the 1980s the search for what could break the hold of representation was in high gear. Fundamental discoveries in modern linguistics and psychoanalysis had radically affected the understanding of how signifying systems operate. There was a growing awareness that a lot was at stake for women in these new assessments of how meaning is produced and organized in all areas of cultural practice. The crisis of authority and value that is symptomatic of postmodernism has itself in large part been instigated by a feminist deployment of laughter. It leveled the playing field for women—and women artists, writers, curators, activists, and cultural and political workers of all kinds began to play in the new authority-free zone. We organized exhibitions, wrote books, arranged symposia, changed university curricula, changed art history texts, changed the history of art, changed history ...

Laughter came to be thought of as a metaphor for transformation, for thinking about cultural change. By providing libidinal gratification, laughter offered an analytic point of entry for understanding the relationships between the social and the symbolic while freeing us to imagine these relationships differently. The revolutionary power of women's laughter does not function like the tendentious joke; this laughter is first and foremost a communal response. The aim is inclusion, not exclusion. By asking for the response of laughter, women artists were engaged in a different and difficult operation. The viewer must want, at least briefly, to emancipate himself from "normal" representation; in order to laugh, he must recognize that he share the same repressions. What is requested is not some private, depoliticized jouissance, but sensuous solidarity. As William Carlos Williams realized: "The tremendous cultural revolution implied by this interior revolution of technique tickles the very heart and liver of a man, makes him feel good. Good, that is, if he isn't too damned tied to his favorite stupidities. That's why he laughs. His laugh is the first acknowledgment of liberation."[12]

The feminist intervention moved from a critique of biological determinism to a consideration of positions occupied in the field of signs. Feminist art practice does not designate the work of a homogeneous group (the disenfranchised) or a fixed site (the margin) but rather an agency of intervention—an ongoing activity of pluralizing, destabilizing, baffling any centered discourse. This work, like all feminist activity, is fueled by calculated optimism; as a consequence, we have been accused of utopianism, or at least participation in what Steven Connor has referred to as "the romance of the margins"—an overgeneralized belief in the subversive potential of marginal conditions.[13] But I think that women are not likely to regard their marginal condition as "romance." Although the romantic notion of the "outsider" artist working alone in his [sic] studio continues to be a romantic role for male artists, it is more likely to be a bleak reality for women artists who so often work in isolation. The Guerrilla Girls rewrote this particular romance in a poster, "The Advantages of Being a Woman Artist" (1989). Among these advantages: "Working without the pressure of success. Not having to be in shows with men. Having an escape from the art world in your four free-lance jobs. Being reassured that whatever kind of art you make it will be labeled feminine. Not having to undergo the embarrassment of being called a genius. Not being stuck in a tenured teaching position. Knowing your career might pick up after you are eighty." If women artists have been working at the margins, it is because that has been the only site available to them. But by the 1980s, woman artists began turning the culturally marginal position to which they had always been relegated into the new frontier.

Writing at the end of the 1980s, Arthur Danto surveyed mainstream contemporary art and acknowledged, somewhat to his surprise, that were he "to select the most innovative artists of this particular period ... most of them would probably be women." This realization caused him, in turn, to ask "whether this particular period, and hence this particular mainstream, was made to order for women."[14] Yet, to question whether the mainstream was "made to order for women," as if the changeover had occurred by some happy accident, is to fail to realize that the very nature of contemporary art has been changed because of the power of the persistent critique that women have brought to bear on key assumptions about art, art history, and the role of the artist. We were interested neither in valorizing a mainstream nor in exploring, validating, and reinforcing hegemony, which, as Raymond William points out, is a process that relies upon the mechanisms of tradition and the Old Master canon in order to waylay the utopian desires that are potentially embodied in cultural production. It was, and will always be, the waylaid utopian desires that we are interested in.[15]

There has been a resurgence of feminist art activity in the United States during the past two years. Exhibitions, symposia, and publications have made 2007–2009 a prolific time for women in the arts; and the June/July 2007 issue of *Art in America* is devoted to covering this surprising resurgence. Most of this activity has been retrospective in nature, recounting or returning to the heyday of the feminist movement. The aim of the historical exhibition *WACK! Art and the Feminist Revolution* (2006–2007) was to examine the international foundations and legacy of feminist activism and art making that occurred during the crucial period 1965–1980.[16] Even the symposium "The Feminist Future: Theory and Practice in the Visual Arts" (at The Museum of Modern Art, New York, January 2007) was redolent of nostalgia for the early days of the women's movement. I understand the impulse to repeat: I did it myself in 1995 with the exhibition *Laughter Ten Years After*, which was a replay of an exhibition I had organized more than a decade earlier—*The Revolutionary Power of Women's Laughter* (1983).[17] Yes, we want to commemorate the past. But we are also anxious that the work undertaken and the progress women have made is often lost or forgotten—that women's history is written in a faint hand and must continually be re-inscribed before it is erased.

However, not all recent feminist exhibitions are replays. In the summer of 2006 I was taken by curators Gaia Cianfanelli and Caterina Iaquinta to see their exhibition *Dissertare/Disertare*. The title of the exhibition was a provocative paradox: "dissertare" means discussing, exchanging views, networking, being mobile and ready to put oneself on the line, while "disertare" means "to desert" or "to adandon" any static position. The exhibition, they explained, was intended to explore the ways in which the current generation of Italian women artists had either engaged with, or turned away from, the issues of the early Italian women's movement, and to see what issues they were currently addressing. Their announcement included a passage from Luce Irigaray's *Speculum of the Other Woman*, in which she exhorts women to "overthrow syntax" and "occupy the places of her exclusion."[18] In order to examine how the new generation of women artists have occupied the spaces in the discourse opened by feminist theory, they invited artists' groups and curators from all over Italy to respond. The manifesto explained the spirit and aims of the exhibition, and they used the Internet to cast what they called a *ragnatela*—a web, a net, a loose supporting network of ideas that enabled these artists to connect. Their invitation ended by saying, "Whoever wants to understand is invited to play."

And play they did! Their invitation was no ordinary "artists' call"; the *ragnatela* turned out to be strong enough to support a large-scale, theoretically coherent group show, as well as elastic enough to transcend the political correctness, dogma, and factionalism that so often plague feminist exhibitions. Twelve cultural associations and 11 independent curators participated. As the exhibition itself expanded, the exhibition site had to be changed to a larger space; the final venue was the Centro Internationale d'Arte Contemporanea, located in the Castello Colonna in Genazzano, a small town south of Rome.

At the entrance of the Castello Colonna the curators placed a large map of Italy showing the location of the cultural organizations, the curators, and the artists who had responded to the invitation. Visitors proceeded into the castle over a narrow bridge and entered an enormous space filled with women's art—more than 60 women artists from all over Italy! There it was—this play, the revolutionary power of humor that enabled this exhibition of feminist artwork to take place with the ease and grace of a natural force. Here was a haven and a laboratory for women artists examining the social realities, cultural myths, and material conditions of women's lives. The heterogeneous activities of the artists in the exhibition did not suggest any homogeneity in the women's art movement in Italy; but the show offered a cogent collective look at the production of women artists in Italy today, both those who reference feminist theory in their work and those who do not. Some works were liberations of fantasy or of repressed or censored material. Some explored the potential of play and pleasure. Others enacted a physical liberation through dance or athleticism. All were happily occupying the places of their exclusion as Irigaray had suggested women might do ... someday.

These Italian artists came together as if they had been working collaboratively for years. The curators and artists shared a talent for converting the difficult or demanding into the pleasurable and engaging, creating cultural and social synergies. In the end, the most amazing and gratifying thing about this exhibition is that it happened: 60 women addressing some of the problems, pleasures, and potential of women today. Whether the style, the message, and the suggestions they offer are useful for feminist artists and organizations in the United States is an open-ended question, since, of course, cultural predicaments figure not only in the way we address problems but also in the very kinds of problems we address. Nevertheless, perhaps we can learn from the pleasure of this exhibition. In my view, an exhibition in which women artists actively enable one another, and are accountable to and for one another, represents a feminist future in the making.

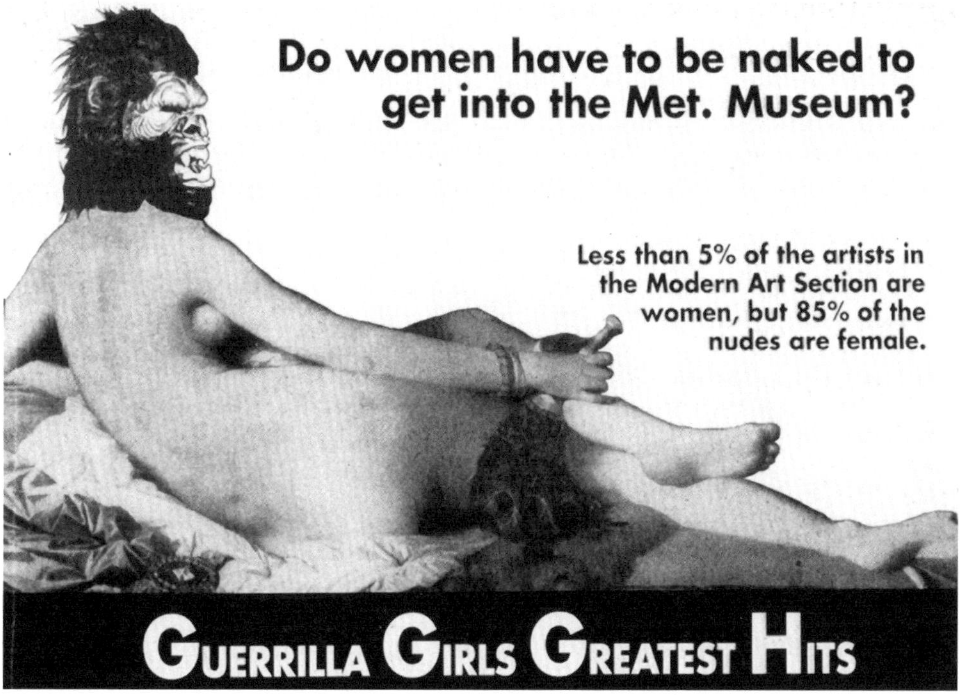

The Guerrilla Girls' poster of a larger than life-size reproduction of Ingres' *Grand Odalisque* appeared in the streets and on New York City buses posing the question "Do women have to be naked to get into the Met. Museum?"

NOTES

1
Faces of Laughter—Female Strategies in Art at the Stedelijk Museum, Amsterdam, in 2001; *Vice-Versa-Vice* at the Jan van Eyck Akademie in Maastricht, Holland, in 1998; and "Virtue and Vulgarity: A Feminist Conference on Art, Science and the Body," held at the University of Reading in Reading, England, in 1997—focused in large part on the body, humor, and the carnivalesque. Even the panel "Trash and the Abject" at the College Art Association in Los Angeles in 1999 focused on women and humor, as did the conference "Representing Hysteria" held at Trinity College, Hartford, Connecticut, in 1988, "Exquisite/Corpse" at Artsite, Burlington, Vermont, 1996, and the discussion of primary narcissism at the CAPC Musée d'Art Contemporain in Bordeaux, France, in 1997.

2
Louis Aragon and André Breton, "Le cinquantenaire de l'hystérie," *La Révolution Surréaliste*, II, Librairie Gallimard, Paris 1928; reprinted Arno Press, New York 1968, p. 20–22.

3
Stokely Standiford Churchill Carmichael (1941–1998), later known as Kwame Ture, was a Trinidadian-American black activist in the 1960s Civil Rights Movement. A leader of the Student Nonviolent Coordinating Committee (SNCC) and later "Honorary Prime Minister" of the Black Panther Party, he separated from Panthers in 1969, and his early advocacy for integrationism gave way to affiliation with black nationalism and the Pan-Africanist movement. His much-debated offhand comment about women in the SNCC was made in 1964.

4
See Sigmund Freud, "On Narcissism" (1914), in *The Standard Edition of the Complete Psychological Works of Sigmund Freud* [henceforth *SE*], trans. J. Strachey, Hogarth Press, London 1957, vol. 14, p. 88–89. In *Feminism and Its Discontents: A Century of Struggle with Psychoanalysis*, Harvard University Press, Cambridge, Massachusetts 2000, Mari Jo Buhle discusses Freud's concept of narcissism as developed in the 1914 essay in the context of his meeting with and fascination for Lou Andreas-Salomé (1861–1937), and her different conceptions of love, narcissism, and sexual difference (see, esp., p. 63–67).

5
Sigmund Freud, "Humour" (1927), *SE* vol. 21, p. 162; also in this volume.

6
Sigmund Freud "On Narcissism" (1914), *SE* vol. 14, p. 89.

7
Sigmund Freud, "Humour" (1927), p. 163.

8
Mikhail Bakhtin, *Rabelais and His World*, trans. Helen Iswolsky, MIT Press, Cambridge, Massachusetts 1968, p. 10. Mary Russo warns that the marginalized position of women and Jews placed them in danger during carnival: "Jews were stoned and there is evidence that women were raped, during carnival festivities." But I would argue that carnivalesque transgressions should not be confused with attacks on women and other marginalized groups which occurs when the public law is suspended. Laughter, as Bakhtin points out, "is an idiom never used by violence and authority" (1968, p. 90). Acts of violence that occur when the Law, that regulates a community and maintains social hierarchy, is suspended, need to be understood as an extension and reinstatement of that same Law. In fact, they are a more blatant

statement of what is understood, but goes "unspoken" in the public Law. Mary Russo, "Female Grotesques: Carnival and Theory," in *Feminist Studies/Critical Studies*, ed. Teresa de Lauretis, Theories of Contemporary Culture vol. 8, general ed. Kathleen Woodward, Indiana University Press Bloomington, Indiana 1986, p. 213–239.

9
Susan Sontag, *On Photography*, Doubleday, New York 1973/1990, p. 178.

10
Sigmund Freud, "Jokes and Their Relation to the Unconscious" (1905), *SE* vol. 8, p. 100.

11
Mary Ann Doane, *Femmes Fatales: Feminism, Film Theory, Psychoanalysis*, Routledge, London 1991, p. 30.

12
William Carlos Williams, "A1 Pound Stein," in *Selected Essays of William Carlos Williams*, New Directions, New York 1954, p.163. Williams is speaking specifically of Gertrude Stein's breakup of patriarchal poetry and prose, but he was among the first to understand her work as part of a broad-based feminists' deployment of laughter.

13
Steven Connor, *Postmodernist Culture: An Introduction to Theories of the Contemporary*, Blackwell, Oxford 1989, p. 228.

14
Arthur Danto, "Women Artists, 1970–85," *The Nation*, December 25, 1989, p. 794.

15
See, Raymond Williams, *Marxism and Literature*, Oxford University Press, Oxford 1977, p.115–117.

16
Curated by Cornelia H. Butler, *WACK!: Art and the Feminist Revolution* was shown at the Museum of Contemporary Art, Los Angeles, and the National Museum of Women in the Arts, Washington, DC; exh. cat., MIT Press, Cambridge, Massachusetts 2007. For an account of some of the ideas and decisions involved in curating this show, see Butler's "LA Now and Then," in *Recent Pasts: Art in Southern California from the 90s to Now* [SoCCAS Symposia vol. 1], JRP|Ringier, Zurich 2006, p. 33–40.

17
The Revolutionary Power of Women's Laughter opened at Protetch/McNeil, New York City, in January of 1983 and traveled in the US and Canada for a period of two years. Included were the works of Mary Kelly, Jenny Holzer, Ilona Granet, Nancy Spero, Barbara Kruger, and Mike Glier. *Laughter Ten Years After* commemorated the earlier exhibition and the exceptionally prolific decade of woman's art production that followed. It included the work of 20 international artists and toured for three years (1995–1998).

18
Luce Irigaray, *Speculum of the Other Woman*, trans. Gillian C. Gill, Cornell University Press, Ithaca, New York 1985; cited in *Dissertare/Disertare*, eds. Gaia Cianfanelli and Caterina Iaquinta, plug in, Rome 2007, p. 13.

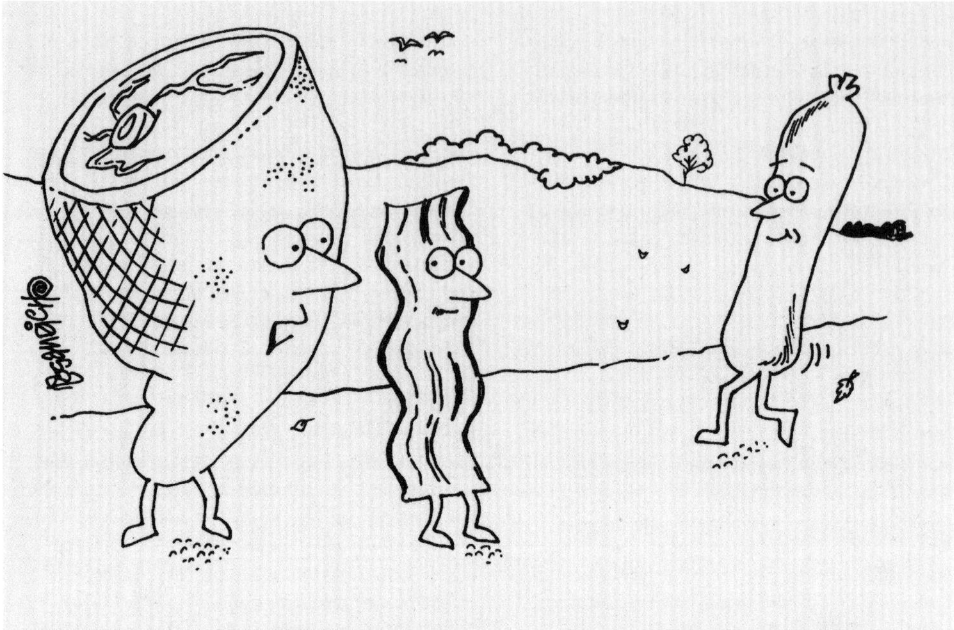

"COOL IT WITH THE ETHNIC JOKES. HERE COMES POLISH SAUSAGE."

Simon Critchley

LAUGHING AT FOREIGNERS: A PECULIAR DEFENSE OF ETHNIC HUMOR

Although I have spent many happy hours thumbing its pages, it is always an open question how much authority one should invest in the Oxford English Dictionary. If one consults the entry on 'humour,' the OED states that the first recorded usage of the word to indicate something amusing or jocular occurs in 1682. This is obviously not to say that there was no humor prior to that date, but rather that the association of the word 'humour' with the comic and the jocular is an innovation that belongs to a specific time and place: the English language in the late 17th century.

Prior to the late 17th century, humor signified a mental disposition or temperament, as in Ben Jonson's play *Every Man in his Humor* (1598). The earlier meaning derived from the ancient Greek medical doctrine of the four humors or fluids that made up and regulated the body: blood, phlegm, bile, and black bile (melan-colia). It is this link between humor and melancholy that André Breton suggests in his notion of *humour noir*, a retrospective category a little like *film noir*, that he used to title his famous anthology. Breton brought the term *humour noir* to prominence in 1940 (a particularly *noir* moment in European history) to describe, or more properly to invent, a tradition that extends from Franz Kafka back to the 18th century—the first entries are on Jonathan Swift and the Marquis de Sade.

Thus, the association of humor with the comic and jocular is specifically modern, and arises in the period of the rise of the modern nation state, in particular the astonishing rise of Britain as a trading, colonizing, slaving, and warring nation after the establishment of constitutional monarchy in the so-called Glorious Revolution of 1689. This dating is confirmed if we turn to Anthony Ashley Cooper, Third Earl of Shaftesbury. In 1709 Shaftesbury wrote a hugely influential treatise on humor: *Sensus communis. An Essay on the Freedom of Wit and Humor* (for a discussion of this work, see Jeffrey Minson, "Resonances of 'Raillery,'" in this volume).

A pupil of John Locke, Shaftesbury was the first theorist of humor. He viewed humor as the expression of sensus communis—which connotes a shared, public sensibility or moral feeling rather than mere "common sense." Shaftesbury thought that humor was an essential ingredient in the life of a free society; and that it should be permitted in the discussion of religion, because there can be no better test of a belief than to see if it can withstand mockery. Not so funny, perhaps, is the fact that Shaftesbury was also a key figure in the establishment of colonies in the Carolinas. Together with Locke, Shaftesbury drafted the Fundamental Constitutions of the Carolinas in 1669, an excessively feudal and restrictive document for these purported champions of freedom.

The modernity of humor is something apparent in French accounts of the origin of the concept. Although the English word is originally a French borrowing, from the Anglo-Norman "humour" and the Old French "humour," it is curious to note that French dictionaries claim that the modern sense of humor is an English borrowing. The *Dictionnaire de l'Académie française* is quite adamant on this point. "Humour" is a "word borrowed from English. A form of irony, at once pleasant and serious, sentimental and satirical, that appears to belong particularly to the English spirit (l'esprit anglais)."[1] Apart from the dissenting voice of Voltaire, who thought that the English had stolen the notion of humor from the comedies of Corneille, French authors in the 18th century and as late as Victor Hugo in *Les Misérables* (1862) refer to "that English thing they call humour."[2]

One finds the same view in Diderot's and D'Alembert's *Encyclopédie*, in a fascinating short article that may have been written by Diderot himself, although the attribution is not certain. "Diderot" writes:

> HUMOR: The English use this word to designate an original, uncommon, and singular pleasantry. Among the authors of that nation, no one possesses humour, or this original pleasantry,

> to a higher degree than Swift. By the force which he is able to give to his pleasantries, Swift brings about effects among his compatriots that one would never expect from the most serious and well-argued works, ridiculum acri, etc. Thus it is, in advising the English to eat little Irish children with their cauliflowers, Swift was able to hold back the English government, which was otherwise ready to remove the last means of sustenance and commerce from the Irish people. This pamphlet has the title, "A Modest Proposal."[3]

We should note the exemplary place of Jonathan Swift in this French history as the *plus haut point* of English humor. This is something continued by Breton, who begins his anthology of *humour noir* with an extract from Swift's "A Modest Proposal."[4] Breton claims Swift as "the true initiator" of *humour noir*, and as the inventor of "ferocious and funereal pleasantry" ("la plaisanterie féroce et funèbre").[5] Of course, the question of ethnicity returns again here, for it is curious, indeed paradoxical, to define humor as something essential to *l'esprit anglais*, and then to give Swift as the highest example of English humor—for Swift was not exactly English. As Beckett replied when he was asked by an American journalist whether he was English: "au contraire." The same response might also apply to Swift, Laurence Sterne, Oscar Wilde, James Joyce, and many other Irish contraries to Englishness. But if Irishness is the contrary of Englishness, then it is important to point out that the antithesis suggests an internal contradiction. Humor is a battlefield in the relation between what Richard Kearney rightly calls those national Siamese twins, England and Ireland, locked together in a suffocatingly close, often deathly embrace.[6]

Jokes are like tiny anthropological essays. If the task of the anthropologist is to revise and relativize the categories of Western culture by bumping them up against cultures hitherto adjudged exotic or other, then we might say that anthropology shares with humor the basic strategy of defamiliarization: common sense is disrupted, the unexpected is evoked, familiar subjects are situated in unfamiliar, even shocking contexts in order to make the audience or readership conscious of their own cultural assumptions. Anthropologists, in fact, are akin to comedians, tricksters, clowns, or jesters. Humor is a form of critical social anthropology, defamiliarizing the familiar, demythologizing the exotic, and inverting the world of common sense. Humor views the world awry, bringing us back to the everyday by estranging us from it. This is what I mean when I claim elsewhere that humor provides an oblique phenomenology of ordinary life, an indirect description and evocation of our life in the world.[7] Humor is a practice that gives us an alien perspective on our practices. It lets us view the world as if we had just landed from another planet. The comedian is the anthropologist of our humdrum everyday lives. So is the comic artist.

Any study of humor, again like anthropology, requires fieldwork and detailed contextualization. It is, finally, only as good as its examples. And what makes humor both so fascinating and so tricky to think about and write about is the way in which the examples continually exceed the theoretical analysis one is able to give of them: they say more in saying less. We certainly don't require a philosophical theory of humor in order to understand what is at stake in humor.

In my view, the lesson to be drawn from anthropology is the humility of a certain cultural relativism, as a strategy aimed at combating the intolerance and racism of Western ethnocentrism. Now, is the same true of humor? Your sense of humor may not be the same as mine—let's hope it isn't for both of our sakes, as mine is extremely filthy—but does the study of humor lead us to embrace cultural relativism, that big bad bogeyman of Western culture? Can we legislate for humor like philosopher kings, coming up with general laws about what is permitted and not permitted? We will see.

With the question of relativism, arguably the most intractable dilemma of humor can be broached: the universal versus the particular. Most studies of humor, jokes, and the comic begin by claiming that humor is universal. Apparently there have never been cultures without laughter, although the varieties and intensities of humor vary dramatically. However, to say that humor is universal is, of course, to say almost nothing, or very little. All cultures laugh, just as all cultures have a language and most of them seem to have some sort of religious practice usually involving a belief in a hidden metaphysical reality and an afterlife.

So what? The fact that all cultures laugh might be a formal universal truth, of the same order as admitting that all human beings eat, sleep, breathe, and take a shit once a day, maybe even more than once, which is even true of Queen Elizabeth II (I don't know if she goes more than once), but it tells us nothing at the level of a concrete context, and that is where matters begin to get difficult, sticky, smelly, and interesting.

Humor is local and a sense of humor is usually highly context-specific. How does one laugh in a foreign language? Anyone who has tried to render what they believe to be a hugely funny joke into a foreign language only to be met by polite incomprehension will have realized that humor is terribly difficult to translate, perhaps impossible. (In fact, I did this with a French friend in New York last Sunday. As usual, it was a joke involving bears.) Although various forms of non-verbal humor can travel across linguistic frontiers—witness the great success enjoyed by the *commedia dell'arte* throughout Europe in the 16th and 17th centuries and the enduring popularity of various forms of mime and silent comedy, such as Charlie Chaplin, Monsieur Hulot, and Mr Bean—verbal humor is notoriously resistant to translation.

The speed and brevity of wit can become tiresome and prolix in another tongue, and a joke explained is a joke killed. In 1921, Paul Valéry noted, "Humour is untranslatable. If this were not the case, then the French would not use the word."[8] But if Valéry is right and the French use "humour" because it is untranslatable, then might it not be the very untranslatability of humor that somehow compels us? Might not its attraction reside in the fact that it cannot be explained to others, and that humorous *savoir faire* always contains a certain *je ne sais quoi*?

Humor is a form of cultural insider-knowledge, and might, indeed, be said to function like a linguistic defense mechanism. Its seeming untranslatability might endow native speakers with a sense of their cultural distinctiveness or even superiority ("No one understands our jokes, because they are so stupid"). In this sense, having a common sense of humor is like sharing a secret code, often an obscene code. Indeed, is this not the experience of meeting a compatriot in an otherwise foreign environment, on vacation, at an art gallery or a public toilet, where the rapid development of intimacy is proportional to both a common sense of humor and a common sense of humor's exclusivity? We wear our cultural distinctiveness like an insulation layer against the surrounding alien environment. It warms us when everything else is cold and unfamiliar.

I argue in my little book on humor that laughter returns us to our physicality and animality. But it also returns us to locality, to what the Greeks would have called an ethos. It takes us back to the place where we come from, whether that is the concreteness of a neighborhood or the abstraction of a nation-state. The word "ethos" must be understood here

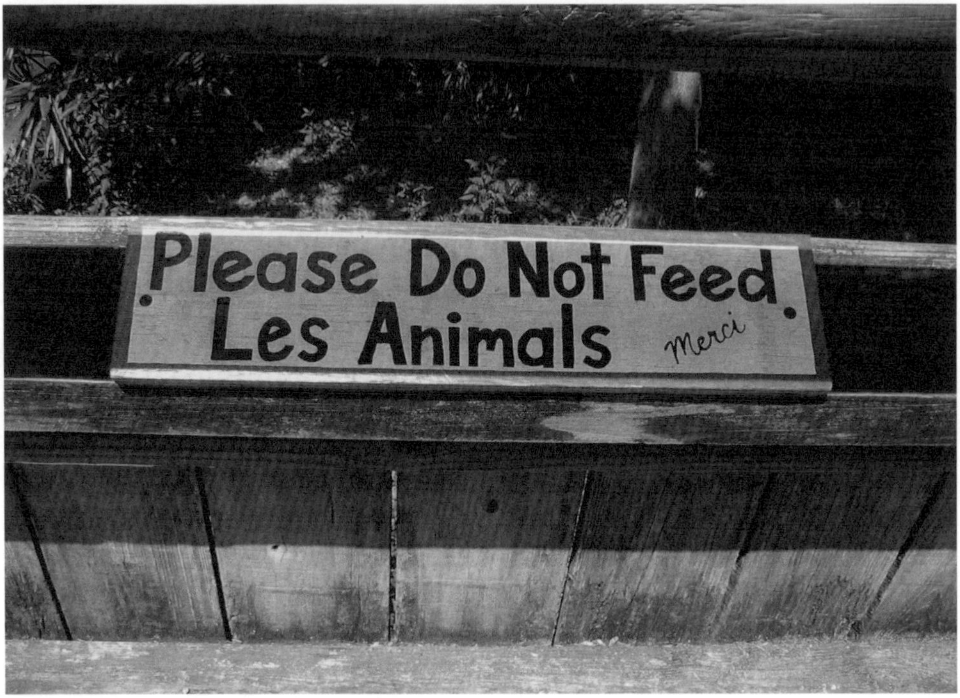
Please Do Not Feed
Les Animals
Merci

in its ancient Greek sense, as both custom and place, but also as disposition and character. A sense of humor is often what connects us most strongly to a specific place and leads us to predicate certain characteristics of that place, assigning certain dispositions and customs to its inhabitants. The sweet melancholy of exile is often rooted in nostalgia for a lost sense of humor. As a voluntary exile from England—which is a dreadful place in many respects, full of cunts with long faces shuffling around and complaining—what I really miss is humor, in particular absurd and extremely obscene humor, the shared effortless sense of the funny that one can share with another cultural insider.

There is a further link to be made here between ethos and ethnos, in the sense of a people, tribe, social group, or, in the modern world, a nation-state. In relation to humor, this is often vaguely expressed in two ways: first, that "foreigners" do not have a sense of humor; and, secondly, that they are funny. Such are the powerful, basic ingredients of ethnic humor. Recall that George Orwell famously said that the British Empire was based on two fundamental beliefs: "nothing ever changes," and "foreigners are funny."[9] In ethnic humor, the ethos of a place is expressed by laughing at people who are not like us, and usually believed to be either excessively stupid or peculiarly canny or clever. The logic of ethnic humor is about the relation to the other, as either stupid or distrustfully clever.

In England, the Irish are traditionally described as stupid and the Scots as canny; in Canada, the Newfies and the Nova Scotians assume these roles; in Finland, the Karelians are deemed stupid and the Laihians clever; in India, the Sikhs and the Gujaratis occupy these places; in the US, it is Mexicans or Blacks who are deemed stupid. It is unclear who Americans find funny, maybe Jews, maybe the English, maybe English Jews. Jews are outsiders because they are suspiciously canny, which is usually run together with being miserly and money-obsessed (this is also how the Scots are seen in English jokes). Either way, as either stupid or clever, the belief is that "they" are inferior to "us" or at least somehow disadvantaged because "they" are not like "us." Such is the menacing xenophobic flipside of a belief in the untranslatability and exclusivity of humor.

The facts of ethnic humor are all too well known: in the European context, with which I am more familiar, the French laugh at the Belgians, the Belgians laugh at the Dutch, and the Dutch laugh right back. The Danes laugh at the Swedes, the Swedes laugh at the Finns, and the Finns laugh right back. The Scots laugh at the English, and the English laugh at the Irish, and the Irish laugh right back. The Germans laugh at the Ostfrieslanders and everyone else laughs rather nervously at the Germans.

In relation to humor, the Germans are obviously a special case and much could be said about anti-German jokes, the history of which stretches back at least 200 years; a case that was obviously not helped overmuch by the events of the last century. German humor is no laughing matter. Ted Cohen relates a splendidly objectionable joke: “The thing about German food is that no matter how much you eat, an hour later you are hungry for power.”[10] This qualifies as what Cohen calls a “meta-joke,” in which the condition for the joke is the fact that you already know the joke about Chinese food invariably leaving you hungry soon after eating. Therefore, this is not just a joke, but a joke about a joke, a sheer play upon the form of the joke. As a hypothesis, I would say that much of the fascinating visual humor in contemporary art consists in meta-jokes, of plays on form that critically address our usual comic reactions, so that the laughter sticks in our throats.[11]

In my view, the intimate connection between the ethnicity of humor and what we might call its “ethnicity” must be recognized and not simply sidestepped. Ethnic humor surely relates to what Thomas Hobbes saw as the laughter of superiority or sudden glory at one person’s eminence measured against another’s stupidity.[12] It is a curious fact that much humor, particularly when one thinks of Europe, is powerfully connected to perceived, but curiously outdated, national styles and differences. There is something deeply anachronistic about much humor, referring nostalgically, as it does, to a past whose place in the present is almost mythical, certainly fantastical. For good or ill, old Europe still has a robust fantasy life, but at least we are not killing each other just at the moment.

Humor, then, is what returns us to our locale, to a specific ethos that is often identified with a particular people possessing a shared set of customs and characteristics. A sense of humor often comprises what it is felt may best be shared with people who are from the same place as we are, and it is this aspect of social life which is perhaps the most difficult to explain to people from somewhere else. That is to say, humor puts one back in place in a way that is powerfully particular and recalcitrantly relative. This point is important because we should not, in my view, shy away from the relativistic nature of humor. When it comes to what makes us laugh, we must, as a teacher of mine put it many years ago, have the courage of our parochialism. As I have claimed, humor puts us back in place, whether the latter is our neighborhood, region, or nation.

Now it can do this triumphantly—which is the basic feature of the overwhelming majority of ethnic humor. However, it need not put us back in place in this manner. It might equally put one back in one's place along with the anxiety, difficulty, and, indeed, shame that can accompany our sense of where we are from. Perhaps one laughs at jokes one would rather not laugh at. Humor can provide information about ourselves that we would rather not have. It reminds us that we are people that we sometimes would rather not be.

This phenomenon is probably most sharply revealed in the gap between what we found funny in the past and what we find funny now. Episodes of Monty Python that had me innocently rolling on the floor in pre-pubescent mirth in the early 1970s, and which we—like so many others—laboriously tried to rehearse word-for-word during lunch breaks at school, now seem both curiously outdated, not that funny, and crammed full of rather worrying colonial and sexist assumptions. Equally, as a right-thinking leftist, I would rather not be reminded of national differences and national styles, yet our sense of humor can often unconsciously pull us up short in front of ourselves, showing how prejudices that one would rather not hold can continue to have a grip on one's sense of who one is. There is an obscene kernel to our subjectivity that we often simply deny and repress in po-faced humorlessness.

In this sense, one might say that the very relativity of humor can function as an (un)timely reminder of who one is, and the nature of what Martin Heidegger might call one's thrownness [*Geworfenheit*], of the fact that one finds oneself always already cast away in a familiar and shared world.[13] If humor returns us to our locale, then my point is that it can do this in an extremely uncomfortable way, precisely as if we were thrown into something we did not and would not choose. If humor tells us something about who we are, then it might remind us that we are perhaps not the people we would like to be. As such, the very relativity of humor might be said to contain an indirect appeal that this place stands in need of change, that history is, indeed, in Joyce's words, a nightmare from which we are all trying to awake. Beneath our easy laughter, it seems to me that the critical function of art is to remind us of this nightmare.

A similar point can also be made in Freudian terms. In *The Interpretation of Dreams*, Freud makes a very perceptive remark about the relation between the comic and repression:

> Evidence, finally, of the increase in activity which becomes necessary when these primary modes of functioning are inhibited is to be found in the fact that we produce a comic effect, that is, a surplus of energy which has to be discharged in laughter, if we allow these modes of thinking to force their way through into consciousness.[14]

The claim here is that we produce a surplus of energy in laughter to cope with our inhibition when repressed unconscious material threatens to force its way through into consciousness. For example, my tight-lipped refusal to laugh at an anti-Semitic joke might well be a symptom of my repressed anti-Semitism; or refusing to laugh at a Mexican gag might be a symptom of my quiet contempt for Mexicans. As Freud claims, jokes have a relation to the unconscious: they articulate and reveal a certain economy of psychical expenditure. In this sense, ethnic jokes can be interpreted as symptoms of societal repression, and they can function as a return of the repressed. As such, jokes can be read in terms of what or who a particular society is subordinating, scapegoating, or denigrating. Grasping the nature of societal repression can itself be liberating, but only negatively. As Trevor Griffiths writes in *Comedians*, "a joke that feeds on ignorance starves its audience."[15]

Contemporary art doesn't starve its audience of humor. On the contrary, at its best it makes any easy laughter stick in our throats. In this way, I think we approach the paradoxical core of the best humor: it is not funny. Rather, it is troubling, unsettling, and disorientating. The joke that one thought was about the stupid or canny other ends up reflexively rebounding on oneself. In great humor, in my view, the joke is always on us. I think the best humor implicates its audience, it grabs hold of us and refuses to let go. Any laughter here sticks in our throats and we begin to choke.

I often sit in diners in New York and look at the yellowing, dog-eared poster about applying "The Heimlich Maneuver" to a choking person. Named after its inventor, Henry Heimlich, the maneuver involves a powerful abdominal thrust that clears any obstruction to breathing. Now, as I'm sure many readers know, the German word "unheimlich" means something uncanny, not at home, strange, or bizarre. At its best, art can produce an *unheimlich* maneuver. We begin to choke and there is no known cure. Funny isn't it?

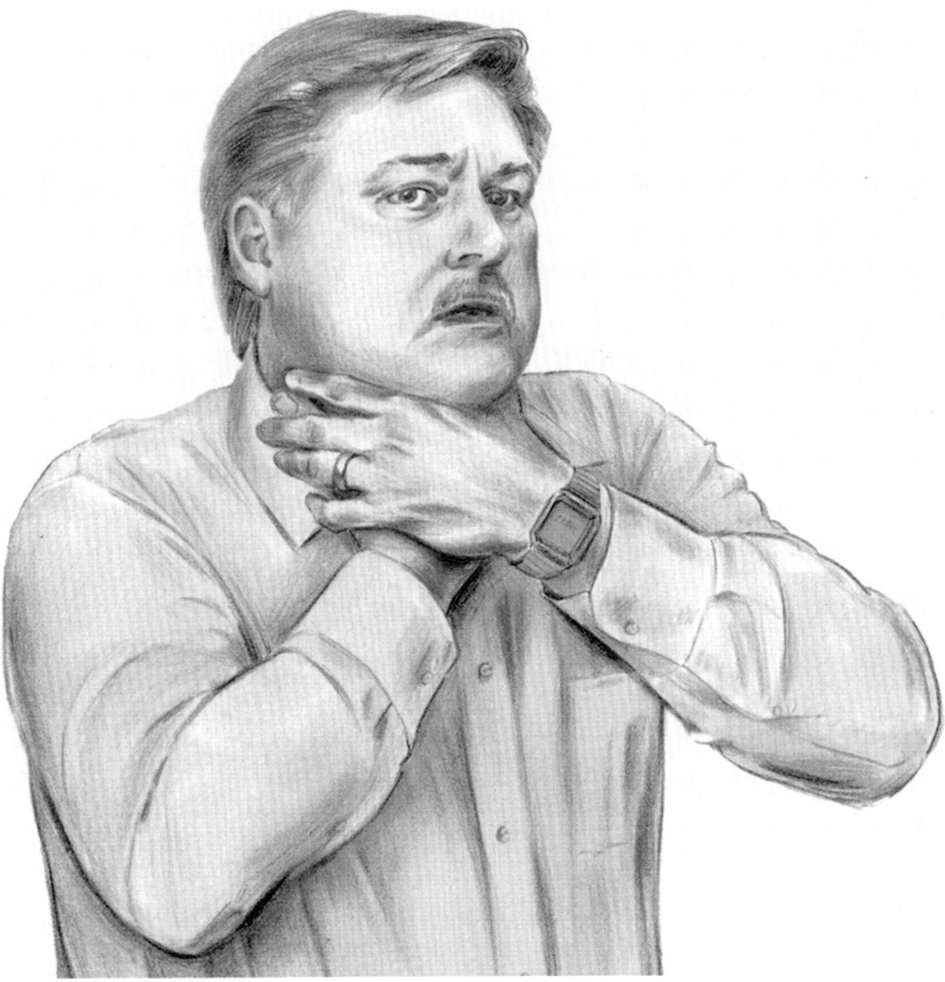

NOTES

1
Dictionnaire de l'Académie française, huitième édition, Hachette, Paris 1935, p. 29.

2
Victor Hugo, *Les Misérables*, vol. 1, Lacroix and Verboeckhoven, Brussels 1862, p. 800: "cette chose anglaise qu'on appelle l'humour."

3
Encyclopédie, Nouvelle impression en facsimilé de la première édition de 1751–1780, Fromann Verlag, Stuttgart-Bad Cannstatt 1967, vol. VIII, p. 353.

4
Jonathan Swift's "A Modest Proposal: For Preventing the Children of Poor People in Ireland from Being a Burden to Their Parents or Country, and for Making Them Beneficial to the Public" was first published in 1729.

5
André Breton, *Anthology of Black Humor*, trans. Mark Polizzotti, City Lights Books, San Francisco 1997, p. 3.

6
See especially Richard Kearney, chapter 8, "Britain and Ireland: A Tale of Siamese Twins," in *On Stories*, Routledge, London 2002; *Postnationalist Ireland: Politics, Culture, Philosophy*, Routledge, London 1997; and *Strangers, Gods and Monsters: Interpreting Otherness*, Routledge, London 2003.

7
See Simon Critchley, *On Humor*, Routledge, London and New York 2002.

8
Cited in *Le Grand Robert de la Langue française*, Dictionnaires Le Robert, Paris 1985, vol. 5, p. 288.

9
"Boy's Weeklies" (1939) in George Orwell, *The Collected Essays, Journalism & Letters*, vol. 1, "An Age Like This, 1920–1940," ed. Sonia Orwell and Ian Angus, David R. Godine, New York 2000, p. 471.

10
Ted Cohen, *Jokes: Philosophical Thoughts on Joking Matters*, University of Chicago Press, Chicago 1999, p. 21.

11
See, for example, *Laughing in a Foreign Language*, exh. cat., Hayward Gallery, London 2008.

12
Thomas Hobbes: "the passion of laughter is nothing else but a sudden glory arising from sudden conception of some eminency in ourselves, by comparison with the infirmities of others ... " in Thomas Hobbes, *The Elements of Law, Natural and Politic*, ed. John Charles Addison Gaskin, Oxford University Press, Oxford 1999, p. 54.

13
See Martin Heidegger, *Sein und Zeit* [*Being and Time*], Tubingen, Max Niemeyer 1972, especially p. 135–136: "This characteristic of Dasein's Being—this 'that it is'—is veiled in its 'whence' and 'whither,' yet disclosed in itself all the more unveiledly; we call it the 'thrownness' of this entity into its 'there'; indeed, it is thrown in such a way that, as Being-in-the-world, it is the 'there.' The expression 'thrownness' is meant to suggest the facticity of its being delivered over."

14
Sigmund Freud, *The Interpretation of Dreams* (1899), trans. and ed. James Strachey, Penguin, Harmondsworth 1976, p. 765–766.

15
Trevor Griffiths, *Comedians: A Play in Three Acts*, Samuel French, London 1976, Act. I, p. 24:

> WATERS (He returns to his desk.)
> A joke that feeds on ignorance ...
> (Points to McBRIAN)
> McBRIAN Starves its audience.

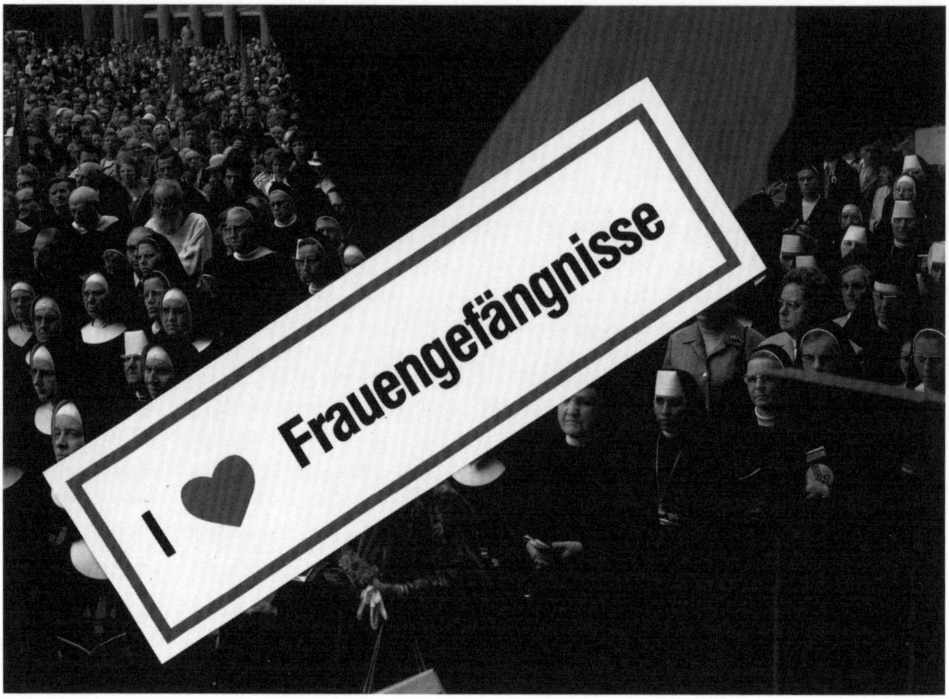

Martin Kippenberger and Albert Oehlen
Page from *The Cologne Manifesto* (Edition Lord Jim Loge, Graz, Cologne, Hamburg 1985), edition of 25 signed copies.
The sticker text reads: "I ♥ Women's Prisons."

Gregory H. Williams

RETREAT TO THE PRIVATE SPHERE: IN-JOKES IN WEST GERMAN ART OF THE 1980S

Thirty years ago a crisis mode had set in among members of the political left in West Germany. The 1970s had been marked by periodic declarations that the transformative events of the 1960s had come to a definitive end. By the late 1970s, various theories attempted to explain a shift in the political, social, and/or cultural climate in West Germany, many of them collected under the rubric of an alleged *Tendenzwende*. Translated as a "shift in tendency," or more loosely as a "cultural turn,"[1] the term began circulating in the mass media around 1973 in the wake of the first oil crisis of 1972, and was then cited with increased frequency as Helmut Schmidt took over from Willy Brandt as chancellor in 1974.[2] There are two dominant meanings of the concept: on the one hand, it refers to a rise in neo-conservatism in response to the late-1960s student revolt; on the other, it suggests a wider shift in consciousness away from public concerns and toward private matters, and is thus associated with the so-called "new subjectivity" that found expression in contemporary West German literature and the visual arts.[3] Jost Hermand has described the resulting climate as prompting "a feeling of helplessness, a lack of orientation, a sense of powerlessness, indeed a hangover."[4]

This uncertain period saw the publication of Peter Bürger's *Theory of the Avant-Garde*,[5] a widely read and highly influential analysis of the historical avant-garde that provided a further indication of the political pessimism of the 1970s. For Bürger, artists working in the 1960s lacked direction after the avant-garde's institutionalization had weakened progressive cultural practice. Despite widespread agreement over Bürger's characterization of the avant-garde as having run its course, subsequent writers have taken Bürger to task for misdiagnosing the situation of what he called the "post-avant-garde."[6] Jochen Schulte-Sasse, for instance, described Bürger as being mired in the same cultural pessimism that had characterized Theodor W. Adorno's negative assessment of art's viability as a socially relevant agent in the postwar period. Adorno's support of art's autonomy and separation from everyday life, or the "social totality," led him to promote the idea that art is "the medium of hibernation in bad times."[7] For Schulte-Sasse, Bürger is similarly burdened by his negative views on art's powers of social persuasion, and his book contains no prescription for an art of the future that might take up where the historical avant-garde left off in seeking to reconcile art and life. Without responding to Bürger directly, West German artists who began showing their work in the late 1970s and 1980s appeared to offer potentially productive correctives to the limitations of his theory.

Working primarily in Cologne during the 1980s, this generation of artists confronted political ambivalence in works that employed humor as both a coping mechanism and a critical tool. When ideologies of all stripes had come to seem suspect, or even completely bankrupt, joking offered a fallback plan for artists who still wanted to address political content but rejected dogma. At the same time, the vernacular quality of jokes could point back in the direction of an avant-garde merging of artistic work and everyday life, opening up space, however limited, for political commentary. Several of these artists had had different experiences with leftist political and social activities during their teenage years. Albert Oehlen, for example, had been involved in the *Mietersolidarität* (Tenants Solidarity) movement in 1972 along with Jörg Immendorff, whose own work had centered on political engagement since his student days with Joseph Beuys at the Kunstakademie in Düsseldorf in the mid-1960s. Under the influence of her older sister, Rosemarie Trockel had taken part in the student protest movement in the 1960s. While Georg Herold, who trained as an artist in his native East Germany before being imprisoned for an attempted escape, was "bought free" in 1973 by the Federal Republic of Germany. Contemporary politics played a distinct role in their formation as artists. Yet in each case direct involvement with political action was more short-lived and experimental than defined by serious commitment. Politics and social critique would find expression in their work, but were almost always observed from oblique, ironic angles.

The turn to humor by these artists was part of a prevalent move away from the public sphere and into the private realm. In an essay for the political journal *Kursbuch*, Johann August Schülein attempted to explain, from a socio-psychological perspective, how the *Tendenzwende* had led many of the individuals in the protest movements to direct their attention toward improving their personal lives outside of the public political arena. Labeling this development the *Rückzug ins Private* ("retreat to the private"), Schülein attempted to identify transitions that had occurred since the early 1970s as street protest turned into rigid dogmatism. This led him to remind his readers that self-examination was indispensable for the process of social critique: "The identity that a subject requires in order to become politically oppositional under the conditions of the *Tendenzwende* must be fundamentally *self-reflexive*. Critical fantasy alone is no longer enough."[8] For Schülein, the attention devoted to the problems of the *Alltag*, or everyday, was not entirely negative. Rather, the return to the private represented a "*historically necessary concentration on everyday problems* that until now hindered and distorted political praxis."[9] The late-1970s crisis mode called for a regrouping, a period in which to seek new strategies that would account for the failings and omissions of the previous decade.

The medium of in-jokes enabled artists to pursue a semi-retreat from the public sphere, opening up a space between public and private communication. In the aftermath of the politically motivated cultural practices of the 1960s and early 1970s, disappointment and pessimism had a paradoxically liberating effect. Adorno's concept of hibernation was to some extent still relevant, but now the artists sought to move beyond the state of immobility that came with such a flight from social engagement. On the one hand, withdrawal was still an operative term as the public-to-private shift motivated in-jokes and group codes. However, as the impact of popular culture on the art of the 1960s only accelerated during the 1980s, the embrace of recognizable images from the mass media meant that true hibernation was never an option. Different forms of public, media-derived language, quite unlike the abstraction of Adorno's hibernating modernism, adhered to the works of many post-1960s artists. Their jokes thus often occupied a middle ground between opacity and clarity, developing a subtle exploration of language that complicates Bürger's schema. Schulte-Sasse has proposed an alternative to Bürger's pessimistic view of a post-hibernation phase within the arts by looking to "the possibilities that inhere in the slippage between society and language."[10] Humor was a productive tool that many West German artists employed in their attempts to locate such flexible spaces. Through the in-joke, artists of the late 1970s and 1980s could simultaneously pay limited allegiance to avant-garde critique while acknowledging the restraining effects of the *Tendenzwende*.

The in-jokes of the 1980s reoriented the collective practices that had grown in prominence and number during the 1960s. As if to point out the difficulties now facing politically motivated artists' collectives, in-jokes sometimes mocked the seriousness of purpose that had once brought artists together. At the same time, 1980s artists could call up earlier moments of group-speak that deliberately avoided clear messages. Whether we look back to the *fumistes* of the 1880s or the Dadaists of the 1910s, jokes helped small groups of artists carve out private space by constructing codes and pseudo-dialects. Renato Poggioli suggests that an essential quality of the avant-garde's "antagonism" toward the older generation and academic tradition was its "use of an idiom all its own, a quasi-private jargon."[11] By the time that postmodernism had, by some accounts, relegated the avant-garde to a historical category, artists from the generation of the 1980s could only play with the suggestion of resistance through obfuscation.

In order to explore the varying levels of accessibility to the codes devised by this generation, one must, following Freud's elevation of the role played by the joke's recipient,[12] attempt to define the joke-makers' audiences. When the works themselves swing wildly from borderline illegibility to hyper-clarity, uninitiated viewers are simultaneously solicited and rebuffed. In such situations, the communicability of humor mingles with the alienation effect of irony, triggering a wide range of responses. Søren Kierkegaard once wrote that humor and irony can be "united in one individual, since both components are contingent on one's not having compromised with the world."[13] One might draw a connection here with the private/public dichotomy in effect during the 1980s: a compulsion to disengage is balanced by a need to stay connected. In another note in which

Kierkegaard referred to humor and irony, he proposed that "life is a constant pendulum-movement between them."[14] While these contrary positions sometimes stand in an oppositional relationship, they are linked as two ends of a "teeter-totter," one continuously giving way to the other.[15] Both modes rely on a virtual contract between humorist/ironist and audience.

West German artists of the 1980s combined irony's tendency toward opacity with humor's potential for playful subversion to challenge the position of the viewer/reader. Kierkegaard's "teeter-totter" effect offers a useful means of understanding how the artists form a bridge, whether secure or tenuous, between the social context of their production and its later reception. The way that the pendulum rotates between humor and irony within a single work of art allows us to distinguish the differing attitudes held by the artists toward the involvement of their public. It is instructive to explore the initial instances of audience formation as they took place in direct communication between the artists themselves. Poggioli's notion of the "quasi-private jargon" that the historical avant-gardes used as a form of resistance had long since lost its truly alienating capacity. Still, the inability of artistic dialects to reinforce estrangement did not mean that artists gave up their hermetic modes of communication. Instead, in-jokes and group-speak were utilized more for their positive generative powers than for their negativity or evasiveness.

One of the most revealing instances of generative insider joking is found in the practice of Martin Kippenberger. In his remarks on Kippenberger's fostering of group dynamics in the studio, former assistant Merlin Carpenter has called the collaborative act itself the "'secret explainer' of the [artist's] aesthetic."[16] Kippenberger's works and titles originated in a situation that to some extent presupposed the place of an audience. Ideas were exchanged, many of which came from the assistants themselves (according to Carpenter, there were phases when they came primarily from the assistants), and the ensuing conversation shaped the final work. As an already partially public encounter, Carpenter argues that the dialogue between artist and assistant enables "others to see the joke."[17] In other words, a degree of semantic transparency would seem to be built into Kippenberger's everyday production activities in the studio. The references may have been obscure, but at least one additional person besides the artist himself had understood the humor at the moment of the joke's inception.

Carpenter's insight reveals the way in which Kippenberger's jokes were committee-generated rather than springing directly from the artist's comedic mind. Assistants, friends, and artist-colleagues were relied upon to launch concepts for visual gags, with Kippenberger participating as much as he needed to, even if this meant only stepping in at the last minute to give an idea his blessing. Yet how are we to locate the "secret explainer"? The term itself incorporates the idea that the explanation is partly hidden away behind the inherent secrecy of studio work. Carpenter seems to imply that if we could only retrace the original conversation, then the first instance of laughter would be revealed and the work's code could be cracked. He implies, in other words, that a kind of archeology of the anecdote is ultimately the best route toward comprehending the workings and effects of the in-joke. This is, in fact, the general condition of most of the in-jokes developed by this group: a tightrope walk between private laughter and public reference, with the joke performing its traditional function of shifting back and forth between familiarity and estrangement. In this sense, Carpenter is right: the group conversation often brings the joke one step closer to general comprehensibility through the collective reliance on (often painfully) familiar codes.

Oehlen once recalled how he and his peers relied—like Picasso and Braque in the Synthetic phase of Cubism before them—on the daily paper to identify their subjects, which "should be truly unpleasantly accessible to everyone."[18] This impression of simplicity, even simplemindedness, can be understood as a test in which the viewer is challenged to puzzle out the separate layers of meaning that are built up out of the object-text relationships in their work. In the introduction to a study of *diskursive Dummheit* ("discursive stupidity"), Uwe Wirth explains that "stupidity is not only a universal phenomenon, but also implies a fundamental philosophical problem: it concerns the power of cognition and judgment."[19] The accessibility of the subject matter is no guarantee of conceptual lucidity. In general, in-jokes, even those possessing the most banal and transparent structure, depend on an audience that is willing to meet them halfway, to retrace the conversation that sparked the idea in the first place.

Kippenberger and Oehlen's appropriation of a coffee-table book of photographs by the photojournalist Ernst Haas is a prime example of a collaborative venture based on the in-joke. The book, *In Germany*, was first published in 1976 and contained photographs from various German regions that attempted collectively to portray a national culture.[20] Kippenberger and Oehlen reworked the book by giving it their own title, *The Cologne Manifesto*, and plastering its pages with their self-made "I Love" bumper stickers.[21] Patently comedic pairings alternate with more absurdist juxtapositions. Such a project clearly leaves behind the declaration of intentions often associated with manifestos of the historical avant-garde, particularly those of the Futurists, favoring instead an idiosyncratic humor generated by the artists' social milieu. Indeed, the book is much closer to the aesthetic strategies of German Dada, in particular Hannah Höch's collages that incorporate the word "Dada" into their chaotic layering of pictures taken from the media and advertising. In both projects, group identity is embedded within images associated with mass culture, thus straddling the line between the private realm and the public sphere.

There is no doubt that, like their Dada predecessors, these young artists had a public audience in mind as they fabricated their in-jokes. Their thirst for art world recognition prevented them from ever retreating into a realm of predominantly private exchange. However, much of their work, and especially what was done in collaboration, retained the appearance of stemming from conversations among friends and close colleagues. Nowhere is this more apparent than in their frequent group exhibitions that led to catalogues in which a kind of collective identity was suggested at the outset, only to be undermined by close reading. Exhibition catalogues offered in-between spaces in which the artists could pursue jointly authored statements while still maintaining their individuality as makers of images and objects with a singular imprint. In his analysis of 19th-century literature and art, Pierre Bourdieu developed a productive distinction between "positions" and "position-takings" that helps us to situate these activities. While "positions" signify the formal aspects of the work of art, "position-takings" are carried out in the social realm in the form of "political acts and discourses, manifestos or polemics, etc."[22] The close relationship between the two categories "obliges us," he notes, "to challenge the alternative between an internal reading of the work and an explanation based on the social conditions of its production or consumption."[23] The collaborative catalogues pair socially motivated group activity with individual objects, and in order to interpret them, one must operate along the boundary that ordinarily exists between internal and external readings. A sufficient number of such projects took place during the mid-1980s to give the impression that the artists saw themselves as participating in a collective endeavor. At the same time, they challenged their audience to identify the source of group cohesion.

The intertextual strategies employed by Werner Büttner, Kippenberger, and Oehlen were taken up most forcefully in their 1984 exhibition *Wahrheit ist Arbeit* ("Truth Is Work") at the Museum Folkwang in Essen.[24] In this publication a jointly authored, three-way essay employs a montage technique, blurring the boundaries between the voices of the artists. All three were responsible for the rambling text that runs alongside the illustrations of works included in the show: pictures taken from the media and popular culture, photos of the artists' mothers and friends, and various other images that emerged out of their collective interests and obsessions. Much of the text has a distinctly anecdotal quality, held together by a veneer of the serious and sober that characterizes Büttner and Oehlen's numerous co-written essays from this period. Their texts are structured around long-winded storytelling with plots and detours drawn from their daily lives, all of which are communicated in a comically dry, almost pedantic mode of address. Assisted by the permissiveness of the exhibition catalogue, the mundane content of these subjective accounts of the artists' social and working lives elevates private, seemingly incongruous, domestic concerns into purportedly notable events. If the "secret explainer" can be located anywhere, one would assume its likely home is somewhere between the lines of the collaborative essay. Yet even in these pages, the verbal joke does not easily translate into the written narrative; the reader is given no guidance for any attempt to trace the recorded events back to their emergence in an instance of collective laughter.

In contrast to the essay's textual confusion, and highlighting its arbitrariness, the artists included in the lower register of the pages a number of "serious" contributions from writers including cultural critic Diedrich Diederichsen, theorist Nicola Reidenbach, novelist Rainald Goetz, and even the venerable philosopher of science, Sir Karl Popper—appearing, one assumes, without his knowledge or consent. Diederichsen and Goetz represent a second circle of involvement with the group dialogue as both interacted closely with the artists at the time of the exhibition. Popper, on the other hand, could not be further removed from the group; a portion of his 1934 essay "Logik der Forschung" ("Logic of Research") is reproduced here in what would seem to be the most inappropriate of venues.[25] Yet a perverse degree of connectivity cannot be overlooked: Popper's essay treats the question of certainty in scientific investigations. He argues that scientific objectivity leads unavoidably to a realization of the provisional nature of scientific knowledge. We can only be certain about any of our observations on a subjective level, an idea that touches, however indirectly, on issues of relativism that crop up in the work of this generation. Ultimately, all of the textual material in the lower register serves merely to enhance the absurdity of the artists' own writings at the same time that it lends them a kind of dubious "credibility."

In his 1992 essay for the catalogue of an exhibition by Büttner, Kippenberger, and Oehlen, *Malen ist Wahlen* [To Paint Is to Choose (or Vote)], Diederichsen describes how names had operated within the tangled web of texts in the *Wahrheit ist Arbeit* catalogue, essentially summing up these artists' working methods during the mid-1980s. He describes how the semantics of the catalogue breaks down under the pressure of name-dropping run amok. Fortunately, we are able to leave the text and move back to painting, which "turns into a language itself that can attain all other effects of language on its own, especially the one that is decisive here: unconditional access for everyone and total hermeticism at the same time."[26] As a critic privy to some of the initial conversations, Diederichsen was in a position to retrace the specifics of the naming process, including the occasionally arcane terminology of in-jokes, while acknowledging how the viewer might experience it all as a hermetically sealed system closed to non-participants.

The highly artificial rubbing of artistic shoulders with thinkers and other cultural producers operating in different spheres does not, of course, convincingly extend the studio conversation beyond the small-group context. One can, however, gain a sense from the invented dialogue that the artists thought of themselves as somehow implicated in a broader network of influences and ideas. The frequency with which they used their collaborative projects as a basis for situating their work imaginatively within a more public discursive space testifies to a need to move beyond the private domain. Their in-jokes functioned as bridges between these realms. Yet for all the moves they negotiated toward a more expansive conception of critical and aesthetic discourse, their group humor always circled back into the zone of the private laugh during this period. And when the laughter was overtly public, it was also conditioned, as Tom Holert has

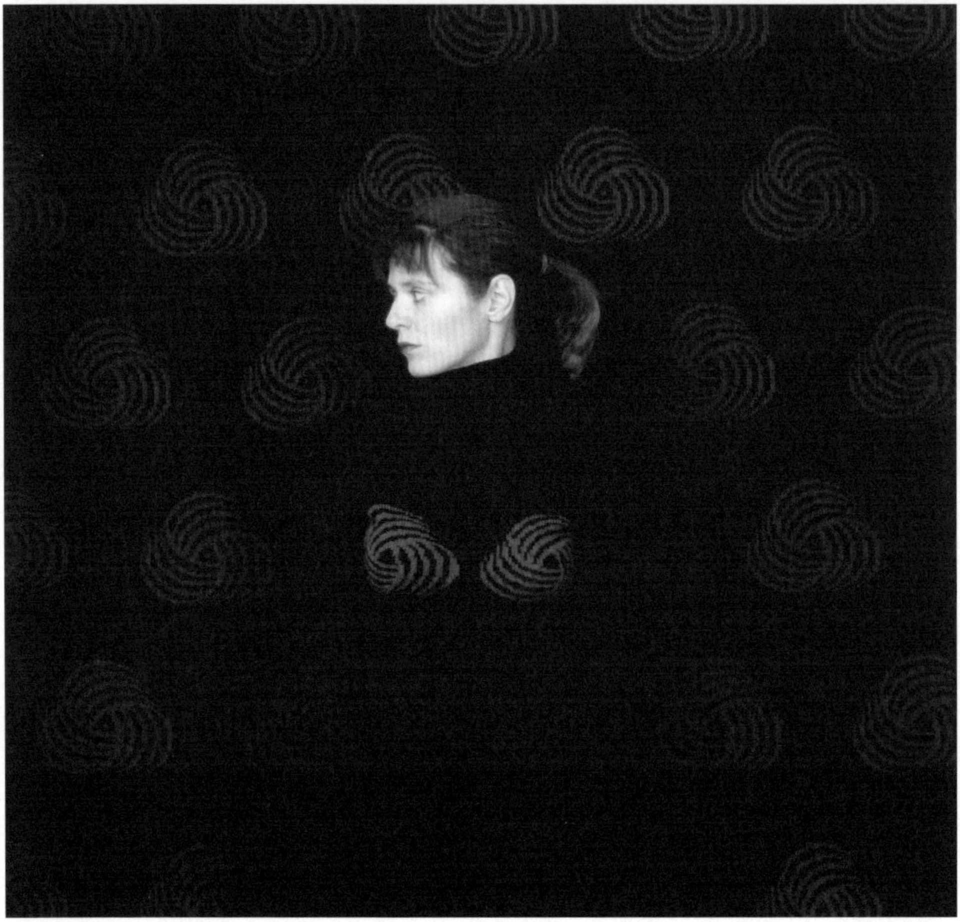

Photograph of Monika Sprüth wearing Rosemarie Trockel's Dress, 1986, wool (standing in front of Trockel's Untitled, 1986, wool)

claimed, by "ironic detachment," as the artists "were putting each collective effort in bold quotation marks."[27]

The catalogues, invitations, and posters produced by these male artists frequently included photographs of Büttner, Georg Herold, Kippenberger, and Oehlen in which each figure maintained a high degree of self-definition. While certainly not a recluse, Rosemarie Trockel, by contrast, cultivated an artistic image always located at one remove from the core of the Cologne art scene. As a result, the boisterous group conversation and in-jokes of Kippenberger, Oehlen, and their peers took on a less rowdy tone in the work of Trockel and her supporters. Her greater emphasis on intimacy and quiet, private utterance stood in opposition to the loud chuckles and backslapping bravado of masculine studio and bar culture. This characterization of Trockel as an outsider on the inside track has been repeated numerous times during the past 25 years. In many ways, it is true that she has consciously and intelligently charted an individual course, but she has done so with considerable help from a tight network of supporters and fellow travelers. Most important has been a long-term relationship with her dealer Monika Sprüth, who had a knack for publicizing the work of her artists and thereby increasing her own visibility.

When Trockel teamed up with Sprüth in the early 1980s, they were conscious of forming an alternative to other recently established galleries run by Max Hetzler (who showed the Büttner/Kippenberger/Oehlen group) and Paul Maenz (who represented artists from the Mülheimer Freiheit group). The kinds of political factionalism associated with the 1960s appeared to transfer to the increasingly market-driven art world of the 1980s, prompting Isabelle Graw to claim that "in the 1980s, everything was still dominated by conflicts between antagonistic camps."[28] At the same time, there were no seriously antagonistic relationships among the different galleries. Sprüth included members of the Mülheimer Freiheit in her first exhibition, held in the studio rooms she shared with Trockel, and a generally cooperative spirit prevailed even as the various players staked out their territories.[29] Jutta Koether suggests that having studied at the Werkkunstschule (School of Applied Arts) in Cologne, Trockel was less inclined to compete with a "master," as was the case with male artists who had studied at the more hierarchical Kunstakademie in Düsseldorf or the Kunsthochschule in Hamburg.[30] The Werkkunstschule, a crafts-based institution, was not known for producing artists who competed in the gallery scene, contributing to Trockel's sense of not belonging to the dominant groups.

An early instance of Sprüth's effective promotion of Trockel and other women artists was the series of three exhibitions, beginning in 1985, called *Eau de Cologne*, each of which was accompanied by a magazine of the same title.[31] In the pages of the magazine, Sprüth and Trockel established a transatlantic exchange with New York artists such as Jenny Holzer and Cindy Sherman, whose works were reproduced. A conversation among international women artists thus ensued, which was thematized in the first issue by a printed dialogue between Sprüth and Trockel. In her comments, Sprüth looks back to 1982, the year she founded her gallery, and explains that the goal was to operate somewhere between the successful women art dealers in New York (who, in her opinion, had too closely followed the male model) and the retreat by feminists in the 1970s into *Selbsterfahrung* (self-awareness). Group dynamics were still actively pursued and shaped, but the previous decade's belief in the personal-as-political had come to seem untenable; a middle course appeared to be the only acceptable option.

A work by Trockel from 1988 seems to address the sense of dividedness that she and Sprüth discuss in *Eau de Cologne*. A modified sweater, *Schizo-Pullover* is wider than the usual garment so that it can accommodate two holes for two heads. Produced after Trockel had already initiated a series of wool paintings in 1985, the *Schizo-Pullover* abandoned the gallery wall and stretcher bars. This more sculptural object could be worn by two people or, at least on a conceptual level, contain the two sides of a single person's split personality. On a page of the catalogue to Trockel's 1991 traveling retrospective, two photographs printed side-by-side illustrate the different possibilities for wearing the sweater. The right image contains two photographs of the head of Esther Schipper—another Cologne dealer and friend of Trockel and Sprüth—who had also founded a gallery in the early 1980s. Her portrait is manipulated to appear as if she were doubly occupying the space of the sweater. This is a recognizable variant of schizophrenic experience, in which the afflicted person copes with multiple versions of the self. Schipper's blank, if slightly bemused, facial expression gives no indication that she finds her predicament either funny or distressing. If anything, she projects an image of self-possession that is comically at odds with the doubling of her subjectivity. The image on the left speaks more directly to the question of Trockel's fostering of group dynamics. She and Schipper are pictured sharing the single, double-necked sweater, their heads floating above the fabric on the same level only inches apart. Their serious expressions, combined with the dark monochrome of the sweater, recall numerous portraits of artists, not to mention dealers and critics, in the 1980s during the heyday of the art market boom. In the catalogue photograph, Trockel and a dealer/collaborator are united physically to form a hybrid figure that might either triumph through their combined powers or implode due to the inherent conflicts that emerge between producer and representative.

Trockel also took advantage of Sprüth's willingness, or desire, to occupy a visibly public position in the artist's other works. Another well-known photograph shows Sprüth wearing Trockel's *Dress* (1986) while standing in front of an untitled wool painting from the same year. The "painting" and the dress are made from the same knit fabric emblazoned with the repeated pattern of the international symbol for wool. In the photograph, Sprüth's head is seen in profile as her body, covered in the fabric with her hands out of view behind her back, appears to merge with the background. Countering the impression of two-dimensionality is the fact that the two wool symbols on the dress are placed strategically over the wearer's chest; Sprüth's head and bosom are the two elements of her body that appear to emerge out of the flatness of the knit painting. The wool logo was appropriated by Trockel and ultimately transformed into a sign that her audience could associate with her extensive series of wool-based works, as well as with German export products. Sprüth takes an active role in the production of the work's meaning and reception, moving beyond the usual activities of selling, distributing, and publicizing it from within the space of the gallery.

There is an easily identifiable undercurrent of lighthearted laughter that defines these images jointly produced by Trockel, Schipper, and Sprüth. One can recognize the bonds of friendship that, as seen in the bar humor of Büttner, Kippenberger, and Oehlen, allowed for day-to-day contacts conducive to brainstorming and the spontaneous execution of ideas. During the years in which Trockel established herself as an internationally successful artist, she experimented with the exposure of portions of the ongoing dialogue that she and Sprüth had conducted since the beginning of the decade. Yet, in spite of a few shared attitudes toward cooperation, their mode of collaboration is quite distinct from the in-jokes generated in exhibition catalogues by Kippenberger and his group of like-minded artists. Trockel's humor moves more in the direction of a stealthy irony, a smart reshuffling of categories and expectations that plays with the language that attends the establishment and nurturing of careers. While humor lies at the heart of this language, it is of a kind that relies less on self-aggrandizement.

The differences between these two groups' in-jokes bring up general questions about the degrees and modes of humor found in their work. An uninitiated viewer may well ask what there is to laugh about. Indeed, many of the jokes they produced are far from laugh-out-loud funny, even for those who can understand the references. As with Breton's black humor, this partly results from the fact that their jokes often leaned in the direction of *Schadenfreude*. On the one hand, the artists occasionally treated themes related to failure and abuse (e.g., alcoholism, pornography, domestic violence). But, perhaps more important, the joke itself was a model that held an attractive veneer of corruption. As many humor theorists since Freud have agreed, the inherent conservatism of jokes means that they are more attuned to the maintenance of tradition than its rejection. Artists in West Germany, as well as several working at the same time in the United States, appear to have found in jokes an appealing *inappropriateness*, an out-of-date quality that made them suited to the obsessive, postmodern recycling of the past.

In 1980s New York and Los Angeles, the two most prominent American manipulators of the traditional joke, Richard Prince and Mike Kelley, shared with their German peers a fascination for the outmoded. Prince's joke paintings, derived from humor books and men's magazines of the 1950s and 1960s, became icons of the postmodern compulsion to repeat, to kill off authenticity and originality through endless replication. "Dumb" jokes about visiting the psychiatrist or marital infidelity, especially when reprinted across one or several canvases, transmit a sense of predictability, even if displayed merely as punch-line fragments. Though his work is generally very distinct from that of Prince, Kelley, too, lifted found texts and images (both artists produced text-only works and image-text combinations) from the same general category of masculine humor publications. In his *Loading Dock Drawings* (1984), part of the exhibition *From My Institution to Yours*, Kelley reproduces raunchy, but harmless, cartoons of the kind faxed between office-workers, such as *Loading Dock Drawing # 4*, captioned "The

Fisherman's Friend," in which a fish performs oral sex on a grinning angler. The jokes of Prince and Kelley operate in at least two communicative registers that are relevant here: first, they precisely and compactly convey the above-mentioned reverence for pathetic and shopworn concepts. In addition, they call upon the traditional, nostalgic power of average jokes, the shared communal space of popular humor. They are truly and uncomfortably transparent. It is especially in this second sense that the Americans tend to operate differently from the Germans, who frequently opted for the obscurity of the in-joke, despite claiming, as Oehlen did, that they aimed for accessibility.

These transatlantic distinctions should not imply that the German artists were not capable of prompting laughter with more straightforward jokes. In *Goethe-Latte* (1982), an early sculpture made with his signature roofing lath, Herold propped up a roughly two-meter length of wood against a wall next to another one less than half its length. "Goethe" is written on the taller one; the phrase *im Vergleich dazu irgendein Scheißer* (which approximately translates into current American slang as, "by comparison, some jerk") appears on the other. There are different ways in which the joke can function. One might focus on the linguistic chasm that is opened up between the glorious prose and poetry associated with the name of Goethe and the vulgar, everyday parlance of his less dignified neighbor. Another reading might center on the notion that in the postmodern era, when the very possibility of greatness and the value of the canon are met with skepticism and derision, the attempt to rise to the level of Romantic genius will invariably fail. The comparison with the shorter piece suddenly loses its impact when the longer piece itself is far from adequate as a monument. Finally, a German-speaking audience would recognize that the word *Latte* is a slang term for an erect penis. There is nothing particularly opaque about this work.

Kippenberger's more overtly comedic works tend to include representations of the artist's body. In 1988 Kippenberger produced a kind of abject pin-up calendar, *Elite 88*, that contained numerous views of him posing in an oversized pair of white, standard-issue men's briefs. For the July scene, the artist is depicted standing in front of a mirror with his hands clasped behind his back, gazing admiringly at the girth of his beer belly. He had already thematized his penchant for addiction and reckless behavior in the painting *Alkoholfolter* (Alcohol Torture, 1981). With a

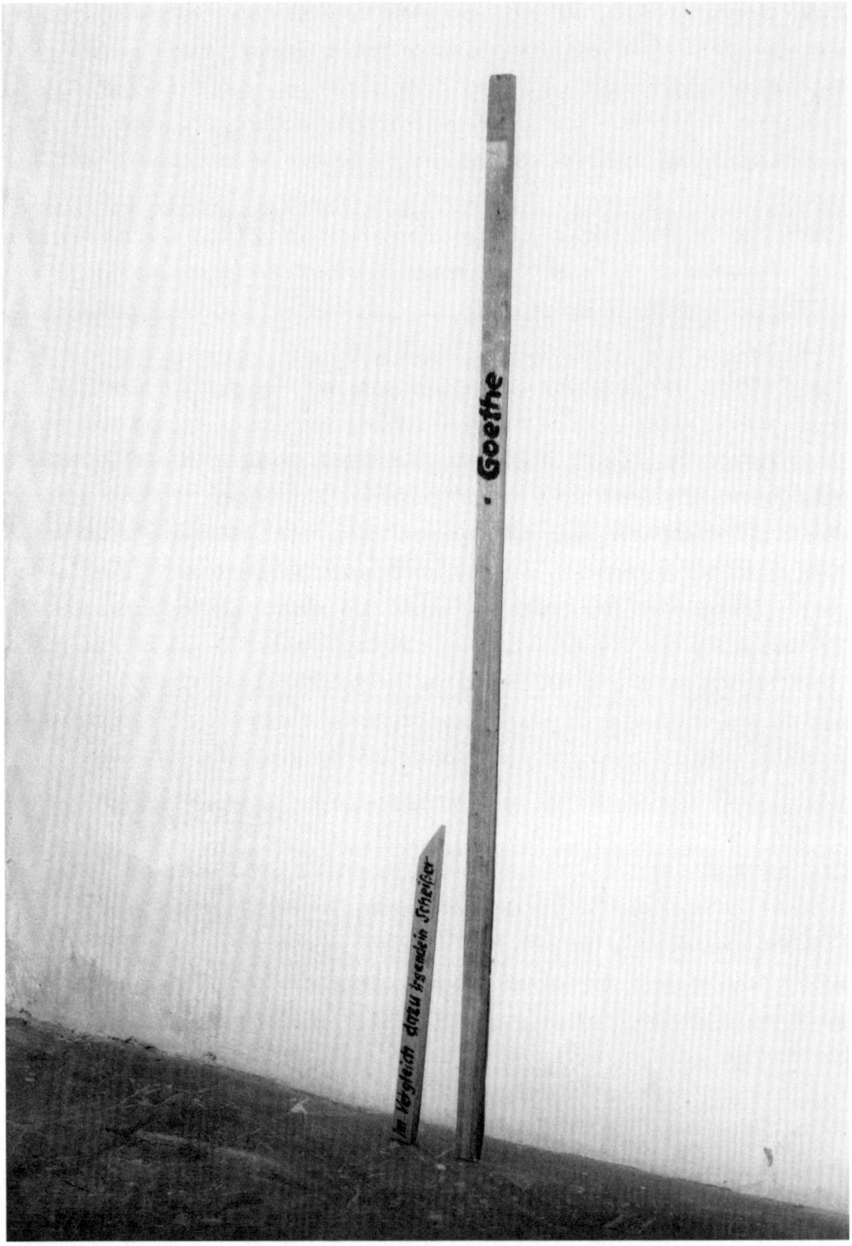

COURTESY OF THE ARTIST | PHOTO: RAINER FICHEL

Georg Herold
Goethe-Latte, 1982
Lath, inscribed text, 2 pieces,
lengths 210 and 60 cm

frightened look on his face, he is pictured holding up his hands, which are caught in two plastic rings on either side of a beer can suspended from the same three-pack holder, a unique packaging device once produced by the famous Schlösser Alt brewery in Düsseldorf. In a move that would become typical of his practice in general, he incorporated the beer-can handcuffs into later works, using them for a magazine cover illustration in 1984 and turning the sculptural object itself into a multiple in 1989. Once he latched onto a source, whether self-produced or appropriated from mass-circulated imagery, Kippenberger ingested and repeatedly processed it until he exhausted its use value.

While Kippenberger operates with the same repetition-compulsion as Prince, he activates it more often through performance, placing him closer to the grotesque, body-centered work of Paul McCarthy. Though Kippenberger was less extreme than McCarthy in his performative self-debasement, with both artists the joke is always also on them, even if they are mocking others (as, for example, with Kippenberger's satirization of Pablo Picasso, or McCarthy's of Willem de Kooning). Kippenberger believed that the joke could be acted out with physical comedy. It was when the verbal element entered the picture, as in his famously endless post-opening-dinner jokes, that Kippenberger's humor moved back in the direction of the in-joke. While McCarthy often seems to exist in a pre-verbal environment, Kippenberger usually could not help using language to deliver his quotient of humor. Given the social nature of his work from the 1980s, it is difficult to separate the individually invented jokes from the group-driven in-jokes. Conversational interaction was almost always an underlying element. In the end, perhaps, we must read all of the jokes spawned by Kippenberger and his colleagues as derived, at least on some level, from in-jokes.

Although their means of publicizing collaboration differed, artists in 1980s West Germany pursued working relationships that ultimately make for a definitively social practice. They responded to the *Tendenzwende* with a retreat to a semi-private space, yet the friendships and collaborations that spawned countless in-jokes never entirely left the public sphere. Nor, however, did they grant full access to their internal dynamics. As Jacques Derrida has written, "Friendship does not keep silent, it is preserved by silence."[32] Remarking on the political nature of such alliances, Derrida explains that friendship only thrives when it does not call attention to itself. Otherwise, the "illusion" on which it is based would become dangerously

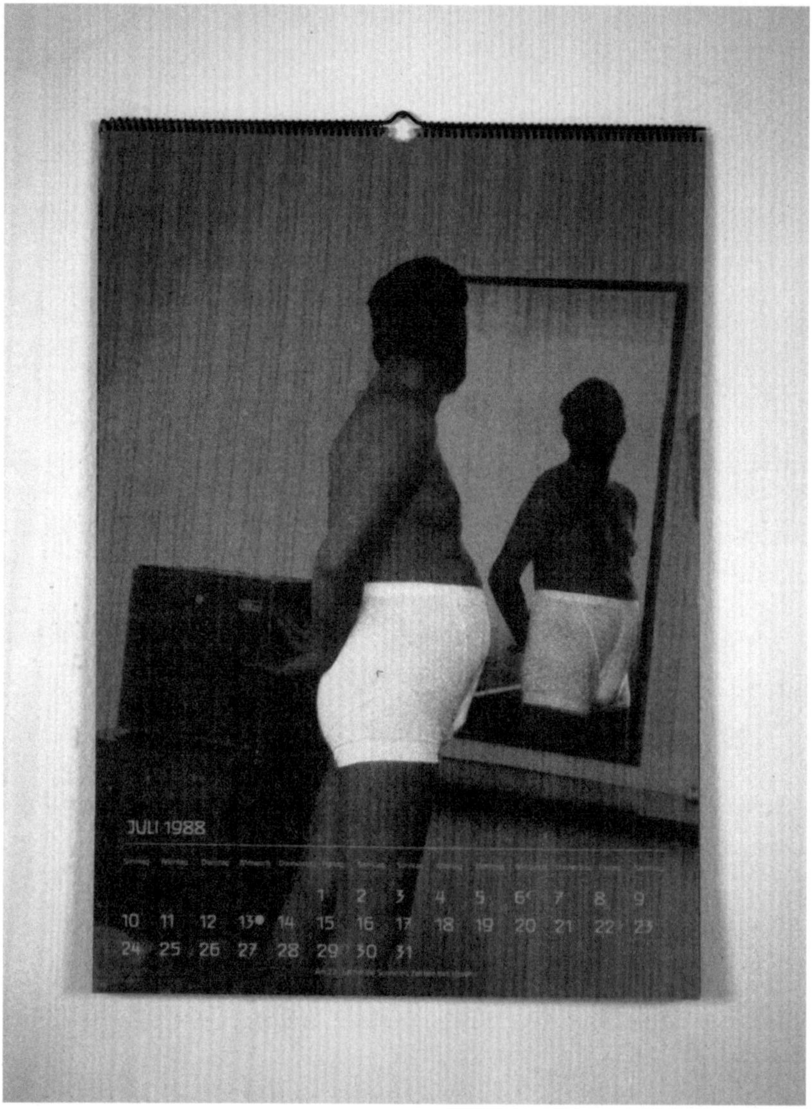

Martin Kippenberger
Elite '88, 1988
Calendar with 24 original silk screens on both sides of variously colored Canson MiTeintes paper 160g, in slipcase, Edition of 27 copies and 5 artist's proofs, numbered and signed
Produced for the exhibition *Elite '88*, Edition Artelier, Graz 1988

apparent.[33] Operating in the linguistic space between hermeticism and transparency, these artists were just about able to keep the bonds of friendship intact by not fully revealing their communicative codes. Nevertheless, they fostered a sense of audience by keeping in play sufficient cultural references derived from commonly shared signs. This balancing act was well suited to a period of political and cultural indecision during West Germany's post-1960s "hangover." It may not have constituted direct action, but neither did it represent a full-scale retreat from the public sphere.

NOTES

1
Russell A. Berman, *Modern Culture and Critical Theory: Art, Politics, and the Legacy of the Frankfurt School*, University of Wisconsin Press, Madison 1989, p. 226.

2
See Jost Hermand, *Die Kultur der Bundesrepublik Deutschland 1965–85*, Nymphenburger, Munich 1988, p. 471.

3
See David Roberts, "Einleitung," in David Roberts (ed.), *Tendenzwenden. Aspekte des Kulturwandels der Siebziger Jahre*, Peter Lang, Frankfurt am Main 1984, p. 7–9.

4
Jost Hermand, *Die Kultur der Bundesrepublik Deutschland*, p. 471.

5
Peter Bürger, *Theory of the Avant-Garde*, trans. Michael Shaw, University of Minnesota Press, Minneapolis 1984 [originally published as *Theorie der Avantgarde*, Suhrkamp, Frankfurt am Main 1974].

6
For a collection of responses to Bürger's book, see Werner Martin Lüdke (ed.), *"Theorie der Avantgarde": Antworten auf Peter Bürgers Bestimmung von Kunst und bürgerlicher Gesellschaft*, Suhrkamp, Frankfurt am Main 1976.

7
Jochen Schulte-Sasse, "Foreword: Theory of Modernism versus Theory of the Avant-Garde," in Peter Bürger, *Theory of the Avant-Garde*, xviii. On the concept of hibernation in Adorno's aesthetic theory, see Irving Wohlfarth, "Hibernation: On the Tenth Anniversary of Adorno's Death," in Gerard Delanty (ed.), *Theodor W. Adorno*, vol. 1, Sage Publications, London 2004, p. 361–390.

8
Johann August Schülein, "Von der Studentenrevolte zur Tendenzwende oder der Rückzug ins Private," *Kursbuch* 48, June 1977, p. 112.

9
Ibid., p. 116, his emphasis.

10
Schulte-Sasse, "Foreword," p. xxxii.

11
Renato Poggioli, *The Theory of the Avant-Garde*, trans. Gerald Fitzgerald, The Belknap Press, Cambridge, Massachusetts 1968, p. 37.

12
See his comments on the crucial role of the "third party" for jokes: Sigmund Freud, *Jokes and Their Relation to the Unconscious*, trans. James Strachey, W. W. Norton, New York 1960, p. 144–145.

13
Søren Kierkegaard, *The Concept of Irony, with Continual Reference to Socrates*, trans. Howard V. Hong and Edna H. Hong, Princeton University Press, Princeton, New Jersey 1989, p. 425.

14
Kierkegaard, *The Concept of Irony*, p. 427.

15
Ibid., p. 426.

16
Merlin Carpenter, "Back Seat Driver," in Thomas Groetz, ed., *Gitarren, die nicht Gudrun heißen: Hommage à Martin Kippenberger*, exh. cat., Galerie Max Hetzler, Berlin 2002, p. 28.

17
Carpenter, "Back Seat Driver," p. 28.

18
Oehlen quoted in Wilfried Dickhoff (ed.), *Albert Oehlen im Gespräch mit Wilfried Dickhoff und Martin Prinzhorn*, Kiepenheuer & Witsch, Cologne 1991, p. 46.

19
Uwe Wirth, *Diskursive Dummheit: Abduktion und Komik als Grenzphänomene des Verstehens*, Universitätsverlag C. Winter, Heidelberg, Germany 1999, p. 1.

20
Ernst Haas, *In Germany*, trans. Lu Fenton, Viking Press, New York 1977 [first published in Germany in 1976].

21
Martin Kippenberger and Albert Oehlen, *The Cologne Manifesto*, Edition Lord Jim Loge, Graz, Cologne, Hamburg 1985, edition of 25 signed copies. The artists produced their own dust jacket that was wrapped around Haas' original book.

22
Pierre Bourdieu, *The Rules of Art: Genesis and Structure of the Literary Field*, trans. Susan Emanuel, Stanford University Press, Stanford, California 1996, p. 231.

23
Bourdieu, *The Rules of Art*. p. 231.

24
Werner Büttner, Martin Kippenberger, Albert Oehlen, *Wahrheit ist Arbeit*, exh. cat., Museum Folkwang, Essen 1984.

25
For the English translation, see Sir Karl R. Popper, *The Logic of Scientific Discovery*, Basic Books, New York 1959.

26
Diedrich Diederichsen, "Virtueller Maoismus: Das Wissen von 1984," in Werner Büttner, Martin Kippenberger, Albert Oehlen, *Malen ist Walen*, exh. cat., Kunstverein München, Munich 1992, p. 38.

27
Tom Holert, "Blood of the Poets: The Tribal '80s," *Artforum* (March 2003), p. 276.

28
Graw quoted in John Armleder, et al, "The 80s Are in Our Midst," in Philipp Kaiser (ed.), *Flashback: Revisiting the Art of the 80s*, exh. cat., Kunstmuseum Basel, Museum für Gegenwartskunst, Basel 2005, p. 35.

29
See Isabelle Graw, "Rosemarie Trockel talks to Isabelle Graw," *Artforum* (March 2003), p. 224.

30
Jutta Koether, "Out of Character: The Strategies for Visual Practice of a Female Artist in Germany," in Gregory Burke (ed.), *Rosemarie Trockel*, exh. cat., City Gallery, Wellington, New Zealand 1993, p. 24.

31
See Johanna Burton, "A Will to Representation: *Eau de Cologne*, 1985–1993," in Rhea Anastas and Michael Brenson (ed.), *Witness to Her Art: Art and Writings by Adrian Piper, Mona Hatoum, Cady Noland, Jenny Holzer, Kara Walker, Daniela Rossell and Eau de Cologne*, Center for Curatorial Studies, Bard College, Annandale-on-Hudson, New York 2006, p. 191–204.

32
Jacques Derrida, *The Politics of Friendship*, trans. George Collins, Verso, London and New York 2005, p. 53.

33
Ibid.

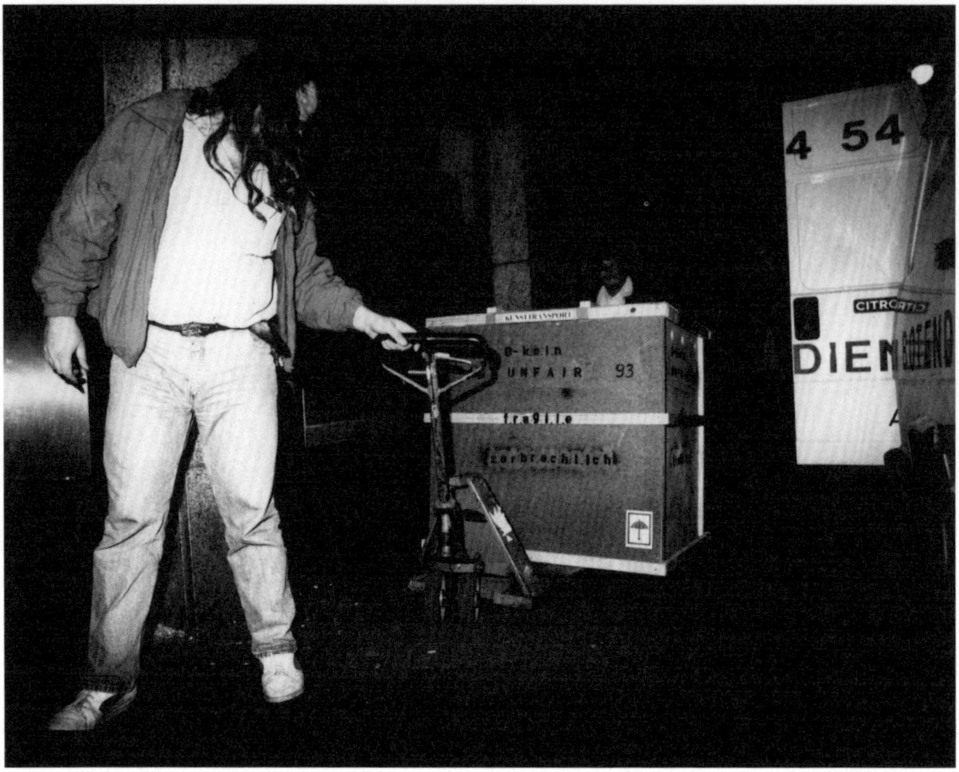

Skip Arnold
Freight, Tuesday, Nov. 9, 1993
I am shipped as an object from Linz, Austria, to Cologne, Germany, to the opening of the *Unfair*

Jan Tumlir

YOUR CONFESSION BOOTH IS MY SOAPBOX: ON SKIP ARNOLD

Breaking Through

I first became aware of the artist Skip Arnold when, as an undergraduate student at UCLA, I attended an on-campus performance of a work of his titled *Marks* (Studio One, Los Angeles, 1984). At the time, Arnold was pursuing a graduate degree, yet he eagerly courted the attentions of his underlings, those of us just starting out. Wandering up and down the halls of the old Dickson building somewhat like a carnival barker, he invited all comers to the show. I recall the impression he made on me then, right when I was most anxious about my own potential to live up to the title of "artist." Arnold's confidence came easily, almost as if he'd simply skipped the stage of radical doubt that precedes, in the narrative of artistic becoming—the *Bildungsroman*, as they say in Germany—the breakthrough. Perhaps his confidence came *too* easily, I thought at the time, attempting to validate my own inner struggle. But I doubted this too: I doubted my doubt. What if it was itself nothing more than a psychological blockage, self-sabotage? What if, by doubting, one was merely deferring a course of action that would have to be taken, at some point, anyway? In this sense, Arnold's breakthrough came down to an absence of any breakthrough due to an absence of doubt. Nothing could have been more troubling to me than this understanding of art as the path of least resistance.

That said, *Marks* was by no means an easy-going piece of work, nor did it suggest that the process of breaking-through, as such, could be simply sidestepped. Here, instead, it was faced squarely. Dispensing with introductions and dramatic development, the artist had seemingly cut through all the twists and turns of a conventional career path to emerge before us in the very moment of climactic confrontation. Basically, the performance consisted of Arnold, naked save for a pair of faded jeans and a crash helmet, hurling himself about in an empty room. The title explicitly refers to the evidential residue of his exertions in dents, scuffs, and stains of blood left behind on the walls, the floor, and maybe even the ceiling. A large part of his effort was devoted to this straightforward "marking" of the space, but there is also a sense in which we, the audience, were "marked" as witnesses to the event. This brings up, in turn, the idea of history, and the relation of a work like *Marks* to other works that either do or do not resemble it. The shock of new art, much like comedy, hinges on the underlying perception of a continuity that is suddenly broken. In order to mark the break, or be marked by it, one first has to recognize the continuity as such. One has to feel oneself to be an integral part of it.

If there was a comedic side to this work, as I now believe, it was lost on me at the time. Certainly, like so many artists in the early 1980s, Arnold was taking a swipe at Abstract Expressionism, and more specifically, at what Allan Kaprow has termed "The Legacy of Jackson Pollock."[1] More pointedly, he was responding to Pollock's studio-bound persona, as it took shape in the various photographs and films that supplement his primary output, and has been compared to that of a "caged animal."[2] All of Pollock's sullen pacing back and forth, his scowling, stopping, and standing still, punctuated by concentrated bursts of action at once violent and graceful—all the sheer existential pathos of it—is here pushed over the top. In *Marks*, Arnold does just what Kaprow suggests, in that he extends the example of Pollock's actions out beyond the painterly frame, beyond the art object as such, and into real space. He follows Kaprow's instructions to the letter, and for this very reason, perhaps, gets them wrong.

Painting Is Dead; Long Live Painting!

The great drama of modernism is motivated, in large part, by a logic of sacrifice: how much of art's traditional ways and means could be relinquished, and yet art would still be art? The pursuit of this degree-zero leads from Pollock, who does away with his brush in favor of an ordinary stick from which paint is dripped onto canvas, to Morris Louis, who does away with the stick, and pours paint directly from the can. Poured paintings then give way to paintings that are sprayed (Ushio Shinohara and the Gutai Group), cut (Lucio Fontana), shot (Niki de Saint Phalle), burned (Alberto Burri), stained, erased, and/or left untouched (Robert Rauschenberg). Approaching more closely Arnold's particular *modus operandi*, in *Marks* are the works of Otto Mühl, Carolee Schneeman, and Paul McCarthy, among others, who dispense not only with the marking tool, but the surface of inscription as well, while keeping the medium—paint itself, or some analogous substance—in play. All of these artists submit their bodies, as "living paintbrushes," to the task of marking their environment.

The term "living paintbrushes" was coined by Yves Klein, in 1958, in reference to the paint-soaked models that he pressed into canvases to produce his *Anthropométries* series. But even more *a propos*, in this regard, is Klein's emblematic *Leap into the Void*, an "assisted" photograph of 1960 which arrests the artist in the midst of an ecstatic swan-dive from the ledge of a single-story brick building and thereby compels us to think forward to the Pollock-style splattering of viscera that will be left on the pavement below. As the "The Legacy of Jackson Pollock" devolves into staged transgressions of physical integrity, such as Andy Warhol's urination paintings (the *Oxidation* series), Piero Manzoni's canned faeces (*Merda d'artista*, 1961), and Gina Pane's public self-lacerations (as in *Le corps pressenti*, 1975), the painterly act is revealed as essentially regressive—and possibly a consequence of poor toilet-training.

Here, then, is the opening through which Arnold enters the art-historical fray; yet his reply to these precedents is remarkably downbeat. No sense of psycho-sexual liberation ensues from his sacrifice of art as objective complement to the artist's subjectivity. It would seem, moreover, that subjectivity "itself" becomes dismally attenuated in the process. Arnold's *Marks* is not quite "expression" any longer in the sense that it does not originate from any particular interior, or interiority. If any residual affect can be ascribed to it, it would have to be frustration—but, again, this is a generalized, free-floating sort of frustration, one that could belong to any artist, even to the making of art in general. *Marks* is "about" the frustrations of art in much the same way that the television show *The Office* is "about" the frustrations of white-collar busy-work. Art is here reduced to the level of a dumb joke about banging one's head against the wall.

I began by thinking about breakthroughs because no such thing occurs in Arnold's work. *Marks* is decisive on this point: it is a physical demonstration of the impossibility of breaking-through. As in so many of his early performances, Arnold dispenses with any sort of narrative arc, to chart instead a course of uninterrupted decline. Initially energized and determined to do some damage, he gradually wears himself out until, like a defeated boxer, collapsed on the spot, he has to be helped out of the arena. In the absence of any other intermediate thing upon which to train one's expressive will, it is simply acted-out in an unfocused and, ultimately, exhausting manner. This acted-out expression is inevitably shadowed by neurosis. One might recall how repetition is linked to mental illness, especially when it is exercised in the hope of achieving a different outcome. In *Marks*, this definition is applied across the board to the practice of avant-garde art.

The figure of the avant-garde artist presented by *Marks* is a figure of fun, even if the work itself does not exactly invite laughter. While the fulfillment of what is, after all, a self-fulfilling prophecy is grim, this should not keep us from finding in it some sort of joke-like levity. If authentic tragedy is guided by the axiom that bad things happen to good people—or, more generally, that life is unjust—then comedy plays instead on expected outcomes, "just desserts." In tragedy, we are tricked by fate right along with the tragic hero, whose downfall is typically caused by some unintended transgression. In comedy, conversely, what happens to a person will be shown to be entirely consistent with who they are. Even if they do not recognize it, we, the audience, do. In comedy, we know that character *is* fate, and vice-versa.

In other words, failure is funny only if and when it is deserved. Humor may well be found in the spectacle of someone so stubbornly pursuing a goal that is unlikely to ever materialize, but only if we believe that this goal is somewhat laughable to begin with. Inasmuch as the goal is equated here with breaking-through—already by this point a laughable romantic cliché—then the utter futility of Arnold's means will be revealed as context-appropriate, and accordingly, as equally laughable. Banging one's head against the wall is funny, in this case, not because it is absurd, but because it is perfectly adequate to the task.

Marks makes a mockery of the avant-garde artist's striving to transcend the context of art through the sheer force of physical presence. Having systematically sacrificed every one of art's traditional media and materials on the modernist altar, all that is left is a bare studio with a bare body in it. That this process of radical reduction has obviously done nothing to curb the artist's aesthetic impulse might itself amount to a statement about the stubbornness of character: art remains essentially a mark-making game. The failure of the artist to generate a new content to suit the new conditions of art is what is at stake here, this now seen against the perhaps over-reaching ambition to do so in the first place. And here is where Arnold's work invites a whole other range of possible readings, no more or less humorous in their implications. That the collapse of "The New" in the person of this stubbornly self-defeating avant-garde artist might have been acted-out in the interest of "The Old" cannot be ruled out. In short, that the outwardly radical *Marks* is actually a work in service to tradition. Painting is dead; long live painting!

Hitting the Wall

If we want to think of Skip Arnold as a comic performer, then he should be grouped among the physical, *slapstick* sort. In this regard, it is worth noting that the etymology of "slapstick" refers the term to an actual device, a theatrical implement made of two lengths of wood that can be knocked together to simulate the sound of a collision between body and body, or body and thing, onstage. One can only imagine how the addition of just this kind of sound effect, improvised on the spot, would have affected the reception of *Marks*. Whatever ambivalence we experienced as an audience would have been swiftly dispelled. The comic motive—to "make 'em laugh"—is one that the public is always prepared to reward, especially in the context of performance art, which is typically approached with some degree of trepidation. It is in this context, precisely, that we are eager for cues to guide our reception one way or another.

In the performances of Arnold's that I actually attended, no such assistance was offered, as the artist's favored mode of gradual depletion seemed to disqualify the sort of short, sharp shock to the system that compels an immediate reaction. Even when Arnold was engaged in frenetic activity, as in *Marks*, the experience of part of the audience verged on a kind of serenity. Once it became obvious that nothing in particular was being asked of us, we were granted permission to revert to distanced, dreamy contemplation. However, this was itself a set-up of sorts, for it was not in spite of this appeal to high-minded connoisseurship, but in direct relation to it, that the slapstick nature of the collision was ultimately determined. Throughout it all, we were continually reminded of what cannot be avoided: the body will surely hit the wall, and just as surely fall.

This sense of suspension between the orders of the imaginary and the real is theatrical by definition, and therefore most evident in works by Arnold that are emphatically staged and visible only from a fixed point of view by a seated audience. However, much the same can be said for works specifically enacted for the video camera, and even those that take place "in the round," where the artist's body takes on a kind of sculptural presence in the open field, as it inserts itself as a quasi-decorative fixture into a landscape, cityscape and/or architecture as such. Almost always, there is an element of endurance that endows these events with a duration directly related to the artist's physical being, his capacities for withstanding the elements, and maintaining an upright posture, or pose. Just as important, though, is the overall deployment of a *mise-en-scène*, the acute attention Arnold brings to the formal details of framing, line and color, dynamism and balance, and so on. Underlying all of these works is a persistent ontological ambiguity: from *Marks* onward, it becomes increasingly evident that Arnold is, above all, interested in the potential of performance to generate a certain kind of *image*.

Bearing in mind that the aims of performance art were initially defined in strict opposition to those of theater and the orders of representation and illusionism more generally, we are confronted, here, by a kind of counter-iconoclasm. By presenting himself as his work, Arnold obviously remains invested in the great avant-garde project of blurring the boundaries between art and life, only not for the reasons we have come to expect. That is, if it was once assumed that life should always be favored in this equation, then Arnold means to reverse it: he performs on the side of, on behalf of, art—with a capital "A." He aims high, over and above the sort of willfully compromised, contingent, and transitory art that defines the postmodern moment, and toward something more wholesome, lasting ... "classical." However, precisely because it is comprised of living things that exist in time, from the outset the work itself is destined to miss its mark.

Ultimately, it is all about the slapstick inevitability of "hitting the wall," even as every effort is made to forestall this end, and to effectively hold the eternal pose of art as the forces of gravity, entropy, and disintegration set in. In this sense, all of the ways that the artist has had himself forcibly fixed into place throughout the course of his career can be seen as both tortuous impositions on the body and as prosthetic aids, artificial means of maintaining the desired condition of stasis. In *The Plague* (1984, Zero One Gallery, Los Angeles) Arnold was hung by the wrists and ankles from a wooden structure reminiscent of medieval torture scenarios; he was clamped between two planks of wood and then leaned against the wall in *Closet Corner* (1987, The Variety Arts Center, Los Angeles); displayed in a Plexiglas cube in *On Display* (1995, Burnett Miller Gallery, Los Angeles); inserted into a custom shipping crate and then transported from Linz, Austria, to the Unfair in Cologne, Germany, in *Freight* (1993); and sealed top to toe in a large plastic bag and hung from the wall in *Specimen* (2003, Tea Building, London). Even so, time and again, the transcendent aspirations of the artist are undermined by an abject temporality. Arnold stages his work to insure this outcome, thereby also coaxing from failure a certain measure of success.

Fulfilling the sacrificial course of the avant-garde in such a way that loops it right back to an origin in religious ritual, Arnold resumes the role of scapegoat and martyr, channeling onto his own physical being a free-floating cosmic pain that ostensibly threatens us all. But this no longer comes down to an exercise in catharsis. On the contrary, it would seem that his suffering has been rinsed clean of its moral dimension. However painful or degrading the trials that he endures, we, the audience, remain relatively guilt-free throughout, secure in the knowledge that we are not their cause. The tortured figure standing (or hanging) before us, center-stage, also haunts the wings; it is he, not us, who pulls the strings. It is

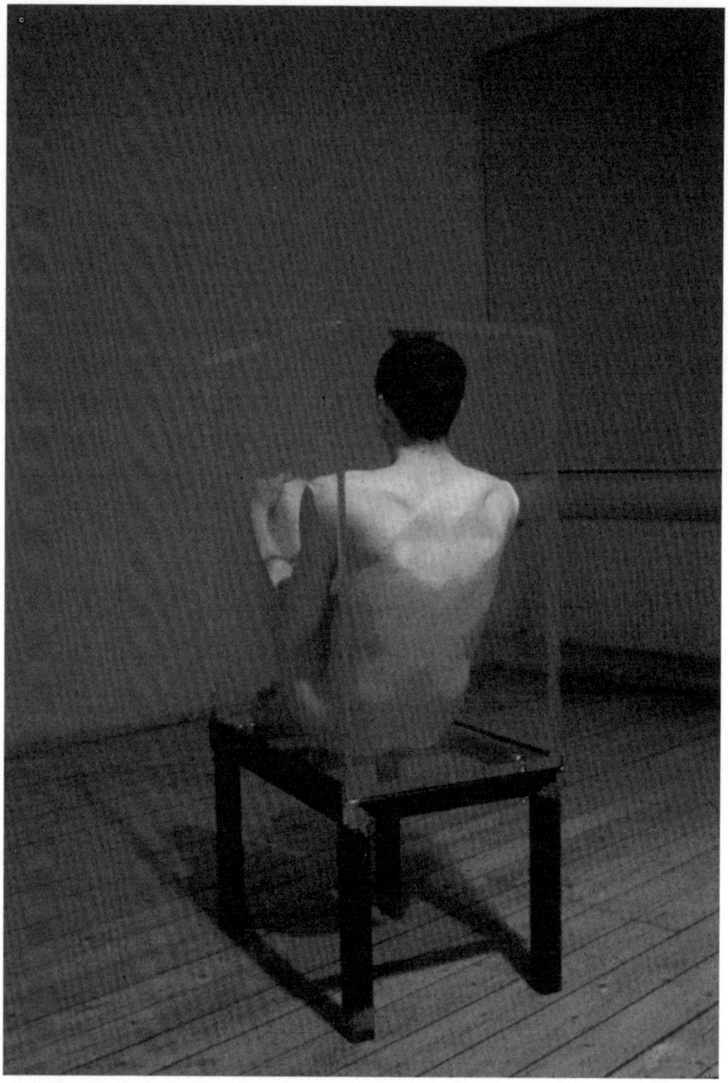

COURTESY OF THE ARTIST AND SPENCER BROWNSTONE GALLERY

Skip Arnold
On Display, OK Offenes Kulturhaus Oberösterreich, Linz, Austria, December 1–18, 1993
I am experienced as a fetish (part of a collection); I offer myself as an object, as something collectable, to be displayed like an object in a natural history museum.
20 mm thick acrylic, steel stand, Skip, 720 mm x 855mm x 470 mm overall

therefore perfectly fitting that in so many of the pieces mentioned above, the artist becomes a marionette and is literally left dangling. And the responsibility is ultimately his: he got himself into this bind.

Here, then, is another distinction that we may draw between comic and tragic figures: what happens to the latter also happens to us, whereas in comedy it tends to happen to someone else. In tragedy, the flaw that ultimately takes down the hero must be seen as inherited, socially imposed, or else originating in the most submerged and occluded recesses of the individual psyche. Our empathetic response is conditioned by a presumption of innocence, which is also the basis of all moral judgment. If no such thing occurs in comedy it is because there we are dealing instead with autonomous beings who are solely responsible for their foibles, which they must accept right along with the troubles these cause them. In comedy, that is, the character flaw is rendered in the light of the "purely aesthetic."

The Dialectics of Inside and Outside

Arnold shows us a body and, moreover, his body. His lanky, mantis-like physical being constitutes his medium just as brushes, pigment, and canvas serve for a painter. He must also be able to work himself as raw material into the form of a compelling object and/or image. Generally, Arnold straddles the line between the two: working in actual three-dimensional space and for a certain period of time, he composes a picture, a *tableau vivant*, with himself at its center. But Arnold consistently downplays the sort of self-mastery that the *tableau vivant* demands on principle; he does not try to subordinate every living, breathing element to the effect of an uncanny—because inert—life-likeness. He inserts himself into the framework of art, but then goes on being exactly who he is.

This last point might seem almost self-evident: since Arnold *is* who he is, how could it be any other way? The moment the artist decides to enter, and thereby also to become, the work, then the work in turn will have to adapt its formal contours to his own. It will have to surrender its formerly unlimited potential to be virtually anything in order to be just this. Arnold not only embraces the fact that the "what" of the artwork is ultimately transformed into the "this"—this person, this body—but he does so in a manner that his long line of historical precedents, from Chris Burden and McCarthy to Kaprow and, finally, Pollock himself, do not. To a greater or lesser extent, theirs remain generalized bodies, stand-ins for everyone and anyone, so that it is only the framework of art that may be conceived as a concrete particular.

All of these historical figures still work under the aegis of the great project of avant-garde expansion; undertaking voyages of exploration into the outlands of the everyday. As the prime movers of this process they themselves automatically become central, as well, to the work's composition, but this does not imply, as with Arnold, a corresponding absorption. Initially, that is, the artist's body is included within the body of the work mainly as an agent of antagonism. The work that this body performs is directed against the work of art that contains it as a host body, and that, for its part, offers only resistance. The avant-garde strains against this resistance; this is its whole *raison d'être*. It wants somehow to cancel the dialectical opposition between the inside and the outside of art, even if this is also the source of its own self-definition. On the proverbial front line of the culture wars, the avant-garde can only fulfill its mission by falling, which is basically what has already happened by the time we get around to Arnold.

The first time as tragedy, the second as farce: the figure of the avant-garde artist is embodied by Arnold as already fallen, a figure of fun. If the bodies of Pollock, Kaprow, McCarthy, and Burden worked from the inside out, straining heroically against the institutional confines of art, Arnold's body works in the opposite direction, comically. It is not in reversal as such that the humor lies, but in the understanding that, because we no longer have any agreed-upon measure, any constant or mean, it is impossible to determine whether one is moving forward or backward, or whether one is inside or outside to begin with. Within this context of total deregulation, Arnold's various "border crossings" between life and art take on a patina of allegory, because they are "about" history, while remaining entirely literal, because this history no longer has any meaningful bearing on the art. What one is left with, finally, is just this literal enactment of history within a post-historical context, which is perhaps just another way of describing the general condition of a body existing in time.

That the body has its own form of memory that it exercises at all times in the processes of walking, standing, sitting, and even lying down—

that basically every action it performs is also a reenactment—is a consistent subtext of Arnold's work. In the absence of any historically mandated mission, the artist rehearses all former struggles with the institution of art as a *coup de théâtre* predicated on the costs of fitting in. In this way, we can join the Plexiglas cube of *On Display* to the wooden crate of *Freight* as well as to the bank vault that is the ultimate destination of Arnold's journey through *Mittel Europa (Living Quarters/Conducting Business)*, (*Unfair*, Cologne, Germany, 1993). All are equally representative of a standardized system of symbolic exchange that now operates on a truly global scale, while at the same time recalling the specific contribution of postwar art to its development. For Arnold, these are just so many variations on the form of the minimalist cube, which is resuscitated time and again as the emblematic limit-object of a late-stage modernism that flirts with ideas of de-differentiation and the all-out adoption of mass-market principles. Here, again, it is clear that this history is being approached from its "other end," as an art of radical reduction and negation is progressively filled back up.

Replenishing the cube's formerly hollow interior with himself, Arnold confirms the suspicion, famously articulated by Michael Fried, of the "latent or hidden ... anthropomorphism" ostensibly always present in this format.[3] The figure returns to the site of its expulsion as a kind of repressed content. Taking the form of a living artist's body, it saps the cube of its aesthetic autonomy and abstraction leaving us with a utilitarian object, a disposable container. Inside this thing, the figure is duly commodified, turned into a thing itself; but these things are not equivalent, nor are they just anything. Arnold occupies the cube or crate in much the same way that he occupies the space of the studio or gallery in *Marks*—that is, as a framework that defines its contents as art. This is a generalized symbolic transaction and, as such, easily understood; however, it is in the specific details that that one tends to get lost. Crammed inside the wooden box, one imagines Arnold's body hunched at 90-degree angles, whereas in the "white cube" this body literally bounces off the walls.

When, in *Gargoyle* (1992), the artist climbs up the facade of the old Otis building in MacArthur Park and crouches for some hours on a narrow pediment overlooking the street like an ancient stone demon, he is literally incorporated into its design. The same goes for *Statue* (1993), for which he posed with arms and legs spread like Leonardo's "measure of man,"

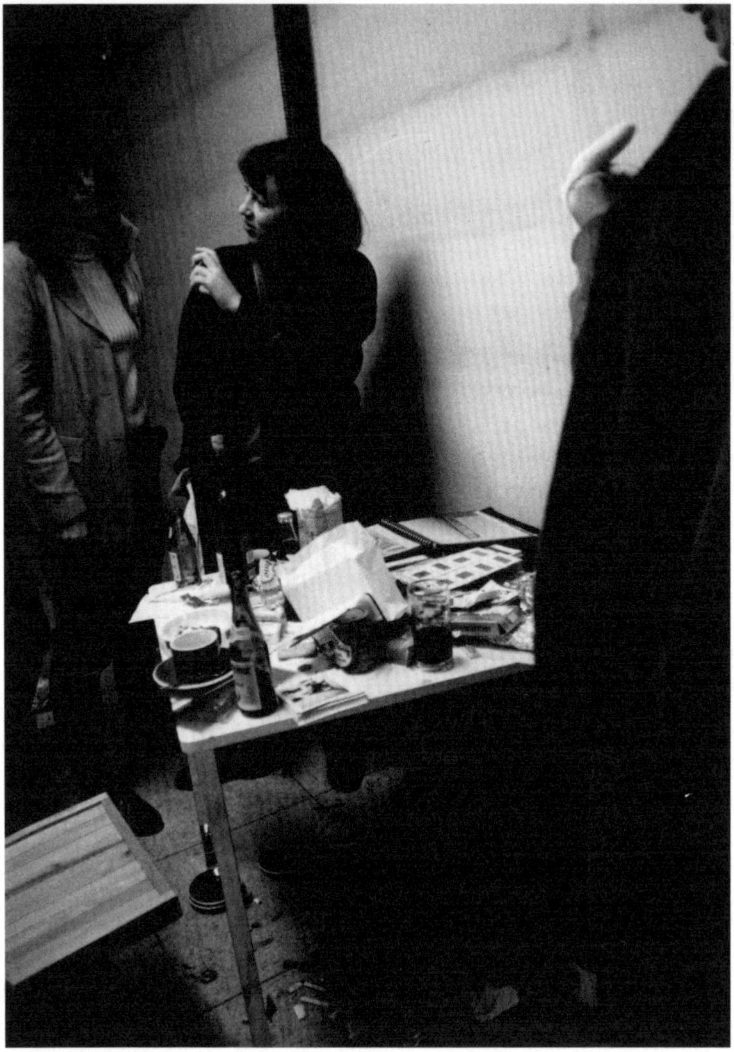

COURTESY OF THE ARTIST AND SPENCER BROWNSTONE GALLERY

Skip Arnold
Living Quarters/Conducting Business,
November 10, 1993, through November 15,
1993; *Unfair*, Cologne, Germany
After being invited to the *Unfair* I was given a room to use. My interest was to live and conduct business for the duration of the *Unfair* in the space I was given; to promote myself and the work I was doing in Europe. I made people comfortable by serving wine and cheese.

standing watch just above the doorway of the Kim Light Gallery in Los Angeles; and for *Marquee* (1999), in which he is wrapped in plastic sheeting and then tied to an awning in front of the Kunsthaus Glarus during a festival of performance art in Switzerland. If the figure is not inside the frame, then he is never far away, hugging its edge, conforming to its shape. Whether inside or outside, Arnold's body is absorbed into an order of things in the manner of those insects and animals that are able to blend in with the scenery either to elude their stalkers or surprise their prey. Arnold similarly conforms his body to the demands of the surrounding landscape, the architecture, and even the objects within it; but he does so for strictly non-practical reasons. A confirmed exhibitionist and aesthete, he asks us only to observe, and therefore not to overlook, what he puts before us.

In this way, all former distinctions between inside or outside are gradually eroded, leaving the viewer in-between, and caught in an implicitly theatrical condition. The stage is a site that has been cordoned-off from the world for purposes of make-believe, but without ever renouncing its hold on the real. This much is evident from the point of view of the audience, whose negotiation between two sorts of fascination, actual and imaginary, is always ongoing. But this is no less the case for the person on-stage who is "actually acting." Arnold milks this paradox for all it is worth. As a real artist who plays the role of an artist on the stage of an art world that has become indistinguishable from the real world, he wields an intermittent presence, continually disappearing and reappearing before us.

Crash Helmet

All of these symbolic transactions between art and life, the make-believe and the real, tend to produce an acutely physical remainder, and it is to this remainder that our attention is finally drawn. What is in play here can be related to Roland Barthes' "third meaning," a semantic order in which what is sought in the form of the work is not confirmation of a purported message but precisely those telling details that derail its delivery.[4] Barthes locates the third meaning in a series of stills excerpted from Sergei Eisenstein's film *Ivan the Terrible* (Part I, 1944). The director's decision to cut short the flow of the narrative is indicative of a desire to isolate the aesthetic dimension of art from any sort of functional relation to the logic(s) of representation. At the same time, however, he strictly refuses to provide us with any assurance that the resulting fragments can be pieced back together into anything like an autonomous modernist totality. Form, in Barthes' thinking, is never self-sufficient or pure; it is what strains against signification, our obligation to read and to understand.

Accordingly, in the image of two courtiers "raining down gold over the young czar's head," we are pointed to such things as "a certain compactness of the courtiers' make-up, thick and insistent for the one, smooth and distinguished for the other; the former's 'stupid' nose, the latter's finely traced eyebrows, his lank blondness, his faded, pale complexion, the affected flatness of his hairstyle suggestive of a wig, the touching-up with chalky foundation talc, with face powder."[5] These are all signs of "a rather pitiful disguise," as Barthes puts it, that plainly speak to their own theatrical construction at the expense of verisimilitude and our suspension of disbelief; and yet, for all this, they do not spoil our pleasure.[6] To the contrary, these "obtuse" details are precisely what we are most drawn to. They pinpoint, in art, "what one loves, what one wants to defend: an emotion-value."[7]

To return one last time to *Marks*, I want to admit that the piece affected me much more than it probably should have. I could not write it off as easily as I'd hoped, but I could not reconcile with it either. Thinking about it years later, one detail began to stand out as a *punctum* of sorts: the crash helmet that Arnold had donned as the sole measure of self-preservation within this otherwise straightforwardly self-destructive exercise. At a time when no such thing was required by law, when the safety standards governing both life on the streets and inside the institution were so much more lax than they are today, the fact that Arnold had decided to buck the freewheeling trend with this show of (at the time, extreme) caution was my first clue that something "funny" was happening in *Marks*. Clearly, his nakedness served to instantly draw all eyes upward toward that crash-helmet, so much so that it is finally this *thing* that is accentuated as the critical element—I want to say, the fulcrum—on which *Marks* is made to teeter between high drama and low farce.

In relation to the harmful actions that this work entailed, the helmet stood out as a vaguely Socratic affirmation of the mind-body split, as well

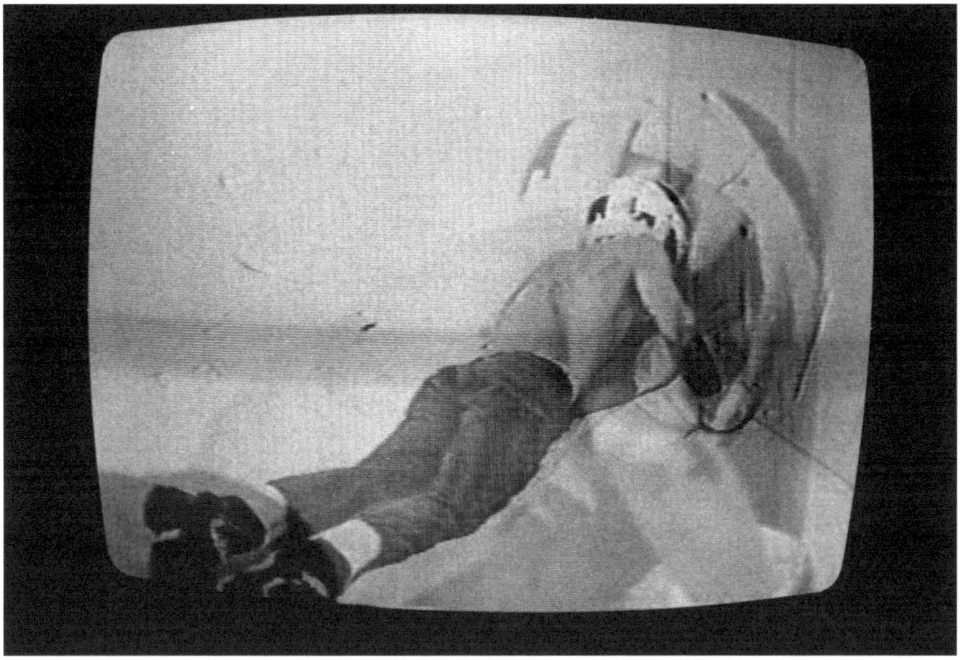

Skip Arnold
Marks, 1984
Live performance made for MP/TV
Los Angeles, CA, on January 1, 1984
I use my body to make marks on the walls of an 8 x 8 x 8' white room while an audience watches on closed circuit TV. The piece ended when I lost consciousness.

as all its implied hierarchies. Ruin the outer shell of the body, but preserve the inner life of the mind. After all, the body is merely the engine, the labor-force that answers to orders from on high. The mind is where art-as-idea takes shape, and as the point of origin for this particular work, it must be given its due. Brains and brawn: one imagines top-rank military strategists gathering in rooms far removed from the front to plot out dangerous maneuvers on paper, estimating their costs, acceptable losses in terms of human life, before sending their lower-downs to certain death. Arnold, likewise, had made a point of exempting the head from the violence that is to be endured by the body below.

This is perhaps a far-flung comparison, but not entirely beyond the pale. Literally "stripped down" to only the most generic elements—a body, a room—*Marks* would nevertheless admit one crucial reference to the socio-political present in the form of that helmet, which appears in the work as an emblematic found object. As a store-bought item, all of the helmet's concrete particulars of style and design were highlighted against the scrupulously uninflected "look" of everything else we were given. As such, the decision to wear a helmet was already strange, but even more curious was the choice of this specific helmet, decorated with the stars and stripes of the American flag and thus serving as both a token of patriotism and a sign of counter-cultural inversion—as with Peter Fonda's "Captain America" character in *Easy Rider* (dir. Dennis Hopper, 1969), for example. If, overall, the work is underwritten by a logic of strict reduction, then the helmet is proposed as its antithesis: something excessive, *de trop*.

Due to their mutual lack of color, Arnold's body, dressed only in faded jeans, and the "white cube" space that it occupies become one—a basically monochromatic backdrop *for* the helmet. Squinting one's eyes, this highly graphic, colorful thing could be made to fly freely about, somewhat like a super-ball rebounding off the walls. Super-balls are in themselves silly, hence funny, but they are sillier and funnier still when they are insinuated into a scenario as ostensibly grave as this one. Imagine a super-ball thrown into a morgue. If this thought strikes a comic note, it is not just because this bouncing thing, simply by virtue of its silly nature, disrupts the decorum that "comes with the territory" of death. What compels laughter is the secondary perception that this disruption of the expected order of things makes sense, that it is somehow "right." A latent symmetry must be found to exist between these two worlds, tragic and farcical.

Bodies that fall do not rise again, and again, and again ... The idea of the super-ball, a sphere of lifeless stuff with seemingly unlimited reserves of vitality, throws every existing limit of physical being into sharp relief. An obnoxious reminder of human finitude, or mortality, it both undercuts and reinforces the grave tone of Arnold's performance—its *gravitas*, which is here directly an outcome of physical gravity. To put it another way: gravity is a force to which the artist-protagonist of *Marks* wholly submits, at the same time making light the submission.

Gravitas

In the opening-out of the work of art to the world that follows from "The Legacy of Jackson Pollock" as Kaprow understood it, there is an insistent element of disenchantment. The work pried from the virtual dimension of the white wall becomes just a thing among other things. Surrendering the armature of its autonomy, art becomes potentially perishable, and this is born out in so many of the movements that succeed Abstract Expressionism and make a virtue of their steadily elapsing life spans. Clement Greenberg's opposition to so much of this work, from Minimalism to Conceptual art, land art, body art, and so on, is raised on the very borderline between anti-illusionism and becoming-real. Fried is even more acute on this point when, in the anti-Minimalist polemic of "Art and Objecthood" he interprets the becoming-real of art as a fall from grace.

Fried opens his essay with a quote from the Puritan scholar Jonathan Edwards, whose thoughts on transcendence, the pursuit of the eternal moment across the bounds of human finitude, he aligns with the experience of modern art as he goes on to describe it. Grace is proposed as a momentary reprieve from the repetitive succession of "one thing after another"—as Donald Judd described the principle of making that underwrote his "Specific Objects." Fried's description is less neutral, more pejorative: he writes of an "endlessness" that ties art *literally* to life, which is oppressive because it does in fact end.[8] That is, by overflowing its former aesthetic boundaries, the work is made subject to the boundaries of existence itself. This once-transgressive permission quickly turns stale, as "being able to go on and on" becomes a mandate for "having to go on and on ... "[9] Just like every one of us, then, art in its endlessness must submit to the durational course of the great countdown clock. The sense of time's passing weighs on every individual instant of post-medium art, so that temporality itself becomes the medium that links it to its audience. The work shoulders the very same weight that bears down on the body of the observer and marks it with age: the weight of gravity, precisely. Grace, as embodied in works of modern art, arises in our release from it. No longer.

Gravity, which draws every paint-laden gesture downward, in drips, from the point of inscription to the bottom edge of the canvas, is a force that Pollock effectively distilled in the production of his drip paintings. When the canvas surface is pulled from the wall to receive the same drips that would otherwise fall away from it, abstraction itself takes the plunge. Descending from the untethered "opticality" championed by Greenberg and Fried toward the studio floor, abstraction itself becomes an experience of low physicality or, in the language of Georges Bataille, "base materialism." Subsequent accounts of "The Legacy of Jackson Pollock" as proposed by Rosalind Krauss and Yve-Alain Bois, for instance, revel in a convergence of high-mindedness and *bassesse* that now becomes Pollock's very *raison d'être*.[10]

Arnold's *Marks* precedes this particular analysis but comes to much the same conclusion. Let's not forget the concept of "formlessness" inherent in Kaprow's argument: he suggests that Pollock's whole practice was directed to this end, "to get rid of the usual idea of form."[11] It is worth noting that Kaprow's definition of form is, from the first moment, bound up with time as a matter of "beginning, middle, and end."[12] He writes: "We do not enter a painting of Pollock's in any one place (or hundred places). Anywhere is Everywhere, and we dip in and out when and where we can. This discovery has led to remarks that his art gives the impression of going on forever."[13] However, as Kaprow goes on to explain, this "impression" is in fact tied to the concrete actuality of the edge where every painting is brought to a stop. It is the particular quality of this stopping that we attend to: Pollock's "abrupt leaving off of the activity" at the edge, his vain "refusal" of that edge as an "ending."

Arnold, like Kaprow, starts out by considering "The Legacy of Jackson Pollock" in a tragic light, so that the refusal of endings in art may have actually precipitated the too-early ending of the artist's own life. In *Marks*, he embodies this "legacy" in the role of the boundary-breaking artist as tragic figure, one who quickly expends his vital supply of energy by banging about the studio in fruitless pursuit of transcendence. The brevity of the performance is telling: the artist grows increasingly sluggish, stooped, until at last he is unable to maintain an upright posture and falls. Accordingly, falling is equated not just with the failure of the avant-garde, but with the larger tragic fate of mankind. Only an art that acknowledges its limits, the edges of the frame, the "beginning, middle, and end" of the act, is allowed to escape this fate—which is, ultimately, just what *Marks* does. This is the punch line: the artist's falling body brings the work to its proper conclusion. It had failed to "tear down the wall," as it were, and done so ... successfully.

NOTES

1
See Allan Kaprow, "The Legacy of Jackson Pollock," in Kaprow, *The Blurring of Art and Life*, University of California Press, Berkeley 1996.

2
Paul Schimmel writes of "the spectacularly theatrical photographs by Hans Namuth that capture an image of the artist as a caged animal in a high-contrast, black-and-white trance of creative, mythmaking action." Paul Schimmel, "Leap into the Void, Performance and the Object," in *Out of Actions*, exh. cat., Museum of Contemporary Art, Los Angeles 1998, p. 18.

3
Michael Fried, "Art and Objecthood," in *Art and Objecthood: Essays and Reviews*, University of Chicago Press, Chicago 1998, p. 157.

4
Roland Barthes, "The Third Meaning," in *Image, Music, Text*, trans. Stephen Heath, Flamingo, London 1984.

5
Barthes, "The Third Meaning," p. 52–53.

6
Ibid., p. 57.

7
Ibid.

8
Fried, "Art and Objecthood," p. 166.

9
Ibid.

10
See Rosalind Krauss and Yve-Alain Bois, *Formless: A User's Guide*, Zone Books, New York 1997.

11
Kaprow, "The Legacy of Jackson Pollock," p. 5.

12
Ibid.

13
Ibid.

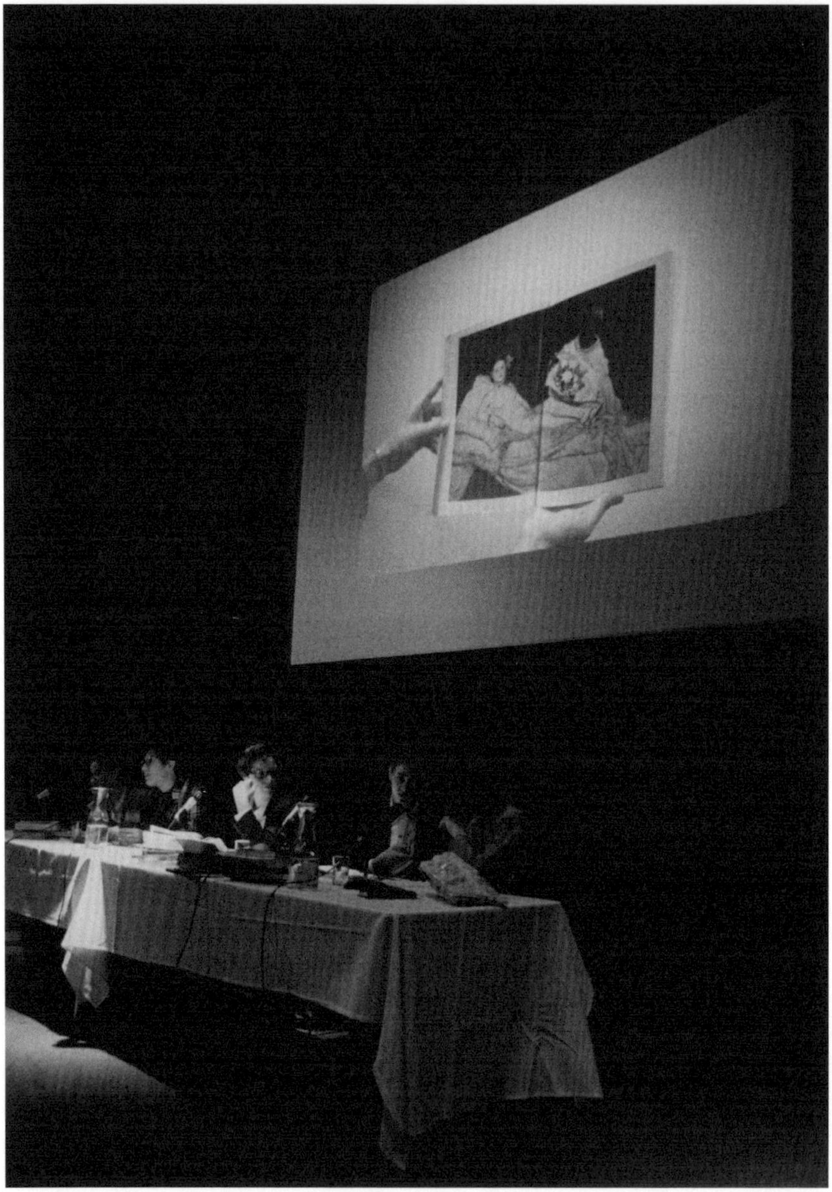

Andrea Fraser, Jessica Chalmers, Marianne Weems, Erin Cramer, Martha Baer
The Question of Manet's Olympia*: Posed and Skirted,* c. 1989
University Art Museum and Pacific Film Archive, Berkeley

Jessica Chalmers

V-NOTES ON PARODY

Introduction

In the 1970s and 80s, US feminists briefly discussed the possibility that there is a revolutionary form of laughter that is specific to women. Pointing to Hélène Cixous' influential essay "The Laugh of the Medusa" (1975) they described a kind of laughter that was not so much funny as it was political.[1] As much as they explained it as coextensive with the body, with *jouissance*, feminine sexual pleasure, as well as with *écriture féminine*, the much-debated notion of a specifically female type of writing, the theory never produced much in the way of art or performance. The problem was not with the idea, which was delightful—who could argue with the notion of a special in-laughter between women, a laughter women were understood already to possess? The problem was in the execution. I, for one, have never been able to laugh in exactly this way. I have tried out several versions of a Medusa-like laugh, none of them very satisfying and none of them resembling anything remotely like orgasm.

In the mid-1980s, with no special laugh or snake-head to ward off the evils of gender, I, along with the other four women who made up the performing group The V-Girls, tried parody instead. The following is a reflection on that effort in the context of feminism's changing relationship to humor. While parody is often portrayed as trivial and glib—as a failure to commit—I try to show its seriousness by sketching our group process and explaining parody's rise in the 1980s as a transformation in feminism's attitude toward female stereotypes. If, by the end of the essay, the reader has not felt evil to have been put at bay, I apologize. Academic exegesis may be edifying, it may add to "awareness," but it is hardly the snake-head we crave—that phallic armour of hissing friends whose mere presence is reassuring because it promises to turn aggressors to stone.

An Unlaughing Feminism

For every group, a lightbulb joke—except, maybe, straight white men, about whose competence, at least in technical matters like lightbulb changing, we are usually, as an audience, easily convinced. Speak for yourself, someone might comment, perhaps ready to describe a hilarious instance of incompetence by one or more straight white man of their acquaintance. That someone is a voice in my head, though she has appeared to me in various human forms over the years. Her voice is female, it is a "feminist" voice. She wants me to laugh with intelligence, though laughter is dumb. She disturbs me with her stern demand for my uncompromising opposition to the state of things. While other voices demand my honesty, she takes a stand against my unconscious, against its ideological conformity. She is grim, this voice, but I understand her. She doesn't want (me) to be taken for *just any woman*.

Laughter is dumb, and a certain feminism has tried to control, redirect or, better yet, suppress it. In the eyes of this radical, yet fearful politics, laughter is a sign of capitulation, of feminine capitulation to the male and to the masculine system for which he stands. Susan Purdie describes comedy and joking as an exchange that creates intimacy between the joker and his audience based on their mutual recognition of the joke's temporary transgression, as well as of the joker's agency in overseeing that transgression. The laughter of the one who listens is thus an assent to the joker's mastery of discourse: he is accepted as the one who has the power to damage, and then repair, the rational flow.[2] Feminism objects to the traditional gendering of this scenario, which has the woman as the appreciative audience of the man's joke, with her laugh as a sign of her lesser status as the receiver rather than teller of the joke. The giggling ninny is also a stock character in comedy, which takes both women and "womanish men" as the butt of its jokes. "We laugh," writes Henri Bergson, "every time a person gives us the impression of being a thing."[3] The offence to feminism in most jokes about women is that they so often make woman into a thing, a sexual thing, but also a fool and a nag.

If feminists are stereotypically grim, it is in order to ward off joking's potential to demean them. Feminists may even be said to nurture anger in order to sustain this energy of negation. Their political identity depends on this slow-burning feeling, this squelching of laughter. It is an anger that has also been celebrated as rebellion. I think of RE/Search's *Angry Women* anthology of 1991, which opens with an unsmiling, leather-clad Diamanda Galas. On the first page of her interview, the music-and-performance artist—known for albums with titles like *The Litanies of Satan*—enthusiastically describes a pet fantasy of revenge, in which a gang of "feminist diesel dykes" rove around castrating male rapists.[4] This is obviously no ordinary woman. She is not *nice*. Like the other angry women in the anthology—Avital Ronnell, Karen Finley, Kathy Acker—Galas is held up as exemplary: anger as non-capitulation to the status quo.

Anger is exciting. In its thrall, one feels clean as a knife, unhesitant, secure. In its wake, though, comes remorse. You may be fierce as a diesel truck when angry. You may be clear about who you are. But the identity forged in anger is a tenuous contraption that needs to be constantly fed. An identity based on anger needs constant reminders to fuel its battle and maintain itself against dissolution. Political identity is the same, attempting to secure itself through anger—a security that boredom or laughter threatens. Georges Bataille and others may have written with appreciation about laughter's subversion of rationality, of laughter as the best medicine for decentering the self—but the "black humor" approach does not apply in the sort of politics I am describing.

My argument here parallels that of Mary Russo, whose notion of the female grotesque, as Celia Marshik notes, "builds on Peter Stallybrass and Allon White's argument that 'the grotesque returns as the repressed of the political unconscious, as those hidden cultural contents which by their abjection had consolidated the cultural identity of the bourgeoisie.'"[5]

Laughter is an aspect of the female grotesque that is repressed by feminism in order to preserve its political integrity. I want to suggest, furthermore, that that repression is carried out through an injustice that is central to the mainstream of feminism. While claiming to stand up for every woman, feminism in fact has made femininity its scapegoat. Discrimination against femininity and against feminine women is a hypocrisy that has perpetuated self-hatred among women. If femininity is understood as a term that applies to all women, then those women who have utterly refused to perform it still cannot entirely escape it. Femininity always threatens to return, especially through the perceptions of others. Laughter might even be taken as a figure for the return of this repressed—not the eternally celebrated laughter of the Bahktinian carnavalesque, not the laughter that is presumed to be jolly and "the best medicine" for pain—but the laughter of girls, the laughter that hides or gives them away. This is the laughter that seduces or curries favor; feminine laughter, whose meanness is legendary, as it plays out, say, from Dostoevsky's manipulative character Grushenka in his final novel *The Brothers Karamazov* (1880) to the vixens of the film *Mean Girls* (dir. Mark Waters, 2004).

One can find in feminism a wholesale rejection of femininity at least as far back as *The Feminine Mystique* (1963), in which Betty Friedan contended against the roles of mother, lover, and wife.[6] Germaine Greer's *The Female Eunuch* (1970) similarly maligned women's feminine aspirations by associating them with false consciousness.[7] While Greer, for example, criticizes men for their inflated sense of self worth and denigration of women, her main argument is that women have been *self*-castrated by their investment in male approval. Akin to a rewriting of Simone de Beauvoir's more tender analysis in *The Second Sex*,[8] the book insists that the problem with gender is, in the main, a problem with women. Women, she complains, have not taken the opportunities they were offered by the suffrage movement. They have squandered their chances, remaining ensnared by the false promises of gender-as-we-know-it. I suspect that Greer—advertised as a "saucy feminist even men like" on my 1972 Bantam copy—is mainly interested in arguing for her own sexual lifestyle. Her most forceful passages accuse women of conforming to traditional morality, thereby losing their sexual freedom.

By the 1990s, the tendency to reject femininity had only strengthened. Despite the rise of a younger generation of women who, remaining purposely outside the academic system, began to propose a new "sex-positive" feminist outlook, the grimness of feminism within it increased. For example, in *Unmarked* (1993), Peggy Phelan upheld "disappearance" as a strategy for living in a world that downgrades those who stand out in any way.[9] To be "marked," in her parlance, is to be downgraded to the status of object, put into circulation on the marketplace of images. Phelan points appreciatively to several examples of performance in which gender is uncomfortable, even tortured, as performers are seemingly caught in the act of revoking it. In *Unmaking Mimesis* (1997), Elin Diamond took this attitude of renunciation a step further by calling for the dismantling of language's symbolic structures.[10] Both books are absolute in their assessment that culture is controlled by patriarchy. Both call for extraordinary measures for unmaking the status quo, defining female identity in idealist terms as a construct of the future, not the present or past. Female identity thus becomes merely fantasy, only fully existing in a realm in which representation, both visual and linguistic, is totally overhauled.

Both books also contribute to a regime of feminist virtue in which women are divided along lines that, ironically, map almost exactly onto the contours of traditional patriarchal morality. While tradition divides women according to their sexual modesty, feminist morality divides them on the basis of their gender display. It is a question of *performance*. In traditional morality, there are the good women who tone down their sexual display and there are the other women who enhance it to get what they want. In parallel, mainstream feminist morality divides women into the good, who do their utmost to renege on gender, toning themselves down, and the others, whose femininity is seen as a ploy for gaining attention.

It is a question of *authenticity*. Femininity has always been suspected of inauthenticity and feminism is no different in its suspicion that those who cultivate their beauty, for example, are in the game for the wrong reason. One has to be or to become some kind of neutral in order to please those who see feminine beauty as a form of submission in and of itself. In this "political" mode, feminism means dressing down. A woman's position on gender is legible in this performance of "unmarking." She should be imperceptible, under the radar—or she should seem to want to be imperceptible, since even disappearance has to be performed. She should evict any trace of "come-hither" in her wardrobe and vocabulary. In this way, she is also performing something very close to normative masculinity. If she is an academic, she knows that her speech must also be unmarked, especially by the first-person, which is often understood as feminine, non-scientific, not objective. And as for laughter? She knows to be very careful, lest she be taken for girlish, in other words for a fool. Nor does she want to be taken for a manipulator, even if she really is one. After all, in the traditional scenario, if the male role is to vie for approval by making a woman laugh, her attempt to gain his approval is through her laughter. As a result, both parties understand that, though her laughter may be authentic, it can also be falsified. Laughter may be an eruption, but—as with every sign of authenticity—an eruption can be performed, and women's reputation for faking both orgasms and laughter have historically been at the root of repeated accusations against their duplicity.

Just any woman, then, turns out to be a tittering whore—in the sense that she "sells" her laughter in return for love. That, at least, is the fear on the part of the men who joke, as well as on the part of feminists, for whom femininity and normativity usually automatically coincide. The male fear has to do with the possibility that, even while she laughs, a woman is secretly despising him. The feminist, on the other hand, fears feminine laughter as one fears betrayal by one's own image in the mirror. She will not laugh if it means that she becomes any kind of whore. She will not be silly. As a result, she has gained a reputation for being grim, shrill, and generally unamused, a reputation that only deepened as feminism moved from the activism of the 1960s to the academicism of the 1980s. The political correctness that began to emerge in the 1980s as a moral "specification of individuals" (as Foucault proposed in a different context[11]) was, in a sense, a self-policing activity that attempted to keep identity free from, among other things, the corruption of feminine laughter. Through a process of specification that identified and categorized women of false consciousness, a certain form of feminism emerged as an ideal form, a pure identity whose laughter is held in reserve.

Q. How many feminists does it take to screw in a lightbulb?

A. That's not funny.

Serious Vs

Parody loves the serious. It needs the kind of commitment to authenticity I describe above in order to thrive. The postmodernism of the 1980s thrived on the idealism of the 1960s. In the period of its decadence, at the turn of the 1970s, that idealism against stereotypes became fodder for the younger generation. While many of their hippie elders accused them of apathy and "post-feminism," the young counter-culturalists were not actually ignoring politics, but continuing them by other means. The V-Girls were in this category of the young who, in the early and mid-1980s, took it upon themselves to further the feminist cause from the rather precarious, mock-presumptuous roost of parody. Defended in theory by Linda Hutcheon and Phil Auslander,[12] parody was the mood of our generation, on a par with the pared-down comic sobriety of the music called "new wave." Authenticity was *out*. Like Warhol, we wanted to be machines—if, that is, by being machines we could distance ourselves from what we saw as the sentimentality of the older generation. The growing fixation on the crime of essentialism in feminism was part of this generational battle. Our generation assaulted our elders by deconstructing them. Our parodies were aimed, in great part, at their melodramatic relation to politics. If the Baby Boomers had bolstered their political identities against the threat of laughter's triviality, we invested in laughter itself. After the stridency of the hippies, the new mood was a balm. Inauthenticity was in.

In such a climate, the mock-panel seemed a perfect medium in which to make a contribution. The V-Girls, a performance group devoted to the impersonation of academics, were: Andrea Fraser, Jessica Chalmers, Marianne Weems, Erin Cramer, and Martha Baer—in that order (we insisted). Between 1986 and 1996 we brought our specific brand of feminist academic humor to various conferences including the CAA and MLA, putting our performances in critical relation to the "straight" panels being presented there. We appeared at the New Museum in New York and at the gallery of the EA-Generali Corporation in Vienna, Austria, as well as at Harvard University, and many other venues. These were not only opportunities to perform, but to continue a private, group discussion of our politics, goals, and methods while on the road. Two scripts were published in *October* magazine, along with an interview that we conducted among ourselves. "The interviewers

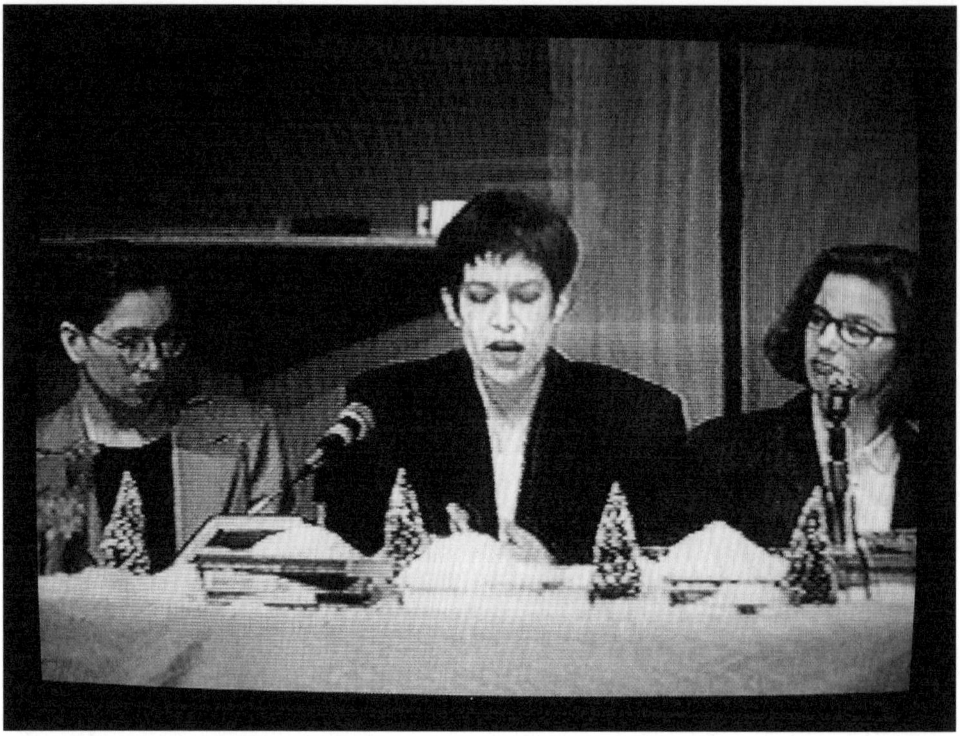

Andrea Fraser, Jessica Chalmers, Marianne Weems in *Academia in the Alps: In Search of the Swiss Mis(s)*, January 5, 1991
Judson Church, New York City

were not present at this interview," we wrote pompously as a footnote to the text.[13] We were almost always pointedly pompous, at least in the initial stages of our performances. Like most comic performers, we did not laugh. We offered stern imitations of women on panels we had seen—and, in the early-to-mid 1980s, the New York art world was a world of panels. We sported what C. Carr once called a "fresh-from-the-Sorbonne" look, by which she referred both to our youth and to our competence in theory.[14] Even though, for example, the table for *Academia in the Alps: In Search of the Swiss Mis(s)* was strewn with piles of books, little Christmas trees, and heaps of artificial snow, we maintained dignity, at least for the first section of the panel. Only toward the end of the show, during what we called the "breakdown," did our carefully woven stream of serenely delivered short speeches become even more broadly ludic, fragmentary, and mutually disruptive.

In successive versions of two mock-panel performances called *Academia in the Alps: In Search of the Swiss Mis(s)* (1988–1991) and *The Question of Manet's* Olympia*: Posed and Skirted* (1989–1992), the V-Girls used personal and parodic voices to disrupt the repressions of academic decorum. *Academia in the Alps* broached topics of women in academia through discussion and mock-analysis of Hannah Spyri's children's classic *Heidi* (1880). The Manet panel took on similar topics using critical discussion of Édouard Manet's painting of a courtesan, *Olympia* (1863), and its crucial position in the history of Modernism, as points of departure. Along with direct parodies of current trends, we used elegy, poetry, lists, opera summaries, and analytical critique.

Our success was, in part, a result of the way we looked. We were relatively attractive as well as smart. We were massively educated, and we all had, as we often pointed out, brown hair. We were *femme* in the butch world of *academe*, seated at a panel table—the type of table, we enjoyed pointing out, whose length and covering in itself denotes expertise—at a time when universities were just beginning to hire women in earnest. Merely sitting there in the position of the-ones-who-are-presumed-to-know, we were a rebuke to the academic system and its cast of old-boy characters. In retrospect, I imagine we also seemed a bit like talking dogs. No one would have suspected just by looking at us that we would have so much to say.

We had a lot to say and we knew how to say it. Using the language of expertise, and pointing to our use and misuse of that language, we were able to mock its stiffness and exclusivity while at the same time accruing a certain power through knowing it. This strategy also worked to create insider complicity with well-read audiences at universities, as well as museums, galleries, and, occasionally, theaters. Delivered in papers with titles such as "Derrida and Dairy: Recovering the Balanced Meal in Heidi," "The Name of the Father: Why Heidi Can't Have One," and "The Representation of Animals and the Animals of Representation," our parodies served to flatter an audience that had worked long and hard to acquire their conceptual capital. At the same time, and just as powerfully, complicity arose through our representations of what I termed "the Insecure." "My paper is really bad," I apologized after reading a title. "Should I go on?"[15]

In the *Manet* panel as in the *Heidi* panel, we begin with Martha's moderator's preface. Introducing The V-Girls as "an informal group of scholars and members, meeting regularly in order to question ourselves and others," she muses:

> I at first thought I might provide some historical information regarding the painting, but on second thoughts, I felt that the background of *Olympia* was probably familiar to most of us, and since our panelists will be interrogating, even, if you will, overworking, the topic, in a sense, beating it into the ground, I decided to address instead the question of the panel itself, the "itself" itself being so compelling. I myself find myself constantly returning to it, returning, returning, returning inquisitively. There's a kind of lovely naiveté about the way I theorize the object.[16]

Later, after other similarly decorous presentations—including my paper, following T.J. Clarke's *The Painting of Modern Life*,[17] called "The Painting of the Modern Wife: Olympia's Druthers," Erin's paper on the "scenic privilege" of panel members, and Marianne's Lacanian feminist take-off, entitled "The Gaze of the Dog"—our style and mood shifts. We open bag lunches. I get up to read out the reports of a "visual literacy test," supposedly taken by the audience. I also do an imitation of a French academic, mangling the pronunciation of a supposedly translated paper. Martha interrupts me, bursting out angrily against the audience in a fit of misplaced paranoia: "I just want to get something clear here: are you laughing at me, or are you laughing at what I'm saying? I mean, maybe we ought to just stop here and consider the issue of slippage and the production of laughter!"[18]

Martha's interruption, which externalizes a feeling shared by all academics to a greater or lesser extent, more than once gave us pause in rehearsal, since what she said about laughter was, in a sense, true. Sometimes it *was* impossible to tell what the audience was laughing at. Sometimes we discovered unforeseen ways in which our performance texts could be interpreted as funny. Sometimes the audience laughed at things we did not want them to laugh at. And sometimes, when we were almost losing our minds trying to prevent ourselves from bursting out with laughter, the audience was as serious as death. It was at times like that that we truly understood the limits of our art form as a political tool. Laughter *is* dumb. Although sometimes it did work exactly as we had planned, laughter, as we experienced it, could not ultimately be controlled.

The chaos does not get reined in. At the out-of-control end of the Manet panel, I stand to give a summary of an imaginary opera that slaps a happy end on the performance. Marianne turns on the cassette player, and the music begins softly:

> ACT ONE Paris, the Bois de Bologne. Edouard Manet, the aristocrat, lounges on the grass, sketching alongside his companions, the penniless artists Marcello and Rudolfo. After lamenting their tragic inability to adequately sketch their luncheon meat, they are approached by a woman, who, although completely nude, manages to make their acquaintance. Her name, she says as she seats herself beside them, is Victorine Meurent, and she is suffering fatally from indisposition ...
>
> ACT TWO Rudolfo's tiny garret, where the three men are eating a meager meal of rancid fish. Victorine, still nude, coughs and weeps in the corner. Suddenly, an angry crowd enters the garret, led by Public Opinion (a red dog with a limp). The crowd, made up of art critics, demigods, and fox terriers, shouts insults at the terrified Edouard as they chop up his furniture and build an enormous pyre, singing "Liberté, égalité, save that shit for another day." But suddenly Victorine lets out a tremendous screech and, donning a silver hat, snatches Edouard

from the flames. The crowd gasps. As the curtain closes, a crown is slowly lowered onto Edouard's head, the lovers embrace, and, as the crowd has finally reconciled itself to modernity, *all is well with the world.*

[The music rises][19]

A Short History of the Politics of Repetition

The path in aesthetics from the 1960s to the 1980s was built on a changing relation to stereotypes. If 1960s movements were based, in large part, on imagining identity as distinct from any form of stereotyping, deconstruction in the 1980s resurrected stereotypes as a means of reducing their power. The result was a series of art practices that exaggerated stereotypical display, first as still life, then as moving picture. The stills of the late 1970s and early 1980s—paintings and photography—that repeated feminine stereotypes, had a melancholy quality that bespoke the death of utopia and the impossibility of escape. Later, the paradigm of performance encouraged a carnival mood. If identity, and specifically gender identity, was still understood as stereotypical—and was constructed, as Judith Butler suggested, through a repetition of stereotypical behaviors—there was nevertheless a sense of flamboyance to be gained.[20] We might still be trapped in Frederic Jameson's "prisonhouse of language," but life was a party, gender a masquerade.[21]

That there is continuity between the aesthetics of the 1960s and 1980s is also undeniable. Amelia Jones, for example, has deftly demonstrated this continuity in relation to the genre of performance art in *Body Art: Performing the Subject* (1998).[22] Yet, "around 1981" —to borrow a title from Jane Gallop[23]—this continuity was not evident, or it was disavowed in the interest of a new beginning. A discursive break was forged through a concerted effort of denigration. The activist enthusiasms of the 1960s—which I understand as lasting until the end of the Vietnam War in the mid-1970s—were reassessed. What is still today occasionally mourned as the "death of the 1960s" was, at the turn of the decade of the 1980s, celebrated as a loss of naiveté. Gallop's book, a historiographic rereading of feminist anthologies from the 1970s, describes this past in terms of the changes within the field of feminist literary study, from the drive to discover forgotten women writers to the drive to critique the ideological underpinnings of mainstream literature. It was a movement that had parallels in other fields, including visual art, where theory was similarly developing as a language of expertise and various forms of "appropriation," including parody, were becoming politicized. If the 1960s can be characterized as a time when femininity became repressed, the 1980s brought femininity back as parody.

Hal Foster's anthology *The Anti-Aesthetic* (1983), a collection of seminal essays on the aesthetics that had begun to be labeled "postmodern," is a good place to look for the forging of this discursive break with the 1960s. Douglas Crimp's "On the Museum's Ruins," for example, describes postmodern culture as making a break with Modernist seriousness. Focusing on the "joke" of Robert Rauschenberg's collage paintings, which reflect the randomness, heterogeneity, and reproducibility of the contemporary, Crimp suggests that "the fiction of the creating subject gives way to the frank confiscation, quotation, excerptation, accumulation, and repetition of already existing images."[24] Crimp's understanding of Rauschenberg's accomplishment is expressed in terms that seem to undermine and rework the sanctification of art and of the artist. Yet, in the end, while Rauschenberg himself is not credited by Crimp with understanding the measure of his own accomplishment, Crimp himself emerges as master of the new discourse of postmodern value. In the cagey language of the emergent paradigm, Crimp describes good art as art that can give its audience an experience of the world as made up not of substance but of copies. The "already existing images" that are silk-screened or photographed or painted on his canvases are described as species of cliché. In particular, Crimp describes Rauschenberg's recycled nudes. The two canvases reproduced in my edition, *Breakthrough* (1964) and *Persimmon* (1964), both integrate 17th-century images of femininity—in both cases, images of Venus looking in a mirror: *Breakthrough* contains part of Diego Velázquez's, *The Toilet of Venus*, known as "The Rokeby Venus" (c. 1647–1651), but minus her mirror; and *Persimmon* contains Peter Paul Rubens' *Venus at the Mirror* (c. 1614–1615). Both include those images among a scattering of objects—car keys and Merce Cunningham dancers, among other seemingly random items. The cliché of feminine vanity and self-objectification is set rather indifferently amid this apparent clutter of images.

The essay that follows Crimp's in the anthology, "Feminists and Postmodernism" by Craig Owens, seems to chastise Crimp. This is because the essay begins with Owens chastising himself for forgetting "the other," something he blames postmodern critics for in general. He describes their eagerness to embrace the bricolage of contemporary art as mere multiplicity. The essay explores the new art of appropriation by women artists—Cindy Sherman, Sherrie Levine, Barbara Kruger—arguing that the multiplicity of voices characterizing postmodernism are hierarchically organized. While Owens suggests that "[w]hat we must learn ... is how to conceive difference without opposition,"[25] his discussion of the artists in question doesn't necessarily illustrate this democratic goal. He focuses, instead, on the way the art reveals the hierarchy of gender from a specifically female perspective, something it does through a repetition of recognizable forms. He writes that:

> Women have begun the long-overdue process of deconstructing femininity. Few have produced new, "positive" images of a revised femininity; to do so would simply supply and thereby prolong the life of the existing representational apparatus. Some refuse to represent women at all ... Most of these artists, however, work with the existing repertory of cultural imagery—not because they either lack originality or criticize it—but because their subject, feminine sexuality, is always constituted in and as representation, a representation of difference.[26]

What else is "existing cultural imagery" than a form of stereotype or cliché? Like Rauschenberg's nudes, the filmic images of Sherman's *Untitled Film Stills*, for example, are somehow recognizable even though they do not reference specific films. Her poses reference clichés of femininity in a general sense, summoning up a mood of watching that is familiar. They invite watching that lingers on the subject's fear, her vulnerability, or her glamour.[27]

It is ironic that such repetitions of cultural imagery are also meant to undo their power. This mingling of pain and pleasure offers a strange notion of politics. Theory brought the pain, with its blunt understanding of life as having been packaged unfairly by a patriarchal Symbolic, Lacan's scientific version of a punishing god. The pleasure came from critique, a quality attributed to some artworks whose reiterations seemed—or were discussed in such a way as—to reveal their own ideological underpinnings. By the same token, feminist art of the period was sometimes indistinguishable from the stock imagery it was meant to critique. Without the aid of theory, such postmodern artworks could well be misunderstood. Owens mentions that Sherman's later pin-up photos had been criticized for this very reason. According to him, her more provocative photos opened "[her] to charges that she was an accomplice in her own objectification, reinforcing the image of the woman bound by the frame."[28] No wonder feminists have remained grim, even while "telling" this joke about their entrapment in representation. Reiterating feminine stereotypes over and over again, the joke they told was somehow also on them.

The V-Girls are a product of a change within feminist art and theory. In the early to mid-1980s, feminist criticism was focused on the dynamics of male spectatorship as described in Laura Mulvey's "Visual Pleasure and Narrative Cinema" (1975).[29] Her description of the fetishistic consumption of the female image as a normative mode of Hollywood film-viewing led to art video, films, and photography by Martha Rosler, Dara Birnbaum, Yvonne Rainer, and others, including Cindy Sherman. These artists were concerned with images of women, clichés of the feminine as they were depicted in popular culture. By the time Judith Butler came out with *Gender Trouble: Feminism and the Subversion of Identity* in 1990, the focus of feminist art and criticism had begun to shift from images of male desire to the construction of identity through gendered behaviors, and from film to performance.

Like the artwork that reiterates female imagery in the interest of deconstructing it, the performance of identity is also a form of reiteration. Identity, itself understood as reiteration—or "iteration" in Butler's terms—was also understood to be susceptible, and could be undermined. The V-Girls' parodies were effective because they exposed professional identity as a performance, using femininity as a means of disrupting the professionalism of the academic conference and, by extension, academic discourse, which was well on its way to becoming the specialized language of expertise that it is today. Parody was also effective for me personally, since our years-long entrance into the halls of academe as pretenders to the thrones of learning—as performers of an identity to which I, for one, also seriously aspired—had given me a way to take part. My graduate-student status, not shared by the other members of the group, meant that I had an intense and specific relation to the university context. My own quest for a PhD was made lighter by my participation in this satirical portrayal of academics as fallible. If womanliness, as Joan Riviere described, is no different than the masquerade of womanliness,[30] then the masquerade of the graduate student-as-professional-academic was no different from the real thing—an attitude that, for better or worse, has given me an unusual sense of detachment from my identity as a professional academic.

Daughters of the ReVolution

By 1994, the notion of parody seemed used up and the Vs were in the throes of what we viewed as a group creative impasse. The performance that came out of this impasse, created during an approximately two-year process of meetings, research, and discussion, did not prevent us from breaking up in 1996, after ten years of working as a group. The process of making of *Daughters of the ReVolution* (1993–1996) was a way for us to negotiate the friction, as well as harmony, between the personal-political feminism of our teens during the 1970s; the theoretical feminism of our schooling; and a feeling that we had, in 1994, of needing to rethink both our relation to feminism and to performance. For the first time, we also began to talk about laughter and the way parody worked. Our power to provoke general hilarity was extremely seductive to us, though we also saw its strangeness. At times the audience seemed strangely hungry for hilarity *tout court*. They seemed poised to accept laughter at any expense. Privately we discussed our discomfort with the fact that laughter was provoked in the audience at someone else's expense—generally someone who, in all sincerity, aspired to say or do something. We considered the idea that our parodic distance from that sincerity meant that we aspired to nothing but distance. We also saw that we had aspired through parody to be special, but that, in spite of our up-to-date commitment to inauthenticity and performance, what we had wanted all along was actually a *better authenticity*. What we wanted was an authenticity that was more authentic-than-thou by virtue of its parodic remove. What we wanted, we found, was

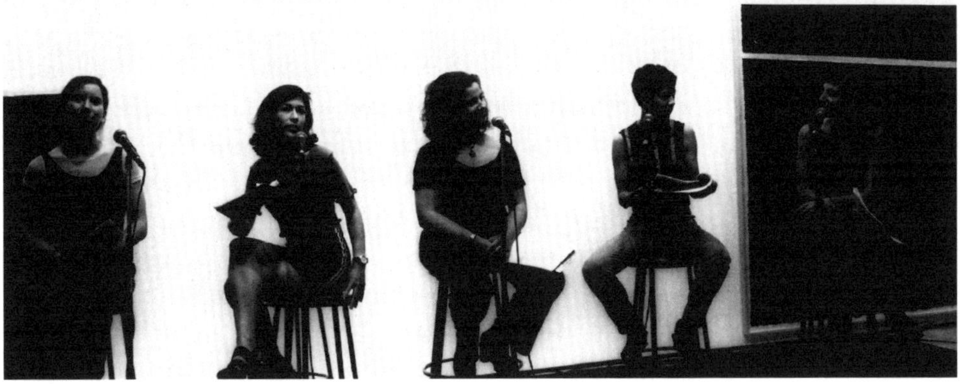

Andrea Fraser, Jessica Chalmers,
Marianne Weems, Erin Cramer, Martha Baer,
in *Daughters of the ReVolution*, 1993
The Drawing Center, New York City

after all really not that different from what the feminists of the 1960s and 1970s had wanted—we wanted not to be taken for *just any woman*.

With its generational emphasis, *Daughters of the ReVolution* was a way of addressing our ambivalence toward what we now understood as our investment in authenticity and uniqueness. The difference of *Daughters* from our previous work was first manifested thematically: we chose a topic that was “nonacademic” in the sense that the texts and acts of 1970s feminism in America seemed to have been elided in the excitement over the experimental narratives of “new French feminism.” In 1992, it seemed a novel idea to examine this heritage. As always when beginning a new project, we began by reading—and immediately ran into the issue that ultimately came to fuel the dialectical energies of the piece. Reading the well-worn paperbacks of 1970s feminism, we rediscovered excitement. We found an optimism that seemed, ultimately, to define our generational difference. If we were the ones with comedy on our side, it was not a light-hearted or hopeful affair. While reading, often aloud, from such works as *The Redstockings Manifesto* (1969),[31] we rediscovered the fervent sense of purpose that was absent from our parody. As we rediscovered it we were also disabused of some of our prejudices against the older generation’s stridency, though it also brought up our inbred fear of being seen as essentialist, in other words as ordinary and naive:

> We identify with all women. We define our best interest as that of the poorest, most brutally exploited woman ... We repudiate all economic, racial, educational, or status privileges that divide us from other women. We are determined to recognize and eliminate any prejudices we may hold against other women ... [32]

It was around the problem of this heartfelt type of language that we built *Daughters* as a progression of framing and self-questioning. The performance begins with our acknowledgment of the power of the now-disputed vision of female union, the maligned “we” of feminist activism. There is a short “go-round” on consciousness-raising topics: Marianne asks us, for example, to “discuss your relationships with other women. Have you ever felt competition for men?” We give an overly brief yes or no answer. Then I say, not as moderator, but as narrator:

> Five girls, V-girls, nice girls, white girls, not boys. They sit before you as daughters, staking a claim to a revolution they only remember barely from childhood ... Of course, they retain certain fragments of the feminist past: a certain vocabulary of consciousness (false or true), of male supremacy, the dialectics of sex, abortion on demand ... memories of mothers and friends in floppy hats, the ironed hair, the hair cropped short, the hairy legs, the bra-less boobs, the embroidered jackets, the granny glasses, the men's pants, those jeans skirts made from pants with the triangles in the middle.[33]

From this point on, however, the representation of difference and dispute takes over, and I am interrupted (interruption remaining a crucial device):

> ANDREA Well, Jessica, that doesn't represent my vision of the early 1970s.
>
> MARIANNE I don't think feminists wore those triangle skirts.
>
> MARTHA My mother only wore these little Jackie Kennedy dresses.

Performing internal dissension allowed us to make an autobiographical representation of the kind of work that went into *Daughters*. Whereas later in the piece we also performed the personal as individual experience, here the attempt was to confess openly to the pains of collaboration. In my view, the public objectification and exposure of what was at times a crippling internal dynamic allowed us to continue as a group, for a time at least. In addition, our group problem, which we tried to understand in part through our reading of psychoanalyst W.R. Bion's *Experiences in Groups* (1961),[34] was also performed as a synecdoche of the generational problem. Although our experience was in many ways "the same" as the factionalism of feminist groups in the 1970s, the disputed issues communicated the historically specific nature of our mainly theoretical training. Whereas groups like Redstockings, Witch, Cell 16, and New York Radical Feminists had splintered over issues of separatism, for example, our discomfort with "ourselves and others" rested, first of all, on the issue of identity. Trained, as we were, by the post-1970s generation, our idea of entertaining psychodrama was to represent tension and confusion between identification and its opposites:

> ERIN What are we doing here? Are we acting out some kinky fantasy of wholeness? ... All right, before we go any further, I want to ask you guys something: Does anybody here actually believe in the self? Could I see a show of hands?
>
> [Finally Martha's hand goes up timidly]
>
> MARTHA Uh, I do. Not *myself*. But I believe in some of yours.
>
> ERIN Let's just say for argument's sake that I did believe in the self. I mean, I do sign my name to checks but that's just a formality, a social convention, really, and I only have a bank account because everyone else does ...
>
> I guess the problem I'm having is if you don't accept the idea of a *fixed* self how do you even begin to think about a *liberated* self? What would that be? Every time I start to think about it all I can come up with is Julia Kristeva singing "Free To Be You and Me." I can't figure it out.
>
> MARIANNE Let's recuperate Kristeva's statement that "on a deeper level, a woman cannot 'be'; it is something which does not even belong in the order of being. In 'woman,' I see something that cannot be represented, something that is not said, something that is above and beyond nomenclatures and ideologies."[35]
>
> ANDREA Girls, why are we making all these academic references? ... Is this what we think our audience knows? Or is this what we *want* them to know? Do they really need to know these things in order to participate in the group?

> MARTHA I think it's what we think the audience wants *us* to know.

Instead of a panel, we created the performance as a re-presentation of a consciousness raising (CR) by first recording ourselves having an hours-long private session using a CR handbook from the late 1960s as a guide, and then editing the transcription and interpolating other items (including Joni Mitchell's 1969 cover of "Both Sides, Now"; a reading on parliamentary procedure from *Robert's Rules of Order*; a discussion of the writer Jane Bowles; a reading in unison from Valerie Solanas's *SCUM Manifesto*, 1968). Our original, private CR session, broadly interpreting the rules we found in Joan Robbins' *Handbook of Women's Liberation* (1970),[36] had ended weepily, with several of us interpreting our personal relation to the group in terms of our intimidation by post-strucuralist theory. However, transcribed and reedited, the session became infused with the irony of performance—knowing ourselves to be seen, judged, and recorded, we altered the content so that, in addition to sincerity (Erin's reminiscences about her all-female dollhouse, Andrea's about marching with her mother in San Francisco's Gay Pride march), there was irony.

"Oh, my fun-filled gynocentric youth, where have you gone, with your mutual back rubs, your hot debates, your berets?" This sentence, which I speak before launching into the particulars of my college history, always provoked laughter in the audience. To my mind, this laughter indicated relief from sincerity, including the intensity of audience-performer identification and the dread of its inevitable rupture. It is also this laughter, which we both wanted and didn't want to provoke, that banishes politics, at least politics in the sternest sense. Representing our dilemma around politics *as, in some sense, our politics*, created a whirlpool effect that led some to criticize us for our "postmodernism." Toward the end of *Daughters*, we also fold *that* criticism into the mix, saying that,

> there is something problematic to me about our reaching back into feminist history and only recuperating the part about subjectivity, where we just change ourselves and defer material inequity to some other agenda ... Why didn't we just organize? There are material conditions out there or, for that matter, in

here. Do you think we think this performance is some kind of substitute? We don't. We don't.[37]

The Dick Joke

Parody offers a place to speak from, though it is not a secure one. It offers "performativity," a kind of academic flamboyance. As the Vs practiced it, it also offered multiple voices from which to speak, though in doing so it eroded the possibility of professing anything like certainty. The multiplicity of this type of performance gave us the freedom of masquerade, but at the same time it masked our insecurity, as performers and as women. Even foregrounding performance anxiety by performing as academic impostors, the Vs never conquered it. We never even really wanted to conquer, only to bring to light the working of the Insecure, that faux-Lacanian register I invented to travesty my own fear. By bringing the Insecure to light as a precondition of subjectivity and identity—of feminine identity—we were not only aiming to show off how much we knew. We also made, we felt, a contribution that included, as it turned out, a joke about straight, white men, though not a lightbulb joke. Lightbulb jokes, which take technical competence as a model for all competence, are unsuitable as vehicles for laughing at men. Instead, we attempted a reversal.

On the Manet panel, Erin launches into the Dick Joke as a joke among women about a male professor who, at a certain point in his lecture, well, just, "takes out his dick"—"You know, just like a guy." Having said this with great hilarity, Erin stops abruptly, reconsidering. Speciously apologetic, she says, "Oh wait a minute, wait a minute. I shouldn't be doing this, I'm sorry. It might be offensive to some of the men in the audience—you know, the real serious ones who don't have a sense of humor. But you women out there, if you want to hear it, come see me after the panel."

As Erin tells it, after the panel performances in which she told this aborted joke she sometimes heard from actual men in the audience, who either asked her to tell them the joke or expressed their annoyance with the whole concept. "It's rather puerile," I remember one young man commenting to me as he handed me his phone number in the hubbub after a performance. "Like junior high humor." I never called him, but I understood where he was coming from. It's hard to play the audience role. You end up either giddy, participating unmindfully in the reactive solidarity of the crowd—or you get grim, fending off laughter in the interest of identity. The guy, choosing identity over participation, also chose to ignore the invitation that parody extends to both performer and audience: the invitation to laugh at oneself and, by doing so, to experience one's own identity from the perspective of both audience and performer.

NOTES

1
Hélène Cixous, "Le rire de la Méduse" (1975), trans. Keith Cohen and Paula Cohen as "The Laugh of the Medusa," *Signs* 1, no. 4 (1976), p. 875–893.

2
See Susan Purdie, *Comedy: The Mastery of Discourse*, University of Toronto Press, Toronto 1993.

3
Henri Bergson, *Laughter: an Essay on the Meaning of the Comic*, trans. Coudesley Brereton and Fred Rothwell, Dover Books, New York 2005; also at *Project Gutenberg*, January 14, 2009, http://www.gutenberg.org/etext/4352.

4
"Diamanda Galas," in Andrea Juno and V. Vale (eds.), *Angry Women*, RE/Search Publications, New York 1991, p. 6–22.

5
Mary Russo, *The Female Grotesque: Risk, Excess, and Modernity*, Routledge, New York 1994, p. 8–9; Celia Marshik, "The Female Grotesque: Risk, Excess, and Modernity," *Modernism/Modernity*, vol. 2, no. 3 (1995), p. 183.

6
Betty Friedan, *The Feminine Mystique*, Norton, New York 2001.

7
Germaine Greer, *The Female Eunuch*, Bantam, New York 1970.

8
Simone de Beauvoir, *The Second Sex*, trans. H. M. Parshley, Vintage, New York 1974, 1952.

9
Peggy Phelan, *Unmarked: The Politics of Performance*, Routledge, London and New York 1993.

10
Elin Diamond, *Unmaking Mimesis: Essays on Feminism and Theatre*, Routledge, London and New York 1997.

11
See Michel Foucault, *The History of Sexuality: An Introduction* [vol. 1], trans. Robert Hurley, Random House, New York 1990.

12
Linda Hutcheon, *The Politics of Post-modernism*, 2nd ed., Routledge, London and New York 2002; and *A Theory of Parody: The Teachings of Twentieth-Century Art Forms*, Methuen, New York 1985; Philip Auslander, *From Acting to Performance: Essays in Modernism and Postmodernism*, Routledge, London and New York 1997.

13
The V-Girls, "A Conversation with October," *October* no. 51 (Winter 1989), p. 115.

14
C. Carr, "Re-Visions of Excess," *Village Voice* (New York), May 30, 1989, p. 91.

15
The V-Girls, *Academia in the Alps: In Search of the Swiss Mis(s),* unpublished book ms., p. 93.

16
The V-Girls, *The Question of Manet's* Olympia*: Posed and Skirted*, unpublished book ms. p. 133–134.

17
T.J. Clark, *The Painting of Modern Life: Paris in the Art of Manet and His Followers*, Thames and Hudson, London 1985.

18
The V-Girls, *The Question of Manet's* Olympia, p. 165.

19
Ibid., p. 174–176.

20
See Judith Butler, *Gender Trouble: Feminism and the Subversion of Identity*, Routledge, London and New York 1990.

21
The allusion here is to Frederic Jameson, *The Prison-House of Language: A Critical Account of Structuralism and Russian Formalism*, Princeton University Press, Princeton, New Jersey 1974.

22
Amelia Jones, *Body Art/Performing the Subject*, University of Minnesota Press, Minneapolis 1998.

23
Jane Gallop, *Around 1981: Academic Feminist Literary Theory*, Routledge, London and New York 1992.

24
Douglas Crimp, "On the Museum's Ruins," in Hal Foster (ed.), *The Anti-Aesthetic*, New Press, New York 1998, p. 18.

25
Craig Owens, "Feminists and Post-modernism," in *The Anti-Aesthetic*, p. 62.

26
Ibid., p. 71.

27
See, *Cindy Sherman: The Complete* Untitled Film Stills, The Museum of Modern Art, New York 2003.

28
Owens, "Feminists and Postmodernism," p. 75.

29
Laura Mulvey, "Visual Pleasure and Narrative Cinema," *Screen* vol. 16, no. 3 (1975), p. 6–18.

30
Joan Riviere, "Womanliness as a Masquerade" (1929), in Victor Burgin, James Donald, and Cora Kaplan (eds.), *Formations of Fantasy*, Methuen, London and New York 1986, p. 35–44.

31
The Redstockings Manifesto was authored by the Redstockings group, founded by Ellen Willis and Shulamith Firestone in New York in February 1969.

32
The Redstockings Manifesto, as quoted in The V-Girls, "Daughters of the ReVolution," *October* no. 71 [*Feminist IssueS*] (Winter 1995), p. 136.

33
The V-Girls, "Daughters of the ReVolution," p. 122.

34
See, W.R. Bion, *Experiences in Groups and Other Papers*, Tavistock/Routledge, London and New York 1961, 1991.

35
Julia Kristeva, "Woman Can Never Be Defined" (1974), trans. Marilyn A. August in *New French Feminism: An Anthology*, ed. Elaine Marks and Isabelle de Courtivon, University of Massachusetts Press, Amherst 1980, p. 137.

36
Joan Robbins, *Handbook of Women's Liberation*, Now Library Press, North Hollywood, California 1970.

37
The V-Girls, "Daughters of the ReVolution," p. 135–136.

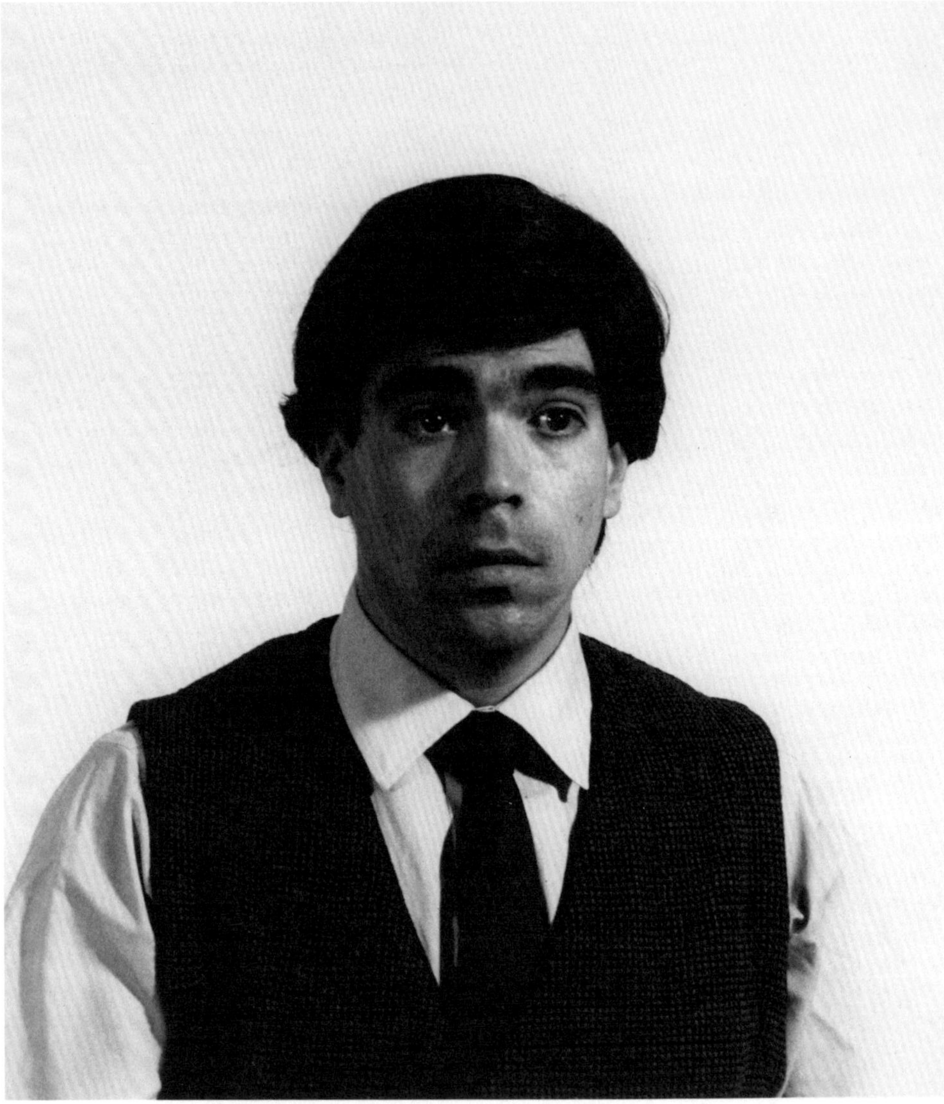

Michael Smith

THE NUT DOESN'T FALL FAR FROM THE TREE: A PIECE OF WORK IN PROGRESS

When making the transition from serious painting to being serious about humor, it was empowering to tell others I was a comic. It sounded cool and made me feel different from other people in a room. During this period, someone I met at a party told me, after hearing about my ambitions, that I was not funny. I quickly responded and said I was a different kind of comic. Some friends were concerned. They thought the audiotapes I was making at this time were distressing. I agreed and said, "They are distressing, but funny." Coming out of Minimalism I was predisposed to repetition and looping shaggy dog stories. I could watch paint dry in the studio, but if I was going to hold people's attention and make them laugh, it was important to remember how easily I got distracted and bored. I became familiar with the Rule of Three, and although I never formalized a plan for myself, I seem consistently to abide by these three unspoken rules.

Rule # 1
Start every performance in boxer shorts

Rule # 2
Always wear briefs underneath the boxer shorts

Rule # 3
No one sees my penis in public

The Rule of Three later also extended into my teaching:

Rule # 1
Clean up after yourself

Rule # 2
You cannot physically harm yourself or anyone else in class

Rule # 3
You cannot jeopardize my job

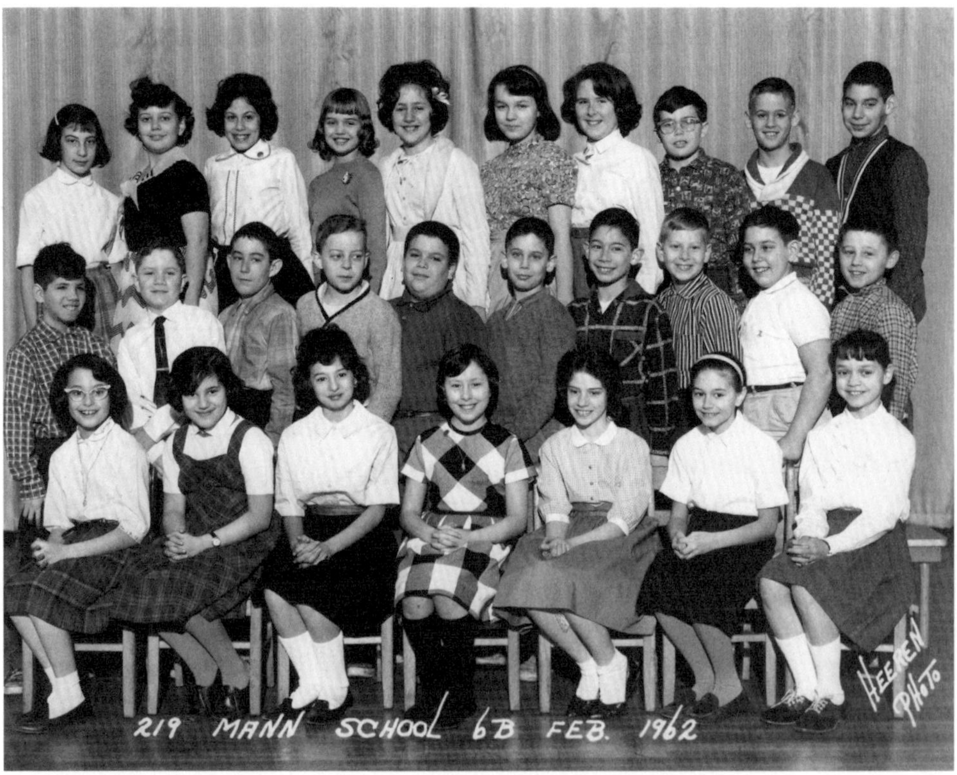

OK, this is not exactly a good example, but there are three rules.

Humor comes to me naturally and I have come to understand it as a natural outgrowth of fear. Like a yapping Chihuahua on the defensive, I learned at an early age that any kind of wisecrack could defuse a potentially dangerous situation in which I may need to reveal my true thoughts or feelings. My performance persona Mike, alias Blandman, a slow, plodding guy caught up in everyday repetitive routines, initially emerged out of my interest in Minimalism, and was an attempt to locate a neutral Everyman with universal appeal. Sure I can say this developed out of my formalist painting background, but more than likely Mike is a cipher who allows me to continue keeping opinions to myself. This repressed character comes from somewhere, and it doesn't take a professional psychologist to figure out that the "nut does not fall far from the tree." Mike is a perfect vehicle to take advantage of *Schadenfreude*. He becomes the fall guy while continually searching for answers in a landscape filled with bad choices. As Mike, I get to re-enact playing a grown-up in the workaday world, a microcosm of what, as a youngster, I imagined my father obsessively participating in. My father was a good provider but not a great communicator. Inadvertently he became the target of much humor in our family, helped along by his incredibly patient, loving wife, my mother. It is no small wonder that my other performance persona is a giant baby called Baby Ikki. The baby came on the scene before Mike and, funnily enough, also developed out of an interest in neutrality. One thing is certain, when a grown man wears a diaper in public, most people do not see it as a neutral image. If I am attempting to re-imagine my father's world with Mike, I wonder what I am re-enacting with the baby. Over the years, in lectures—and on the couch—I've searched for answers to why I do what I do.

When asked to contribute an essay to *Black Sphinx*, I figured I'd transpose the notes from my slide lecture at the Hammer Museum, since on that occasion I attempted to continue my investigation of the sources and psychological underpinnings of my humor. Unfortunately, I realized that I had not only lost those notes; I was also allowed only a limited number of images to accompany my essay. I immediately went into May Day mode. I then thought about Jackie Vernon, a low-key stand-up comic whom I first saw on *The Ed Sullivan Show* sometime in the 1960s. Vernon became famous for his uninflected delivery and self-deprecating humor. One routine, the vacation slideshow, made a lasting impression on me, one reason being my father was a slide-taking maniac on all of our trips. The odd thing was we never looked at them later. I was never sure if it was a problem organizing the slides or the family. Vernon's slide show was much more economical and used only a clicker, which he clicked to indicate the changing, non-existent slides. In his inimitable monotone and with minimal props, he'd describe each slide, setting up a series of jokes, often at his own expense.

Hi there fun seekers
I can't tell you how thrilled I am to be here
Thought I'd show you some slides from a recent trip

Click
This is the first day of my trip entering the Holland Tunnel

Click
Second day of my trip coming out of the Holland Tunnel

Vernon's voice, tone, and cadence mesmerized me. His self-loathing, zero energy, overweight schlemiel persona remains embedded in my memory. I felt a certain affinity with his act. In my family, humor and food ran neck and neck in importance as the twin bonds that held us together. Not surprisingly, humor became my default response to most embarrassing situations. The joke was an effective way not only to avoid responsibility, but to deflect the looks or comments of the non-orthopedic, loafer-wearing kids for being a little different: fatter, shorter, or slower.

> *To look at me now you'd never know I was a dull guy. People point at me, and say, what a personality he ... needs. Everything about me was dull. My idea of a wild time was Kool-Aid and oatmeal cookies. At parties I'd stay in the room with the coats ... [and] memorize [the] labels ...*

After considering my options, I decided I'd use a similar strategy with my PowerPoint presentation, to pay homage to Jackie Vernon and to meet an imminent deadline.

(Click) Image 1

A simple pen study for an unrealized fresco project I made circa 1999, entitled *The nut doesn't fall far from the tree*

This is a drawing of a barren tree set with a lone sad acorn hanging from a scrawny limb. Next to the tree is written, "I like you, you like me, we're a happy family," the first line from Barney the purple dinosaur's signature song. The drawing encapsulates what I hope to get across in my talk.

(Click) Image 2

A recent watercolor, drawn from memory, of my Jewish, middle-class family

Pictured next to me, as a young chubby boy, are my creative big brother, my angry dad, my nice mom, and my older sister. Please note that my drawing style has not changed since I was 8 years old.

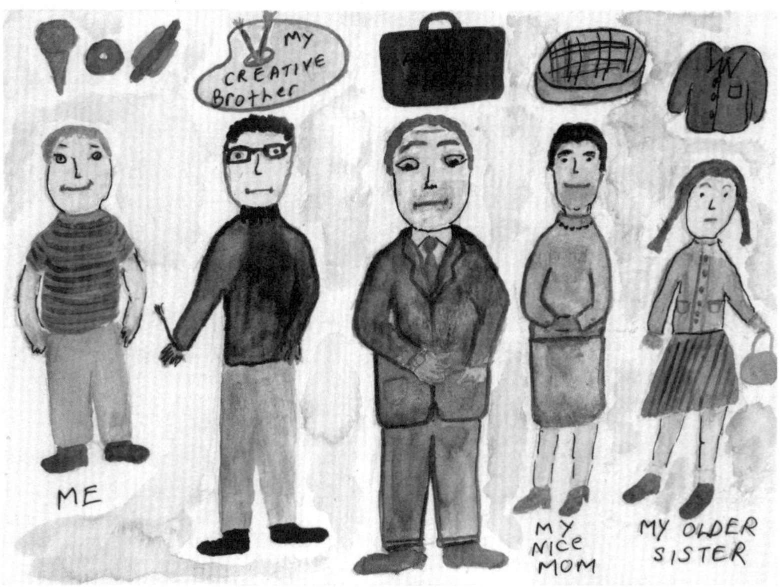

(Click) Image 3

The Smith Family Crest

A colorful, official-looking insignia one could imagine on a shield or banner.

(Click) Image 4

A black and white photograph of Ellis Island, most likely taken at the end of the 19th century

I am pretty sure my grandparents came to the US sometime in the early 20th century, probably at the urging of their neighbors in Poland and Lithuania. Perhaps you wonder how I got the name Smith. I asked my father what our family name was before Smith and without missing a beat, he replied, "Sutton."

(Click) Image 5

The Sutton Family Crest

Similar to the Smith Family Crest; both are colorful and have a knight's helmet in the design. Evidently, my father's father, either before or after leaving Lithuania, changed his name to Smith. The story goes something like this: he hit the rabbi over the head with a candlestick and stowed away on a ship headed to South Africa where he met an older passenger named Smith. Mr Smith later became his partner in a Johannesburg livery business. It is unclear if the name Smith came from his partner or the word "smite," as in "to smite the Rabbi," or from smith, as in a smithy who hammered out shoes for horses. Legend has it that my grandfather lost all his money gambling on ships while sailing around the world. All this happened before he married my grandmother, an orthodox Jewish woman living in Chicago. Together they owned a boarding house where supposedly there was an ongoing card game. Later they owned one of the last livery stables in Chicago, where they leased horses to peddlers.

(Click) Image 6

A crayon drawing of my mother that I made when I was 8 years old

It is of a very large head on a very small body. The head is sporting a checked Tam or beret and some kind of kerchief. At the top of the page, written in pencil is: "My Mother is Gorgeous."

My mother, Fern R. Smith, was born a Rosenberg. To say the least, I was very, very attached to my mother. When my mother was an infant, her mother died in the flu epidemic of 1917. She went to live with a foster family on a farm in rural Michigan.

(Click) Image 7

A photo of the Hatfield Clan, from the infamous Hatfield/McCoy feud (1897)

When my mother was 13, her foster mother remarried a Mr Hatfield from Kentucky. She did not realize her birth name was Rosenberg until her foster mother, en route to Kentucky, left her in Chicago to live with her real family. Mother mentioned she felt different from the other people living in Michigan. Some of them had nicer fruit trees and houses, and others were just different. Marrying my father worked well for her. She adjusted nicely to fitting in and being just another Smith.

(Click) Image 8

A table set for high tea with fine china, cakes, and assorted finger sandwiches

Teatime was an important event at our house. My mother always made sure there were fresh cakes, cookies, or brownies around. She once told me about a dream she had with the Queen of England stopping over for a cup of tea and the only thing my mother had to serve were Pop Tarts. She described it as if it were a nightmare.

(Click) Image 9

A picture of my mother in a hospital bed shortly after I was born

The doctor visited my mother in her room as she was coming out of sedation. The doctor said to her, "Fern, you had a baby boy."

FERN I already have a boy.

DR DALE And you have a daughter.

FERN Then ... it will be my pet.

(Click) Image 10

A drawing from when I was 8 years old with an accompanying essay written at the same time called "Fun at Home"

Fun at Home

In my picture my dad is giving me my allowance. I'm always

happy to get my allowance. When my birthday comes I'm going to ask my dad for a raise. Most kids I know get an allowance. When I get to be ten I hope I get a dollar for an allowance. Most people I know like money very much. I like money too. I like the green kind most people do.

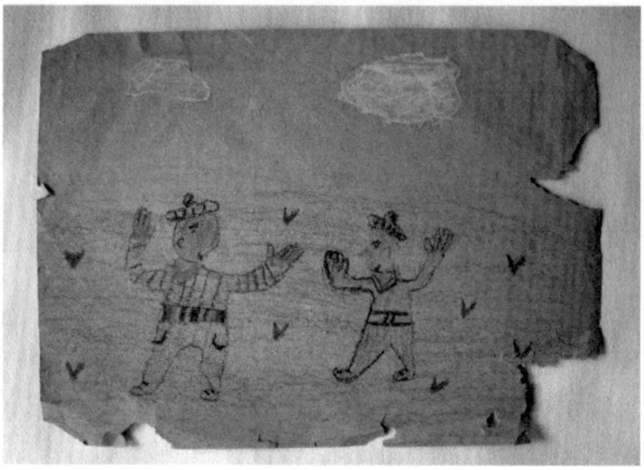

(Click) Image 11

A Timex watch

Besides being generous, my father was interested in time. He wore a special watch to bed.

(Click) Image 12

A wrist wearing some sort of sport watch

He had another watch for yard work.

(Click) Image 13

A gold wristwatch with a gold band

He also had another watch he wore in the bathtub.

(Click) Image 14

More watches

My father wore a different watch to the office and for going out at night.

(Click) Image 15
Even more watches

My dad's life was driven by time. He judged peoples' character according to their punctuality. W.F. Smith was not a patient man. While he was alive, I never wore a watch. After he died I was given a watch with a light. I played with the button so much that it broke within a couple of weeks

(Click) Image 16
A shot of my mother, brother, sister, and me in the foreground looking at my father standing by a window holding a hammer

The only thing my father disliked more than tardiness were mosquitoes.

(Click) Image 17
A shot of my mother, brother, sister, and me in the foreground looking on at my father holding a hammer in front of a broken window

When this happened it produced much merriment for the family.

(Click) Image 18
A picture of me when I was a cute, chubby 8-year-old

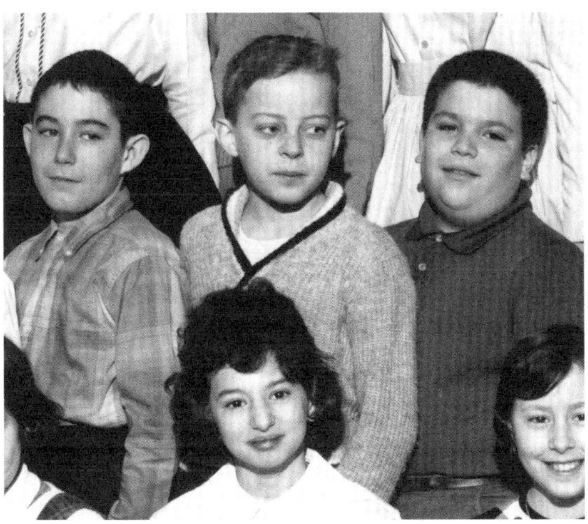

(Click) Image 19
A picture of me when I was a fat 10-year-old

(Click, Click) Images 20, 21
Various pairs of brown and gray husky pants

(Click, Click) Images 22, 23
Various pairs of brown lace-up shoes

If you were young and fat with flat wide feet during the 1950s, there were not a lot of options in clothing and footwear. I bought all my clothes at the Pow Wow Husky Shop and my extra wide corrective shoes from Baron's Shoe Store.

(Click) Image 24
A picture of the Beach Boys from the early 1960s

Whenever I'd hear or see a picture of the Beach Boys, incredibly mixed feelings of envy, fear, and insecurity would well up inside me. They represented everything I would never have: blond hair, a sports car filled with girls, and the chutzpah to wear a swimsuit on the beach.

(Click) Image 25
A portrait of the Three Stooges, Larry, Moe, and Curly, all three dressed in formal attire

It was incredibly comforting to come home after school, go directly to the rec room to watch the Stooges, and suck my thumb. It was like looking at a mirror of my family; Moe was angry, Larry was low-keyed, and Curly offered me hope. He was fat, funny, and resilient to abuse.

(Click) Image 26
A child's drawing

Another crayon drawing I made when I was 8 years old. This one is a cross section of a house with five figures, a male and a female standing on the top floor (my parents?), one female on the middle floor (my sister?), and two males on the bottom floor (probably my brother and me). All the figures are facing forward. This is an accurate depiction of my family. We'd spend some time together at dinner with very little talking. My father finished eating within 10 minutes and immediately retired to his chair to read the paper. Soon after, everyone would go to his or her respective bedrooms or respective nooks.

(Click) Image 27
My 6th Grade report card

My grammar school report cards were divided into two sections, grades and habits. Habits were necessary for the "personal and social improvement of the child." I received a lot of checks in "Social Habits" and "Work and Study Habits." I got average grades in most classes, except for Art, where I received three Ds and an F. In Social Studies, a "course designed to increase the understanding of history, geography, human relationships, and citizenship in a democracy," I performed slightly better. I did, however, receive numerous As in music. The same year, I performed a duet with Nancy Seren in front of the PTA. I sang the high part.

(Click) Image 28
A map of South America

My report card pointed to two things that are still true to this day. I never learned how to read a map and I do not have careful work habits. It's funny that most of the outlines for my projects resemble a map of South America, wide and top heavy at the beginning with a lot of information and descriptions, and narrow at the bottom with little or no resolution.

(Click) Image 29

Contrary to the findings of my report card I developed a keen interest in art. I became a very earnest abstract painter who made formal grid paintings. There was nothing funny about them.

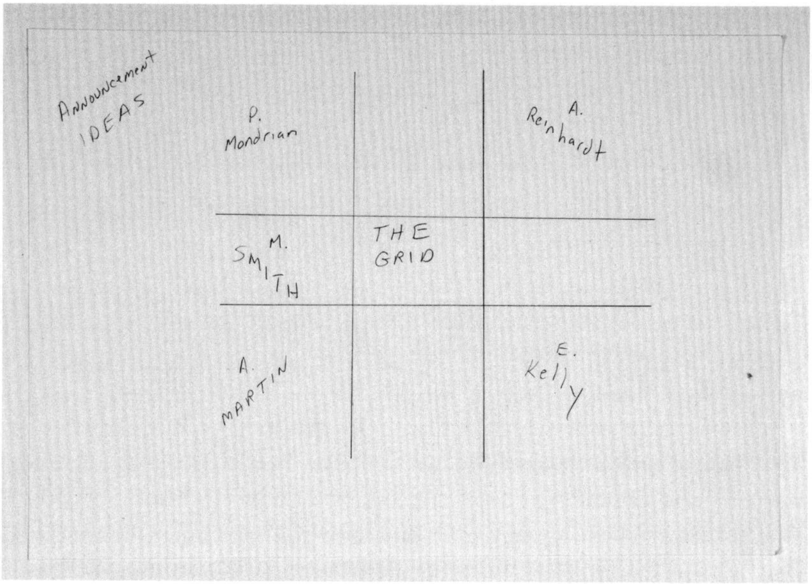

(Click) Image 28

A picture of me and my analyst sitting in a very dark, brown office

I am sitting on a brown leather couch and he is sitting across from me in his brown leather chair. I was there for a couple of reasons. At the time the US was deeply involved with the Vietnam conflict. I was living at home with my parents, trying to be a serious artist and seeing the shrink with hopes of getting a convincing letter to get me out of military service. Conditions at the time were conducive for a very good letter.

(Click) Image 29

Another picture of my analyst and me in his office

I am sitting on the couch looking at him sleeping in his chair. I had planned to work in my father's business to earn enough money, and then retire to the studio and paint. It did not quite work out that way. My painting eventually became so reductive that I did not know what to paint anymore. I stopped painting, stopped working for my father, and made a lateral move to delivering pizzas.

(Click) Image 30

A black and white photo of the Three Stooges with Larry banging his head against the wall as Moe looks on with a perplexed expression on his face

Moe interrupts Larry and asks, "Hey dummy, Why you banging your head against the wall?"

LARRY *It helps my headache.*

MOE *Huh?!? ... How does that help your headache?!?*

LARRY *Every time I stop, it feels better.*

(Click) Image 31

A man eating a carrot in a circle of five people

Part-time delivery work and fear of facing the blank canvas kept me out of the studio and left me with extra time on my hands. I started attending a lot of performance art events.

(Click) Image 32

A woman lying in the middle of a parking lot

It was the early 1970s, so many of the performances I'd see were minimal, process-oriented, endurance works. Often, I'd be the only one laughing in the audience. I was not sure if it was because of the material or my discomfort.

(Click) Image 33

A brick wall with a sign that reads, "Comedy!!!"

One night in 1974, I ended up at a comedy club to watch comedians do their routines. I went back each week and became familiar with their material. A friend suggested I put together an act. I had no idea what to do but I learned that I did not want to make jokes at other people's expense, be it a woman driver, some ethnic group, or mothers-in-law. If a joke was to be at anyone's expense, it would be mine. I also learned about non-sequiturs, and how they could help you out of a failed joke or a lull in a routine and take you anywhere, like going from the northern part South America down to the southern tip of the continent.

(Click) Image 34

An empty, narrow nightclub, filled with empty chairs and tables; the view is from the rear, looking toward a stage with a lone stool and microphone

I eventually put together a routine, but when I got to the club it had closed. Probably a good thing considering that what I came up with was indebted more to John Cage than Henny Youngman. My pacing was slow and plodding and what I thought humorous, others found to be excruciating. Once again, it seemed best to go outside for inspiration. I started rummaging through the garbage.

(Click) Image 35

A picture of me wearing a powder blue leisure suit, a child's cowboy hat, and a holster loaded with a notebook, a whisk-broom, clothespins, and a reflex hammer

Props when repurposed added some absurdity and play to my process, and my attempt at humor became more apparent to others. Unfortunately, the more props I accumulated did not necessarily secure more laughs.

(Click) Image 36

A black and white photo of me dressed as a baby, wearing a white bonnet, white T-shirt, a white diaper, white suspenders, a pacifier in my mouth and a pair of dark children's sunglasses

This is a picture of Baby Ikki. The baby recently turned 33 years old. He has not developed much beyond a normal 18-month-old child. He is able to walk, make noises, and respond to stimuli but still lacks verbal skills.

(Click) Image 37

A fireplace decorated for Xmas. There are four red stockings hanging in a row; three are hand-stitched with the names, Howie, Susie, and Shadow. The fourth stocking is a red liquor bag

Every Xmas, our family would hang stockings. My brother and sister had their own customized stockings. After Shadow, the family cocker spaniel, died, I inherited her stocking. The red liquor bag belonged to Fluffy, the family cat.

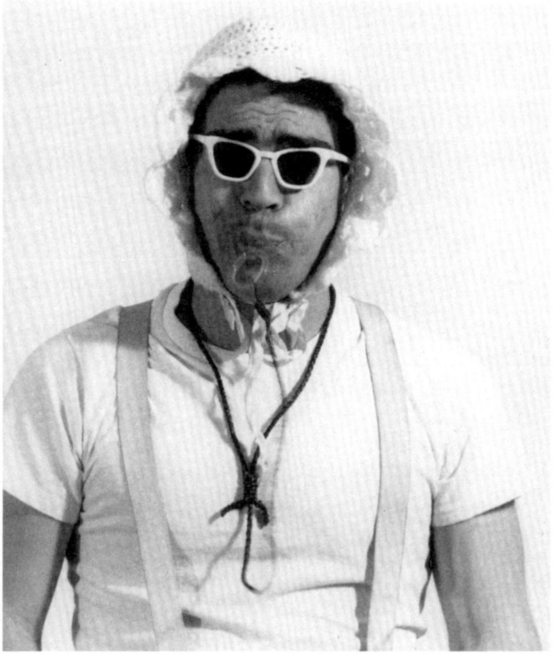

(Click) Image 38
A video still of me sitting in a stuffed chair holding a pillow at arm's length in front of my face, as a woman looks on from another stuffed chair

Some 20 years after seeing the analyst I started going to a Gestalt therapist. Even though I needed a pillow for sleeping, I was never comfortable talking to one in front of the therapist.

> *The reason I got into show business is because I couldn't find a job in my line of work ... I'm a Viking ...*
> —Jackie Vernon

(Click) Image 39

Although Baby Ikki was great for catching people's attention, I thought it important to develop a character that could talk and benefit from my day-to-day experiences. Also, I did not want to be known as the "baby guy."

Mike, alias Blandman, seemed to be the perfect vehicle to utilize lessons learned from years of watching television sitcoms and from my mother who was a master at "passing" and "fitting in." The name Mike, at one time the most popular name in the English language, combined with Smith, seemed custom-made for my purposes. Mike believes everything and understands very little. He probably has an inner life, but he does not seem to be in touch with it. My relationship to Mike is deeper than I like to admit.

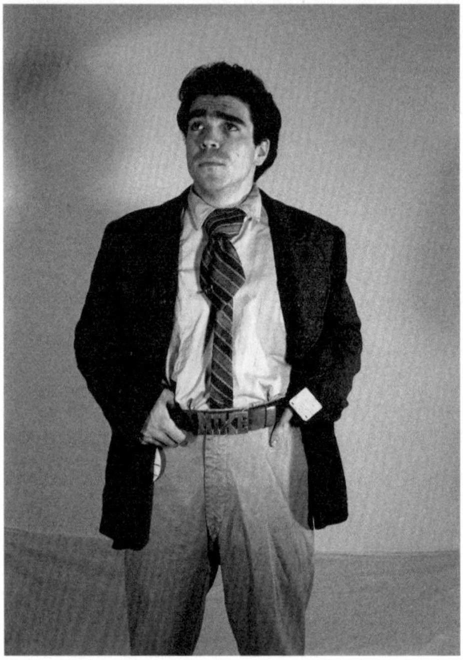

(Click) Image 40
A picture of me and another therapist, sitting in office chairs in a small non-descript room. She has short, thick hair that looks like a wig and is wearing a longish wool skirt. The cheeriest thing in the room is a box of Kleenex.

Some 15 years after I went to the Gestalt therapist I saw another therapist whose name I did not know for several weeks. I thought she was an orthodox Jewess because her hairdo looked like a wig and her skirts always seemed to cover her knees. Months into therapy, she was taken aback when I mentioned that I thought she was orthodox.

I stopped seeing her shortly after this incident and I do not remember her encouraging me to stay on to work out more issues.

(Click) Image 41
A map of South America

(Click) Image 42
A map of Peru

(Click) Image 43
My father, mother, sister, and I are waiting in a long line at the Lima airport with a large group of American tourists. My father and the other American tourists are each holding erotic Moche ceramic vessels.

In 1978, three years after Baby Ikki was born and the same year that Mike, alias Blandman, came into the world, my parents took my sister and me on a 10-day junket to Peru. I realized my father must have gotten a good deal on our Peruvian vacation when, after arriving in Lima, I saw tanks on the streets enforcing a midnight curfew. A major highlight on the trip for me was a visit to the Rafael Herrera Museum, devoted to erotic Moche pottery depicting sexual practices, some rather imaginative. It was funny to see a large number of typical American tourists wearing permanent press clothes and fanny packs, coming out of the gift shop holding handles depicting couples in the doggy style position. Seeing my parents with the same souvenir in hand was, to say the least, confusing.

I am not quite sure which continent the printed text for this talk resembles, but what I do know is that I have written over 4000 words, and I was told to keep it around 4000. Simple math tells me I need to end this text. There is a showbiz adage that goes something like this, "come in and go out with a bang." Too bad my exit bang is the result of a crash landing.

I'm feeling kind of cocky tonight. It must be the handsome blue sports jacket I'm wearing. A present from my wife ... came home early the other night, and there it was hanging on the chair ... I get a lot of my clothes that way ...

—Jackie Vernon

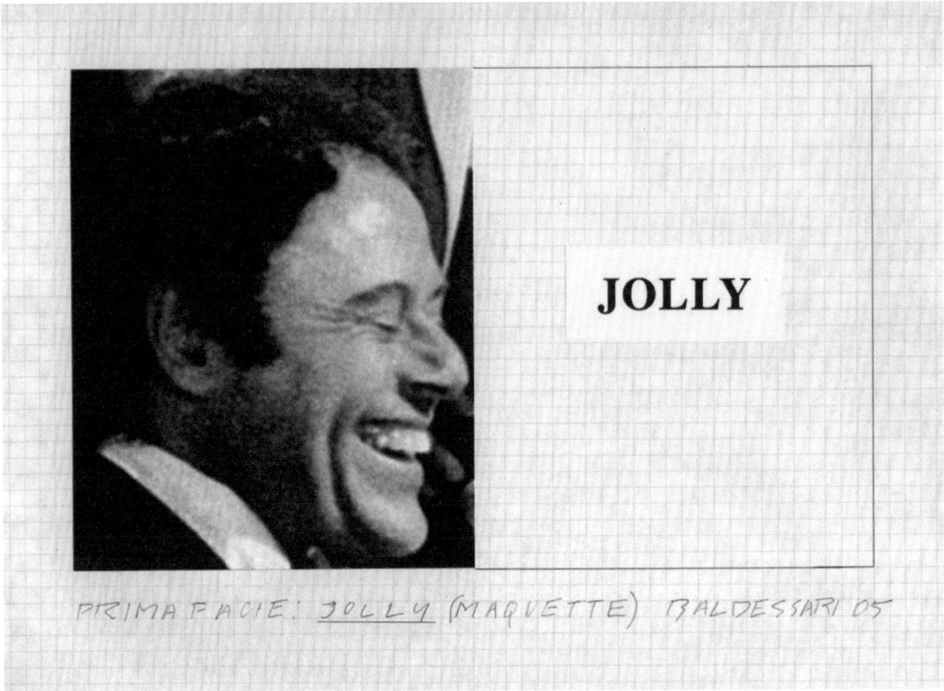

COURTESY OF THE ARTIST

John Baldessari
Prima Facie (Second State): Jolly (Maquette),
2005
Archival digital print, pencil on graph paper,
11 x 15 inches

John C. Welchman

"DON'T PLAY IT FOR LAUGHS": JOHN BALDESSARI AND CONCEPTUAL COMEDY

> I prefer humor in the sense let's say ... of Freud or Wittgenstein.
> —John Baldessari [circa 1990][1]

Of all the contributions made by John Baldessari to the wide world of Conceptual art, none is more celebrated—or iterated—than his association with that spectrum of the comedic caught up in irony, parody, and, above all, the absurd. So pervasive, and apparently contagious, is this affiliation, that when an honorary doctorate was conferred on him in 2006, the presiding Dean (of Burren College of Art in Galway, Ireland), carefully specified the artist's distinct and interrogative "sense of humor and love of the absurd" as leading indicators of his "greatness"; only to challenge the correlation—clearly overwhelmed by the counter-academic implications of a possible category confusion—by intimating that his own sense of judgment might have been infectiously impaired by the creative but confounding absurdism of his honoree: "can I really stand here and say that John Baldessari is a great artist, or am I too engaging with the absurd, albeit in my own way?"[2] Whether we understand this as a backhanded compliment, a case of special pleading, or a form of hapless self-implication, this incident is instructive, as it points to the widespread bafflement and critical confusions so often occasioned by Baldessari's signature brand of humorous debunking. One reason for these misconceptions arises from the constitutional difference between Baldessari's sense and administration of the absurd and the forms of creative absurdity that emerged in the later 19th century, soon to become part of the very definition of visual avant-gardism (several of which are discussed in other contributions to this volume).

If we return to one of the most vibrant comedic constellations developed in apposition to the avant-garde art world—the myriad genres of visual and textual wit generated in the Chat Noir and other cabarets in Montmartre during the 1880s, or by the Hydropathes and affiliates of the Incohérents exhibitions, for example—we will find that it turned on numerous essentially literary affiliations. Humor here was based on puns (visual and verbal), on homonyms and *double entendres*, and aimed at a coterie of knowledgeable insiders. One of the most characteristic aspects of Baldessari's humor, by contrast, is that the forms of social consensus assumed in Montmartre have already been built into his images, photographs, and phrases, arriving there not so much as the consequence of readily available social or political contexts, but as a by-product of consumerist over-production and signifying excess. The work depends, therefore, not on the exchange of repartee and bon mots, as in the avant-gardist clusters and micro-groups of bohemian Paris, but on the unending labor of popular archival sifting, assemblage, and selection, done by the artist himself while walking or driving solo around the streets of Southern California. What eventuates is the product of an environment already saturated with signs, captions, and labels, and flooded with images of all kinds, but especially photographic. Its referents are literally lost in circulation, so that the pressure points of Baldessari's humor run in essentially the opposite direction to the solicitous insider trading of the Incoherents or the Dadaists. Baldessari's preference is to abstract texts or images from their social contexts, set them deliberately aside, and variously to reallocate their semantic focus by fostering appositional over-coding, or stranding them in new, art-inflected, generalities.

As avant-garde humor reached its most perfervid alliance with the cultivation of absurdity in the Dada movements active in Zurich, Germany, and Paris during the heady half-decade from the middle of World War I to the early 1920s, it was characterized above all by the advent of a distinct clamorousness and calculation under the direction of a new breed of charismatic, entrepreneurial ringleaders such as Tristan Tzara, Francis Picabia, André Breton, and—in a somewhat different context—Futurist kingpin Filippo Tommaso Marinetti. The absurd took center stage amid a seemingly endless flow of squibs and evaporations, which layered the para-semantics of the nonsensical over the dissipations of the non-sequitur. This category of experience and production attracted comment from virtually all of the major protagonists of the Dada movement. Hugo Ball proclaimed in June 1916 that Dada was "a farce of nothingness ... [that] loves the extraordinary and the absurd."[3] In "The Dada Spirit in Painting," Georges Hugnet cites the entry in the *Larousse du XXe siècle* as the headtext for section four of his essay, "Dada in Paris," which includes the following propositions: "Aside from humor and mystification, which had a large part in it, we may consider Dadaism as the extreme limit of the possible divorce between words and meaning. 'Sense,' [it] has [been] said, 'is not a property of words that is assured.'"[4] While in a characteristic bout of paradoxological indulgence that put the savior of absurdity between the thieves of death and resurrection, Tzara ventured that: "Dada is dead, Dada is absurd. Long live Dada."[5]

While aspects of Baldessari's humor are also paradoxical and performative, in neither idiom is the effort that animates them forced, precious, or even voluble. The comedic energy that results is almost never shrill or bombastic as with the earlier avant-gardes; so that to the brash willfulness of his predecessors, whose words and actions were often accompanied by melees or fisticuffs, Baldessari retorts with an almost tranquilized mobilization of oddity. To this end, he uses popular, sometimes folksy formats (like the 35 popular tunes used to accompany Sol LeWitt's conceptual statements in *Baldessari Sings LeWitt* [1972]); he drains away much of his own characterological or stylistic self-presence by sub-commissioning amateur painters or commercial sign makers (as in the 12 *Commissioned Paintings* from 1969, in which we encounter a signature conjunction of deadpan withdrawal and situational absurdity)[6]; and he submits to the generalized anonymity of the found photograph in preference to the declamatory dramas of unraveling selfhood preferred by Tzara, Ball, Hugnet, and company.

There is, of course, another, more contemporary, context in which Baldessari's comedic predilections seem out of kilter with prevailing taste, and this is his dissident relation to the Conceptual art movement as it developed and was defined by its more vociferous protagonists in New York in the later 1960s and early 1970s. As is well known, Baldessari was virtually excommunicated from the Conceptual congregation by the most bookish and rebarbative member of the group, Joseph Kosuth, in 1969. While the toughest implication of Kosuth's put-down held that Baldessari's work was, in both literal and metaphorical senses, a joke, the grounds of the dismissal conjugated the LA artist's commitment to comedic outcomes for his art with the attribution of a larger failing. Kosuth pointed to what he saw as the inadequate and retrograde forms used by Baldessari to stage his work. His remarks were predicated on the secondariness of Baldessari's practice, on its putative resemblance to the illustration, or diagramming, of ideas, rather than to their immediate or first-hand production. For Kosuth, still wrestling with an inflected variant of modernist purity inherited from Donald Judd and Ad Reinhardt, Baldessari's use of painted words presented on a canvas was still visibly and materially pictorialist (as in a sense it clearly was).[7] As we will see, however, it is precisely Baldessari's strategic holding back, his refusal to stage-manage his work's delivery, and his intercourse with common objects and procedures (including painting as it appears on the streets not in the gallery)—all processes caught up with a resistant "secondariness"—that pass through his work and generate its humor.

The precise language used by Kosuth is instructive, as it produced, in its way, a subtle, abstruse and loaded indictment. His reference is closed in a parenthesis at the end of a paragraph listing "other artists" (Mel Bochner, Jan Dibbets, Eric Orr, Allen Ruppersberg, Dennis Oppenheim, Donald Burgy, Saul Ostrow, Adrian Piper, Perpetua Butler, Ian Burn, Mel Ramsden, and Roger Cutforth) whose work "within the past year" has taken on a "more 'conceptual' form"; though some relate only "peripherally." Kosuth writes: "(Although the amusing pop paintings of John Baldessari allude to this sort of work by being 'conceptual' cartoons of actual conceptual art, they are not really relevant to this discussion)."[8] In this formula Baldessari's work is subject to five descriptive qualifications, governed by the first of these, the put-down contention that his paintings are "amusing" (amusement stands in degraded relation to humor, one might suggest, as charm does to beauty). At the same time his works are described as "pop," allusive, cartoon-like, and irrelevant. It is clear that this assemblage of characteristics summarizes the very attributes that threatened Kosuth's notion of conceptual purity, and that the danger they posed warranted their further sequestration within the brackets of the parenthesis. By using the term "cartoon," for example, Kosuth associates Baldessari—in a single dismissive sweep—with popular graphic culture and its high art interlocutors—the Pop artists from the preceding generation; with Hollywood and the entertainment industry, in an elitist caricature that partitions a West Coast aesthetic from the more serious and established East Coast center of art world gravity; and with a genre of art-making that would be colorful, fast-moving, fun, and frivolous (and perhaps nothing more). This rhetoric catches Kosuth at his most Greenbergian, for a similar list of contaminating interests might be generated from that critic's diatribes against the Pop art movement.

One of the more interesting aspects of Kosuth's comment is that his attempt to exclude humor from the conditions of possibility proper to Conceptual art is historically indefensible—even, it transpires, in relation to the turn in his own practice, in train at precisely the same time he wrote "Art After Philosophy." Kosuth's move from the dictionary definition pieces commenced in the mid-1960s (which had secured his reputation, and would continue to define it) to the new round of appropriations based on the thesaurus that informed the *Second Investigation* (1969), was actually accompanied by a species of covert humor recognizably contiguous with the avant-gardist tradition of opaque, insider reference that stretches back to the Incoherents, and includes the machinic portraits of Francis Picabia, among many examples. As I discuss elsewhere, Kosuth's correlation of thesaurus entries with places of exhibition (entries under "Class Six: Intellect" are allocated to "Oxford University"); with the interests, real or imagined, of the newspapers and journals in which his extracts appeared (the opening sections of the Synopsis, under "I. Existence" of "Class One: Abstract Relations," were reserved for use in New York-based publications: "Abstract" was marked for *The New York Times*; "Concrete" for *Museum News*; "Formal" for *Artforum*; and, in another instance, "Indeterminate" with *Woman's Wear Daily*); or with wider themes and issues ("Color" is associated with TV)—was, in fact, informed by a wry, even quietly gleeful, sense of locative and historical irony. The matrix of semantic exchanges taken on in the *Second Investigation* is, then, "simultaneously whimsical and critical—though never one without the other. It offers a kind of grounding system seemingly at odds with the sustained anonymity, generality, and abstraction engrained

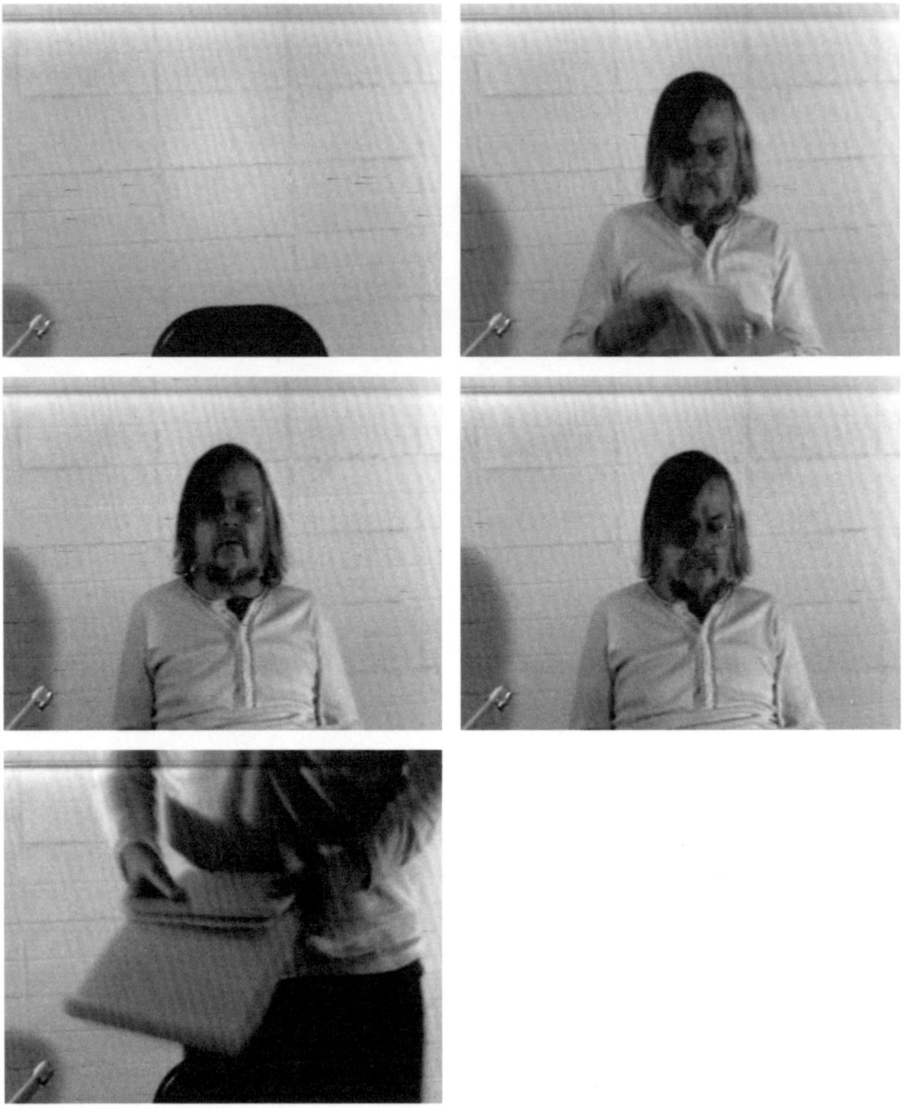

COURTESY OF THE ARTIST

John Baldessari
Baldessari Sings LeWitt, 1972
Black and white video with sound, 19 min

in the program of the *Second Investigation*, acting as a trip wire of opinion and critique, of personal and social investments in the institutional parameters of the art world."[9]

Of course, it's not just the work of Kosuth among the Conceptual generation that engaged with different aspects of humor, whether covertly or otherwise.[10] Droll comedy is a key ingredient in the quizzical investigations of Doug Huebler—who, unlike Baldessari, actually used the form of the cartoon to stage his interventions.[11] Viewed by Huebler as an outgrowth of his *Variable Piece # 70 (In Process) Global* (1971), *Crocodile Tears* was begun in 1981 and published as a comic strip in the *LA Weekly*.[12] In his essay on Huebler, Mike Kelley points to the in-your-face embarrassment and irony-laced utopianism of this project. He also observes that much early Conceptual art was a kind of "parody ... of dominant modes of the presentation of 'knowledge'—rendered somewhat more poignant by the fact that its 'standard fare' of poorly punched typewritten text, black and white snapshot photography, and spare, informational addenda (diagrams, charts, lists, maps etc.) was produced at the same moment that witnessed the rise of psychedelic, counter-culture graphics—effectively becoming a humorously "pathetic version of them."[13]

But as with Kosuth, comic potential also arises in places where it might be least expected. Anne Rorimer contends of Eva Hesse that "if there were nameable content in her work, it's the total absurdity of life ... absurdity is the key word. It has to do with contradictions and oppositions."[14] Baldessari himself noted the "special sense" in which the "obsessiveness" of "Sol LeWitt is hilarious": "I sometimes think he is getting a big laugh too. It's about being obsessed with an idea of the world or seeing paradoxes in the way the world is."[15] And for LeWitt the humorous is often leavened by the absurd: "As this retrospective [at the San Francisco Museum of Modern Art, 2000] confirms, [LeWitt's] oeuvre includes humor and flirtations with the absurd."[16] Robert Smithson spoke of his awareness of a "cosmic sense of humor" which has the uncanny capacity to makes things "tolerable ... not a depressing impasse."[17] While the cumulative attenuations of form and material that characterize Robert Barry's early work from the mid-1960s to the early 1970s have been associated with a more down-to-earth variant of "slyly provocative humor."[18]

Even the shifting institutional parameters of the art world at the turn of the 1970s, and the pressures applied to them by Conceptual artists and some of their gallerists, were subject to a form of comedic review. This is most visible in the reflections of Seth Siegelaub, whose attempt to recallibrate and partly to dissolve the commodity-based system of showing, buying, and selling gave rise to an ironic amusement, which he clearly counted as one of his general commitments and wider contributions. Siegelaub's reflections during an interview in April 1969 on the notion of the gallery and artists' affiliation with it in the "stable" system ("What gallery is he with?"), provoked an outburst of almost existential comedy: "That doesn't mean anything anymore. It's a totally meaningless thing. It's very funny. I just thought about that now for the first time."[19] He likewise poked fun at the disembodied "voids" of the art world to which the new work of the Minimalist and Conceptual generations had given rise, likening his own interventions to "sort of making trouble in a sense." "I mean that's my own private joke," he continued, "for just going ahead and doing something—shows, bringing some people over there."[20] These attitudes correlate with the manner in which Siegelaub highlights, and reiterates, the "absurd" conditions of the new conceptual work and its contexts, when measured by traditional art world standards.[21]

That, in retrospect, the vein of humor running through Conceptual art has become almost arterial is evidenced by the routine attestations of its comedic propensities that have now become staples of most critical discussions: "a pronounced strain of Conceptual art," as one of the most recent of these puts it, "is very funny, or at least absurd."[22] Something similar holds true for the post-Conceptual generation of media- and text-oriented artists on whom Baldessari exercised a significant influence, both as a professor at the California Institute of the Arts, Valencia, and as a wise, witty, and permissive mentor in the wider art world. Sherrie Levine notes of her appropriation pieces, which she commenced in the late 1970s, that, "For one thing, I think this work is very funny. I'm always surprised when people apologize to me for thinking it's funny. I want the work to be funny, but that doesn't mean I'm not serious."[23] Cindy Sherman's serial self-representations, on the other hand, are characterized by a "mocking" inflection that, in the artist's view, might disguise their more obvious humor: "My critics just don't get the joke or see who or what I'm referring to. I suppose it's a built-in defense just so long as it's entertaining somebody out there." Of the body of work employing prostheses and bodily supplementations, Jeanne Siegel notes that Sherman's "black humor [is] connected ... with the exaggeration of fakeness—the big asses, the false breasts."[24] There are many other symptoms of the return back to black humor among artists of this generation, including, *Another* (2008), a recent site-specific installation by Barbara Kruger, which cites a dark aphorism from Voltaire among 33 other quotations: "Those who make you believe absurdities can make you commit atrocities."[25]

In light of these contexts, then, how can we take stock of the signal place of humor in Baldessari's work over the last 40 years? I want to suggest that the answer to this question can best be formulated by thinking through a number of overlapping categories and propositions, the sum total of which will account for his interaction with a unique constellation of comedic resources. We should begin in the most unlikely place, with a principle that is clearly first among equals, but, at the same time, turns Baldessari's alliance with the comedic on its head. This is the notion to which he has alluded in numerous interviews over the years: that his address to humor is neither voluntaristic nor intentional. Baldessari draws this out in a discussion in which he contrasts the methodology of William Wegman's "conscious attempt at humor" to his own strategy of disavowal.[26] Wegman's work is characteristic of a purposeful solicitation of comic effects, "whereas I don't try for humor," Baldessari states. "I enjoy humor a lot and in the art world I'm considered a great repository of jokes and funny stories, but if I were trying for humor the works would be much different."[27] Baldessari separates himself from an intentionalist brand of humor with its literalist proclivities and physical implications, making it clear that his detour around purposeful comedy takes aim, in part at least, at a wider agenda that might be offered by the willful solicitation of amusement: "I think when there's humor it's as a result of something else, and I think when I say something else that I'm trying to get beneath the veneer of the world and trying to understand the world."[28]

One of the implications of an address to humor that "doesn't try" for it, is that the comic in this dimension is more often found than invented. It is deeply situational—tied to, almost trapped by its contexts—rather than artfully contrived or otherwise acted out. If we want to understand the sense of absurdity that arises so palpably in Baldessari's work we will find that it is firmly embedded in the textures of his life and career, in places and purposes that were already inflected by the offbeat and the incongruous. An incubator for all this was the non-descript suburb of

National City, near San Diego, California, the "cultural blank spot"[29] where Baldessari was born (in 1931), came of age, and in—and about—which he made his first "conceptual" artworks in the mid-1960s.[30] While outwardly staid and unremarkable, the experience of this quotidian cul-de-sac just off the freeway to Tijuana, Mexico, populated by servicemen, retirees, and immigrants (like Baldessari's parents, an Austrian-born handyman and builder and his Danish wife), was, nevertheless, doused with intimations of otherworldliness as Baldessari syncopated the steady drumbeat of its inexorable normalcy. The 32 snapshots combined in *The Backs Of All the Trucks Passed While Driving From Los Angeles to Santa Barbara, Calif., Sunday 20, Jan. 63* (1963), is, in large part, a wry reflection on the artist's own behindness in the contemporary art world. The blank, dirty backsides of the working vehicles—encountered, photographed, and then passed-by—act as an allegory for the aesthetic journey on which he was embarked.

The unlikely launch-pad for Baldessari's career was so far off the art world's radar that even routine forms of engagement with the New York mainstream—such as taking out a subscription to "follow the writings of Don Judd in *The Nation*," prompted the artist to reflect on the categorical oddness of his geographical and professional contexts: "I mean, if you consider the absurdity of the situation," he noted in conversation with Los Angeles critic Christopher Knight in 1992, "this guy teaching high school, whatever, down in National City, subscribing to *The Nation* to read Don Judd, it is pretty bizarre [laughter]."[31] While it now takes quite different forms, the absurd continues to play a significant role in Baldessari's everyday life, migrating, for example, from locative to economic conditions. In the context of the sale for $4.4 million at Christies in May 2007 of a painting from the late 1960s inscribed, "Quality material – Careful inspection – Good workmanship. All combined in an effort to give you a perfect painting," the artist offered the wryly unruffled comment that "I used to sell them for a hundred bucks each. Luckily I have a sense of absurdity."[32]

If the situational disavowal to which Baldessari has long been committed can be related to any conceptual format for the comedic, it is to the venerable, and distinctively American, notion of the deadpan. Introduced in the later 1920s to describe a turn in the style of film comedy at the height of the silent era, deadpan offered a striking metaphor for a kind of humor that eschewed expression, emotion, or motile physicality—aided and abetted by distinctively filmic resources such as the close-up and reaction shot—in favor of physiognomic reduction and impassive restraint. Humor was engendered in the deadpan mode by a general economy of means antithetical to the slapstick and vaudeville genres that dominated the earliest years of film comedy. The origins of the term itself are still disputed. Some sources attribute it to the general assimilation of "firearm phraseology" so that "pan" refers to the pan of a musket, and "dead" to the failure of the powder it contained to ignite ("keeping one's powder dry" arrived in the language from the same context). Another etymology has "pan" as "face," a sense apparently in circulation since at least 1833. So that the expressionlessness signified by deadpan "would mean literally 'dead face.'"[33] Whatever its precise origins, however, there is unanimity that the deadpan idiom was given its coup de grace in the films of Buster Keaton, the great "Stoneface," whose unsmiling, immobile features and unreactive demeanor have been celebrated by James Agee and other commentators as one of the definitive contributions to the comedic repertoire.[34] "Keaton's deadpan," noted Wes Gehring, in an assessment that brings together the leading concepts under consideration here, "is a 20th-century defense against the absurdities of the modern world."[35]

While Baldessari's work has been casually described as deadpan with almost as the same frequency as it has been correlated with absurdity, this condition too reaches into and across his oeuvre in a manner that exceeds superficial association. There are times, to be sure, when his counter-auratic performative articulations are quite literally drained of inflection, as with the "deadpan voice" he uses to intone into the camera: "I'd like to sing for you some of the sentences Sol LeWitt has written on Conceptual art" in *Baldessari Sings LeWitt* (1972);[36] or numerous works which establish and literalize formal photographic or social arrangements with comic denotative insistence: *Alignment Series: Arrows Fly Like This, Flowers Grow Like This* (1975), *I will not make any more boring art* (1971). But the reticent awkwardness of the artist's declarations of unedited selfhood, so at odds with the embellished artifice of the airbrush and re-take generations, represent just one dimension of the more general enmeshment of Baldessari's work with the expressive minima of deadpan.[37]

This becomes more apparent if we consider the special attention Baldessari has paid throughout his career to the expressive arena through which most comedy antithetical to deadpan restraint has been played out: the human face. While Baldessari has certainly kept his own face "straight"

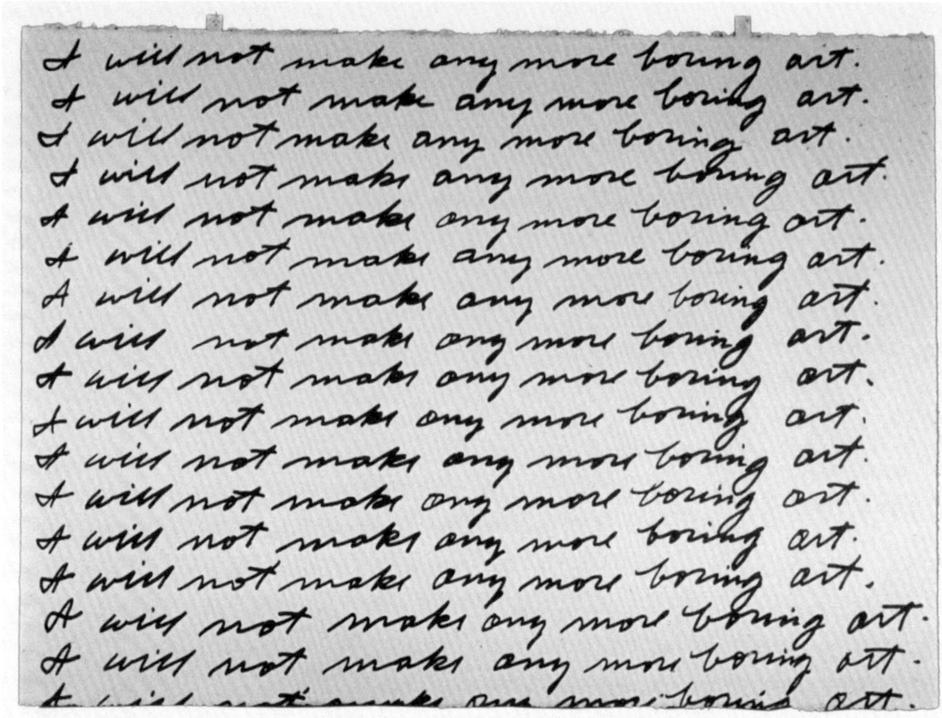

COURTESY OF THE ARTIST

John Baldessari
I will not make any more boring art, 1971
Lithograph, 22.5 x 30 inches

in his video work and occasional self-portraits, his inquiry into the social function of facial expression and the part-objects that constitute its arena of signification—nose, ears, eyes, mouth, etc.—opens up new questions about a whole regimen of short-circuits and detours that compromise the simple relay between self, identity, and disposition so often calibrated through various forms of reckoning with facial amplitude. Most obvious are the refusals of physiognomic particularity brought about by his use of discs of primary color to eclipse the faces populating the appropriated film stills and press photography with which he worked beginning in the early 1980s. But these are part of an inquiry into the wider conditions of facialized deferral, that includes cropping, cutting, altering, masking, and otherwise relegating the face—including his own in works from the mid-1970s such as *Portrait: Artist's Identity Hidden with Various Hats* and *Portrait: (Self) # 1 as Control + 11 Alterations by Retouching and Airbrushing* (both 1974)—even as he worked to investigate the analogizing logic of para-physiognomic reference.

Baldessari has answered to the unflinching blankness of Keaton and subsequent declarations of facial reduction with a startling array of visual deconstructions that lend depth and contour to expressive suspension in the deadpan idiom. His interests meet those of Gilles Deleuze and Félix Guattari, articulated at much the same time, who famously declared that, "the face has a great future, but only if it is destroyed, dismantled." Deleuze and Guattari elevate the scene of such destruction as a privileged method in a "program ... of schizoanalysis" that posits a way "out" of "the black hole of subjectivity."[38] Building on this platform of absence and obliteration, Baldessari has in recent years attempted to reconvene facial signification by attending to various conjugations among the part-objects that make it up; and crossing these with reflection on the often spurious—and sometimes overtly comic—relays brokered between faces, identities, colors, and language. The five states of *Prima Facie* (2005–2006) proffer a series of singular, text or color-coded faces coupled with emotional correlates that somehow label and govern them.[39] The sequence of exhibitions returns multiple instances and subtle variations of its defining format, so that the viewer is constantly reading from one work or series to the others, continually recalibrating and cross-matching between images and texts, colors and appearances.[40] Evacuated or deadpan expression is now replaced by a hectic shuttle of over-coded meanings, which Baldessari humorously returns to a general point of origin in the abstracting, near monochrome, pieces with which the fifth and final iteration of *Prima Facie* ends. Here the face is eclipsed once more, leaving only the bizarrely connotative names of commercial paint hues.

Baldessari has even offered, unconsciously no doubt, a meta-commentary on the possible origins of the word "deadpan" in firearm vocabulary. His frequent resort to gun images—as in the *Thaumatrope Series: Two Gansters (One with Scar and Gun)* (1975); *Violent Space Series: Two Gun Situations (One Threatening)* (1976); *Kiss/Panic* (1984); *Gun-Badge-Knife* (1988); *Flying Saucer: Rainbow/Two Cyclists/Dog/Gorilla and Bananas/Chaotic Situation/Couple/Tortoise/Gunman (Fallen)* (1992); *Noses & Ears, etc.: Couple and Man with Gun* (2007)—collides intimations of popular celluloid culture and formal orientations, such as pointing or loading, with everyday social violence. The prevalence of the gun-related images in his work relates, in large part, to the archival sources in Hollywood movies and popular magazines from which Baldessari assembled the archive of images that funds his practice. In a conversation with Jeremy Blake in 2004, for example, the artist lists "people with guns" as the first item among the countless stacks of images he amassed in "huge folders, each one classified according to subject matter or genre."[41] But perhaps the prominence of gun iconography in Baldessari's work is not merely fortuitous, for it is directed by the artist's encounter in dumpsters and photo bins with an unending series of images precipitated by a fetishization of personal weaponry in the US quite at odds with the place of firearms in other Western nations. This is Baldessari's measured retort to the extraordinary and insidious longevity of the insemination of the gun into the North American popular unconscious, borne out by its omnipresence in film, comic, and now online cultures, and its inflection of the very language that we speak. By crossing rifles and Magnums with deadpan appropriation, of course, the artist also offers guns a measure of control, rendering them mute or inert, robbing them of their capacities to fire ... leaving the powder their pans—in one sense at least—to go dead.

Baldessari also runs the language of deadpan deliciously astray as he tracks it into the deepest canyons of aesthetic seriousness; and then, like those trucks on the California freeway, nonchalantly overtakes it. Nothing better exemplifies his fearless spelunking into domains reserved for straight-laced earnestness or poker-faced delivery than the part he

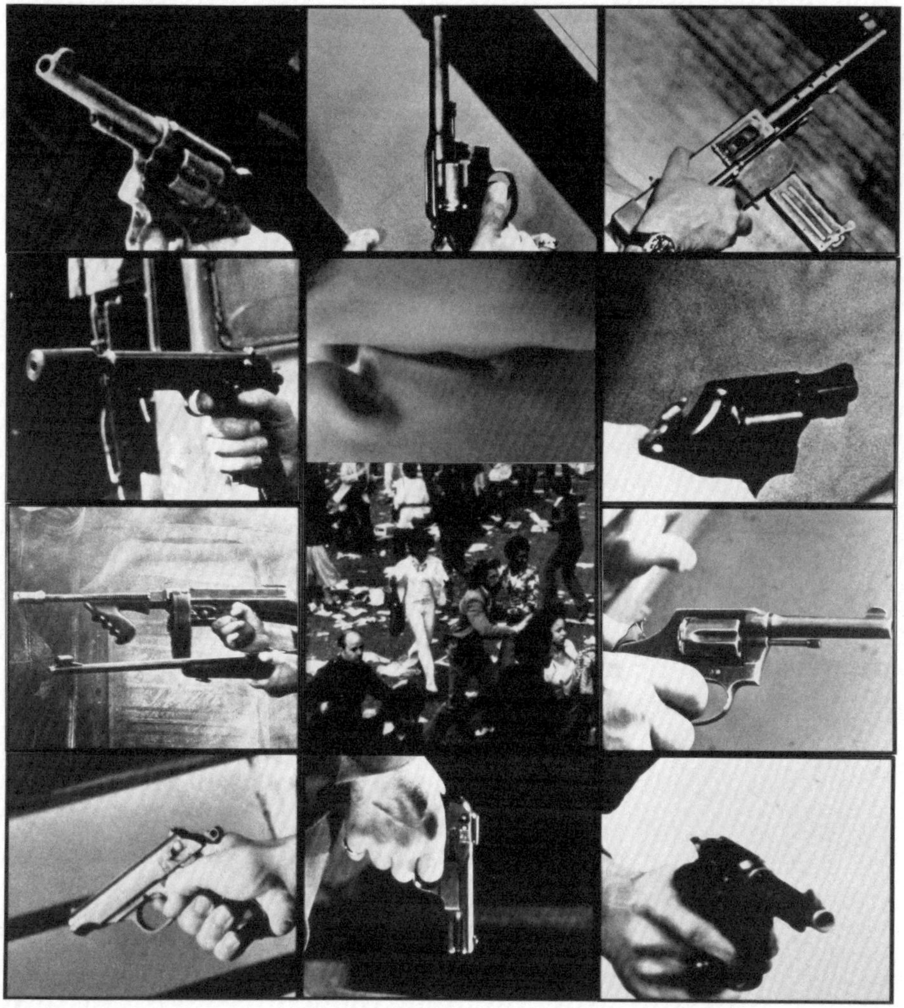

John Baldessari
Kiss/Panic, 1984
Black and white photographs, 2 tinted
80 x 72 inches

took in the explicit turn by many artists associated with the Conceptual movement, including Kosuth, Art & Language, Mel Bochner, and others, toward newly voguish structuralist methodologies and analytic philosophy in the early and mid-1970s. In *Blasted Allegories* (1975), for example, Baldessari offers a wicked "parody of the activity or simulacrum of the structuralists."[42] Here, randomly shot TV images are arranged through the intervention of an intervalometer, with black and white pictures below and monochrome images above. Baldessari's friends selected one associative word for each image and then the various series were organized alphabetically—with the color images arranged in the order of the color wheel: Y[ellow] O[range] R[ed] V[iolet] B[lue] G[reen]. Baldessari scrupulously separates the "structure" of a structuralist model, the self-made "rules" of which he follows unflaggingly, from the message or content level that might underwrite or "explain" it. What results is a manic over-determination of structural congruence that has achieved little more than to lend specious and momentary order to a set of randomly populated variables. Yet, Baldessari pointed, at the same time, to the caprice of pseudo-universality that underwrites structuralist discourse, delivering viewers to an epiphany of judgment, personal choice, chance, and accident that foregrounds everything the structuralist method set out to foreclose.

Like other works from the mid-1970s, the *Strobe Series* (1975–1976), is also deeply engaged with Baldessari's investigations of structuralist theory and his related readings in linguistics and anthropology.[43] While explicitly focused on the relations between diachronic and synchronic temporalities and the emergence of what the artist termed "a 'timeless' time," Baldessari paraphrases the object of his investigation as "an interlude in which magic might occur."[44] The interlude, or space between, is a musicalized punctuation in time, activated, perhaps, by the afterimages and visual intensities created between the beats of a strobe light, which gives rise to referential incongruities such as the issuance not of sound but of flowers from the mouth of the female subject in *Strobe Series/Futurist: Girl with Flowers Falling from Her Mouth (for Botticelli) # 1* (1975). We catch the artist, here, in the process not simply of scrambling the formalized precipitates of written language—words and letters—but taking on the recalibration of the associative spaces that govern the physical delivery of sound or speech—mouth and lips, tongue and teeth—so that human sound-production is not only made visible, but humorously displaced into a metaphorical conjecture founded on the beguiling florality of speech. At the same time, the metaphor turns on another visual pun as the photograph is read as a comic literalization of florid, or flowery, delivery.

The rhythmic play of muteness and expression that comes together in deadpan is so engrained in Baldessari's work and reflection—and the new spaces they negotiate for humor—that they engage, not just with the concepts of counter-facial identity reached for by Deleuze and Guattari, but also with some of the definitional parameters laid down for comedy itself. In *Le Rire* [*Laughter*], Henri Bergson notes a certain dependency of the mechanisms of laughter on disinterested withdrawal, or what he terms a momentary "anasthesia of the heart." Bergson describes the generation of comedic effects through processes of subtraction or partial withdrawal, as in the silencing of music by stopping-up the ears during a dance. Running interference across the signifying planes of representation—and participation—Baldessari's trademark address to humor is also organized through the interruption of code-based practices, so that that their structures and actions become over-literal and, by implication, exaggerated, off-beat, and funny. His work, in fact, harmonizes with various antitheses to the procedures Bergson defines as "*mechanical elasticity*," which the comedic sets out to scramble and rearrange. Bergson mobilizes another musical analogy when he describes the effects of a lack of elasticity as "like a song which lags behind its accompaniment" giving rise to conditions in which "we continue to see what is no longer visible, to hear what is no longer audible, to say what is no longer to the point."[45] He surely reaches here for precisely the kind of jumbled spacing and constitutional secondariness that informs the stutter, opening up possibilities for the comedic that are formed in the signifying gaps around the presentness of an image or phrase, and thus engendered by the momentum of their performativities and afterlife.

Bergson, of course, famously correlated the core orientations of laughter with both the work of art itself and with personalities that might be artist-like—specifying, for example, that the conditions of humorous inelasticity are most clearly visible and ostentatiously funny in the "absent-minded person." For him the greater purpose of laughter "comes into being," however, "just when society and the individual, freed from the worry of self-preservation, begin to regard themselves as works of art." While Bergson's association is a general one, the life-defining parameters of "tension" and "elasticity" he proposes as the founding dialectic of bio-social organization, find their most beguiling conjunction in gestures of "social masquerade" and appropriation. In his terms—and Baldessari's work—in fact, "any form or formula is a ready-made frame into which the comic element may be fitted"[46] and its base assumptions rhythmically, stutteringly, transformed into comedic gold.

Both artist and comedian are invested with the ability to unveil and then reactivate the almost infinite potential of events and customs made ready by the social. The stacks and swirls, compressions and metronymic repetitions of Baldessari's photo-pieces, in particular, accentuate that "uniform rhythm of the bending and release of a spring"[47] which, for Bergson, makes laughter resound. The core of Bergson's philosophical vitalism, partly digested by Deleuze into his counter-organic ontology, is actually founded on the "unbroken melody" of the "inner life" and an "original harmony of forms and colors" that are diminished by utilitarianism and the discordant weight of the symbolic.[48] Baldessari releases a comic corrective to Bergson's suspicion of the everyday by working at the interface between commonplace objects and events, and art genres and forms, and diverting the implications of the former through the latter. From improvisational jazz he learned to foreground "processes of 'itinerative following' rather than 'iterative reproducing.'"[49] And by crossing concept-production with found photography, stuttering language and compositional assemblage, he achieves a signature version of that "non-segregation" and "reversibility of the senses composing amongst themselves"[50] which defines the reinvention of synaesthesia after modernism. Perhaps this is the final destination of Baldessari's comedy: an assemblage based on multiple senses—and in recent works organized through a sounding out of the individual instruments that send and record them (mouths, eyes, noses, ears)—within which each sensory type keeps its own powder dry. They are ready to explode, but this will not be part of the artist's work. His final act of restraint is to put them into contact zones, but hold off on their ignition; and with this gesture he takes us to the very limits of the deadpan, the place where anaesthesia and synaesthesia are about to come together ... but the spark that sets them off is defiantly deferred.

NOTES

1
Jeanne Siegel, "John Baldessari: Recalling Ideas," in *Art Talk: The Early 80s*, Da Capo Press, New York 1990, p. 45.

2
Text of the Introductory Address delivered by Professor Timothy Emlyn Jones, Dean of the Burren College of Art, and Adjunct Professor of NUI Galway on April 18, 2006, at the Burren College of Art, on the occasion of the conferring of the Degree of Doctor of Fine Arts honoris causa, on John Baldessari.

3
Hugo Ball, *Flight Out of Time: A Dada Diary*, trans. Ann Raimes, University of California Press, Berkeley 1996, p. 65.

4
Georges Hugnet, "The Dada Spirit in Painting," first published as a serial in *Cahiers d'Art*, Paris, 1932 and 1934; reprinted in Robert Motherwell (ed.), *The Dada Painter and Poets: An Anthology*, Belknap Press, Cambridge, Massachusetts 1989, p. 126–127.

5
Tristan Tzara, "Dada Manifesto on Feeble Love and Bitter Love," first published in *La Vie des Lettres*, no. 4, Paris, 1921; reprinted in *The Dada Painters and Poets: An Anthology* (1951), ed. Robert Motherwell, 2nd ed., Belknap Press, Cambridge, Massachusetts 2007.

6
Ken Johnson's review of *The Commissioned Paintings* at Sonnabend Gallery, *New York Times*, Friday, October 3, 2008, notes that, "what's most engaging is the deadpan comedy, the exacting, methodical seriousness with which the artist carried out his absurd project."

7
Kosuth twice invokes the notion of "a *purer* form of 'conceptual' art," and in its first appearance italicizes "purer," in the sentences that antecede the reference to Baldessari, reserving it for the work of Saul Ostrow, Adrian Piper, Perpetua Butler, and the group constituted by Ian Burn, Mel Ramsden, and Roger Cutforth (see following note).

8
Joseph Kosuth, "Art After Philosophy," "Part II: 'Conceptual Art' and Recent Art"; first published in *Studio International* (London), 178, no. 916 (November 1969), p. 160–161; reprinted in *Art After Philosophy and After: Collected Writings, 1966–90*, ed. Gabriele Guercio, MIT Press, Cambridge, Massachusetts 1991, p. 29.

9
John C. Welchman, "Ideas Being Given: Joseph Kosuth's Media and Public Projects From *The Second Investigation* (1969) to 2006," lecture delivered at Die Akualitat der Conceptual Art, Kunsthistorischen Instituts der Rheinischen Friedrich-Wilhelms-Universität Bonn, Kunstmuseum Bonn, Bonner Kunstverein, July 6 and 7, 2007; publication in progress.

10
Baldessari notes that "Mel Bochner called some Conceptual art 'joke art.' I always suspected I fell into that category"; John Baldessari, "In Conversation: John Baldessari & Jeremy Blake," *Artforum*, March, 2004. As evidenced by his reference to an essay he was preparing with Smithson on the planetarium at the American Museum of Natural History in New York, Bochner himself took up with jokes: "Buried in my text were also a number of inside jokes. For example, a graphic of a pointing hand based on an actual sign hanging above the main staircase was a tongue-in-cheek nod to Marcel Duchamp. But the most personally significant gibe was my parody

of Judd's writing, a homage to his influence but also an assault on the 'specific object'"; "Secrets of the domes: Mel Bochner on 'The Domain of the Great Bear," http://www.thefreelibrary.com/Secrets+of+the+domes:+Mel+Bochner+on+%22The+Domain+of+the+Great+Bear%22.-a0152514804 [based on a presentation at the Robert Smithson symposium, Whitney Museum of American Art, September 2005].

11
Huebler, of course, was another artist who received special mention in Kosuth's "Art After Philosophy," in this case a somewhat ageist put down that also depended on Kosuth's adjudication of conceptual purity: "It is not my intention to point out a negative aspect of the work, but only to show that Huebler—who is in his mid-40s and much older than most of the artists discussed here—has not as much in common with the aims in the purer versions of 'Conceptual art' as it would superficially seem." *Art after Philosophy and After: Collected* Writings, 1966–1990, p. 26.

12
Commissioned by the Los Angeles County Museum of Art as part of their "In Context" program of monographic exhibitions and originally published in the *LA Weekly*, excerpts from *Crocodile Tears* appear in the catalogue for Huebler's show at the La Jolla Museum of Contemporary Art, *Douglas Huebler*, May 27-August 7, 1988, p. 14–18.

13
Mike Kelley, "Shall We Kill Daddy?" in John C. Welchman (ed.), *Foul Perfection: Essays and Criticism*, MIT Press, Cambridge, Massachusetts 2002, p. 184.

14
Anne Rorimer, *New Art in the 60s and 70s: Redefining Reality*, Thames and Hudson, London 2001, p. 25.

15
Jeanne Siegel, "John Baldessari: Recalling Ideas," in *Art Talk: The Early 80s*, Da Capo Press, New York 1990, p. 43–45.

16
Andrea Miller-Keller, "Sol LeWitt and the Arts Community," in *Sol LeWitt: A Retrospective* (San Francisco Museum of Modern Art, February 19–May 30, 2000; Museum of Contemporary Art, Chicago, July 22–October 22, 2000; Whitney Museum of American Art, November 30, 2000–February 25, 2001), exh. cat., Yale University Press, New Haven, Connecticut 2000, p. 77.

17
Alexander Alberro and Patsy Norvell (eds.), "Robert Smithson: June 20, 1969," in *Recording Conceptual Art: Early Interviews with Barry, Huebler, Kaltenbach, LeWitt, Morris, Oppenheim, Siegelaub, Smithson, and Weiner*, University of California Press, Berkeley 2001, p. 134. In an interview with Moira Roth (ed. and annotated by Naomi Sawelson-Gorse), Smithson notes that some of the activities of the Conceptual artists related to "what Mel Bochner might call Joke art—you know playing little jokes like the Dadaists." See *Robert Smithson*, exh. cat., University of California Press, Berkeley 2004, p. 85.

18
Ken Johnson, "Robert Barry: 'Early Works 1966–73,'" [Gasser & Grunert Gallery, Chlesea, New York], "Art in Review," *New York Times*, April 20, 2001: "A slyly provocative humor runs throughout Mr. Barry's work."

19
Seth Siegelaub in "Seth Siegelaub: April 17, 1969," in Alberro and Norvell (eds.), *Recording Conceptual Art*, p. 51.

20
Ibid.

21
Siegelaub uses the term "absurd" some five times in the interview with Norvell (see note 19 above), p. 37, 40, 42, 45, 46.

22
Pamela Lee, "'If Everything's Good, Then Nothing's Good Anymore': Martin Kippenberger, Conceptual Art, and a Problem of Definition," in *Martin Kippenberger: The Problem Perspective*, exh. cat., Museum of Contemporary Art/MIT Press, Los Angeles/Cambridge, Massachusetts 2008, p. 186. There are numerous other examples, see, e.g., *The Last Picture Show: Artists Using Photography, 1960–1982*, exh. cat., The Hammer Museum, Westwood, Los Angeles, February 14–May 9, 2004: "The broad scope of the exhibition includes diverse and unconventional photographs that demonstrate how artists have used the camera to frame critical explorations and overarching themes. These include architecture and seriality, the body, self-portraiture and identity, found images, appropriation, interventions in natural and built environments, conceptual strategies and the absurd, among others." http://hammer.ucla.edu/exhibitions/detail/exhibition_id/121.

23
Siegel, *Art Talk*, p. 252.

24
Ibid., p. 278.

25
Part of the ongoing Stuart Collection, Barbara Kruger's *Another* (2008) is an installation in the new Price Center East, on the campus of the University of California, San Diego.

26
Siegel, *Art Talk*, p. 43–45: "I told him [Wegman] once ... 'You're somewhere a cross between James Turber and Matisse' ... Bill is like Matisse trying to be funny."

27
Ibid., p. 45.

28
Ibid.

29
Christopher Miles, "Nine to Five" [on John Baldessari], *Tate Etc.* Issue 13, Summer 2008; http://www.tate.org.uk/tateetc/issue13/ninetofive.htm.

30
On Baldessari's life and work in National City, see Hugh Davies, Anne Rorimer, Andrea Hales, *John Baldessari: National City*, exh. cat., Museum of Contemporary Art San Diego, 1997. There is of course a minor industry of autobiographies and academic research devoted to the absurdist impact of the American suburbs, see e.g., Mark Salzman, *Lost In Place: Growing Up Absurd in Suburbia*, Vintage, New York 1996.

31
Oral history interview with John Baldessari, April 4–5, 1992, Archives of American Art, Smithsonian Institution [Interview with John Baldessari conducted by Christopher Knight at the artist's studio in Santa Monica, CA April 4, 1992] at http://www.aaa.si.edu/collections/oralhistories/transcripts/baldes92.htm.

32
Ben Bamsey, "John Baldessari," *ARTWORKS Magazine*, Winter 2007; see http://artworksmagazine.com/?tag=john-baldessari.

33
Merriam-Webster dates the first appearance of deadpan to "circa 1928." For the etymology, see "Lexicons of Lost Lifestyles: Firearm Phraseology (part 2)," *Corona Genealogical Society*, vol. 5, issue 1 (March 2006) at http://www.coronapubliclibrary.org/CGSNewsletterMarch2006.pdf."In the previous article, we looked at the front-loading musket that used a pan to hold the powder, which was ignited by a spark. As already covered, sometimes there is nothing more than a 'flash in the pan'; one might wonder why such an action would be so unproductive. One possibility is that the powder used was wet, thus extinguishing the 'fire' before it really caught. For this reason, a man going forth to shoot game for the evening meal or to fight in a war, even as recent as the War of the Rebellion (1861–1865), would be admonished to 'keep his powder dry.' This advice, now meaning, 'be prepared,' was then a matter of life and death; if the powder was wet and didn't ignite, the enemy could easily get the upper hand (Drake, p. 171–172; Feldman, p.74). This might also take us to the origin of the expression 'dead pan.' Drake seems to tentatively attribute it to the pan of the musket (p. 85), but others are not so sure. Holt states that 'pan' is another word for face (as of 1833) and, since 'dead pan' (sometimes spelled as one word: 'deadpan') means 'expressionless,' it would mean literally 'dead face' (p. 73; Hendrickson, p. 195)." The references are to P. Drake, *What Did They Mean By That: A Dictionary of Historical and Genealogical Terms Old and New*, Heritage Books, Bowie, Maryland 2003; D. Feldman, *Who Put the Butter in Butterfly? ... And Other Fearless Investigations Into Our Illogical Language*, Harper & Row, New York 1989; Alfred H. Holt, *Phrase and Word Origins: A Study of Familiar Expressions* (1936), rev. ed., Dover Publications, New York 1961; and R. Hendrickson, *The Facts on File Encyclopedia of Word and Phrase Origins*, rev. and expanded ed., Checkmark Books, New York 2000.

34
James Agee, in fact, complicates received opinion on the operation of Keaton's deadpan, referring it back to his work on the stage ("he had got the deadpan habit in variety; on the screen he had merely been so hard at work it had never occurred to him there was anything to smile about"); and crossing the notion of uninflected blankness with Keaton's regimen of micro-expressive gestures: "much of the charm and edge of Keaton's comedy ... lay in the subtle leverages of expression he could work against his normal deadpan"; cited in Richard Warrington Baldwin Lewis and Nancy Lewis, *American Characters: Selections from the National Portrait Gallery, Accompanied by Literary Portraits*, exh. cat., National Portrait Gallery Smithsonian Institution/Yale University Press, Washington DC/New Haven 1999, p. 366. These sentiments are echoed by later critics, see, e.g. Gilbert Perez, on Keaton and Chaplin from "The Material Ghost" (1998), in Leo Braudy and Marshall Cohen (eds.), *Film Theory and Criticism: Introductory Readings*, Oxford University, Oxford 2004, p. 595: "It is Keaton's genius as an actor to keep a face so nearly deadpan and yet render it, by subtle inflections, so vividly expressive of inner life." See also, Peter Krämer, "The Making of a Comic Star: Buster Keaton and *The Saphead* (1920)," in *The Silent Cinema Reader*, ed. Lee Grieveson and Peter Krämer, Routledge, London 2004, p. 27–89.

35
Wes D. Gehring, *Personality Comedians as Genre: Selected Players*, Greenwood Publishing Group, London 1997, p. 5.

36
Barbara London in *Video Spaces: Eight Installations*, exh. cat., The Museum of Modern Art, New York 1995, p. 13.

37
Little attention has been paid to the conditions of deadpan in the art world, one exception being the exhibition *StoneFace* curated by Sarah Lehrer-Graiwer and Stacy Bengtson Fertig, September 6–November 9, 2007, at the Fellows of Contemporary Art in Chinatown, Los Angeles, which assembled work by Baldessari, Dan Graham, Jesse Aron Green, Lee Lozano, Rachel Mason, Richard Prince, Mark Roeder, and Maya Schindler. Defining deadpan humor as a "method of critique enacted through pleasure," the curators point to the "critical ambivalence of blankness that allows conflicting positions to co-exist." They trace the origin of deadpan in the art world to Duchamp and Pop art. See, http://www.focala.org/project_detail.php?id=5. Steve McQueen's video/film work *Deadpan* (1997), in which scenes from Keaton's films are re-enacted, was shown at The Museum of Modern Art, New York, in 1997. Allan Kaprow made several references to deadpan techniques in his collected writings, see Allan Kaprow, *Essays on the Blurring of Art and Life*, ed. Jeff Kelley, University of California Press, 2003, p. 67, 86, 198, 246.

38
Gilles Deleuze and Félix Guattari, *A Thousand Plateaus: Capitalism and Schizophrenia II*, trans. Brian Massumi, University of Minnesota Press, Minneapolis 1988, p. 171, 188. Deleuze and Guattari repurpose the forms and implications of the face with the notion of "faciality," which realigns its signification in a matrix of possibilities set out between a "white wall" of "signifiance" and the black hole of "subjectification"; see, "Year Zero: Faciality," in *A Thousand Plateaus*, p. 167–191.

39
Beginning with an exhibition at Margo Leavin in Los Angeles (April 9–May 14, 2005), *Prima Facie* was seen in four further iterations: "Second State" at Mai 36, Zurich, June 11–July 30, 2005; "Third State" at Galeria Pepe Cobo, Madrid, September 14–November 10, 2005; "Fourth State" at Galerie Meert Rihoux, Brussels, December 16, 2004–January 28, 2005; and "Fifth State" at Sprüth Magers Lee, London, April 28–June 24, 2006. The project was also show as *John Baldessari: The Prima Facie Series*, Museum Dhondt-Dhaenens, Deurle, Belgium, September 17–December 3, 2006.

40
I discuss Baldessari's relation to facial representation at greater length in "Art Subjects: Physiognomy Without a Face," in the exhibition catalogue for *John Baldessari*, Los Angeles County Museum of Art, 2009; on which this paragraph, and a number of other references, draw.

41
John Baldessari, "In Conversation: John Baldessari & Jeremy Blake," *Artforum*, March, 2004: "I had these huge folders, each one classified according to subject matter or genre: people with guns, people kissing, Indians and cowboys falling off of horses, getting shot, getting shot with arrows—almost every plot device."

42
Hal Foster, "John Baldessari's *Blasted Allegories*," *Artforum*, vol. 18, no. 2 (October 1979), p. 54.

43
This paragraph, along with concluding remarks about the relation between Baldessari and Henri Bergson, draw from my essay, "Spherical Music: John Baldessari and Synaesthesia After Modernism," in the exhibition catalogue, *John Baldessari: Music*, ed. Stefan Gronert, Bonner Kunstmuseum, 2007

44
Baldessari, cited in Coosje van Bruggen, *John Baldessari*, exh. cat., Los Angeles Museum of Contemporary Art/Random House, Los Angeles/New York 1990, p. 35.

45
Henri Bergson, *Le Rire* [*Laughter*], in *Comedy*, ed. Wylie Sypher, Johns Hopkins University Press, Baltimore 1980, p. 67.

46
Ibid., p. 90.

47
Ibid., p. 110.

48
Ibid., p. 158–159.

49
Eugene Holland, "Studies in Applied Nomadology: Jazz, Improvisation and Post-Capitalist Markets," in *Deleuze and Music*, ed. Ian Buchanan and Marcel Swiboda, Edinburgh University, Edinburgh 2004, p. 25.

50
Jean-Godefroy Bidima, "Music and the Socio-Historical Real: Rhythm, Series and Critique in Deleuze and O. Revault d'Allonnes," trans. Janice Griffiths, in *Deleuze and Music*, p. 179.

LIST OF CONTRIBUTORS

JOHN BALDESSARI

John Baldessari is one of the pioneers of Conceptual art; his work has been featured in some 120 solo exhibitions in the US and Europe, and over 300 group exhibitions. His oeuvre includes artist's books, videos, films, billboards, and public commissions. Recent projects include books, films, a commission at the Deutsche Guggenheim Berlin (2004), and retrospectives at the Museum Moderner Kunst Stiftung Ludwig Vienna, Austria (2005); the Kunsthaus, Graz, Austria (2005); the Musée d'art contemporain de Nîmes, France (2005); as well as Tate and the Los Angeles County Museum of Art (2009–2010). *John Baldessari: Music* opened at the Kunstmuseum Bonn and the Kunstverein Bonn in May 2007. Baldessari taught for many years at The California Institute of the Arts and at UCLA.

JESSICA CHALMERS

Jessica Chalmers is a scholar and performance artist. In addition to being a founding member of The V-Girls, a feminist performance group active between 1986 and 1996, she has worked extensively as a playwright and dramaturge for The Builders Association theater company. Most recently, she has taught Women's and Performance Studies and Theater at the University of Notre Dame, Indiana.

SIMON CRITCHLEY

Simon Critchley has been Professor of Philosophy at the New School for Social Research, New York, since 2004. He has also served as President of the British Society for Phenomenology (1994–1999) and Chief Philosopher with the International Necronautical Society. His books include *Continental Philosophy: A Very Short Introduction* (Oxford University Press, 2001); *On Humour* (Routledge, 2002); *Things Merely Are* (Routledge, 2005); *Infinitely Demanding: Ethics of Commitment, Politics of Resistance* (Verso, 2007); *The Book of Dead Philosophers* (Vintage, 2008); and *On Heidegger's* Being and Time (Routledge, 2008).

SIGMUND FREUD

The pioneer of psychoanalysis, Sigmund Freud (1856–1939) was born in Austria-Hungary, lived in Vienna from 1860 to 1938, and died in London shortly after the outbreak of World War II. Having studied with Jean-Martin Charcot at the Salpêtrière Hospital in Paris in 1885, he opened a private practice in Vienna the following year and later commenced a series of writings that still define the field of psychoanalysis. These include *Studies in Hysteria* (with Josef Breuer, 1895); *The Interpretation of Dreams* (1900); *Three Essays on the Theory of Sexuality* (1905); *Group Psychology and the Analysis of the Ego* (1921); *The Future of an Illusion* (1927); *Civilisation and Its Discontents* (1929); and *Moses and Monotheism* (1939).

JO ANNA ISAAK

Jo Anna Isaak is the Marion Chair in Art History at Fordham University, New York. Her research and writing focus on modern and contemporary art, feminism and critical theory, and more recently on environmental issues. Her books include *The Ruin of Representation in Modernist Art and Texts* (UMI Research Press, 1986); *Feminism and Contemporary Art: The Revolutionary Power of Women's Laughter* (Routledge, 1997); *Mobile Fidelities: Conversations on Feminism, History and Visuality* (KT Press, 2006); and *pressPLAY: Contemporary Artists in Conversation* (Phaidon, 2005). As a curator she has organized exhibitions such as *The Revolutionary Power of Women's Laughter* (1982); *Laughter Ten Years After* (1995); *Looking Forward, Looking Black* (1999); and *H20* (2002).

LOUIS KAPLAN

Louis Kaplan is Director of the Institute of Communication and Culture and Associate Professor at the University of Toronto. His research embraces photography, new media, 20th-century art history, humor, Jewish studies, and visual culture. He is author of *The Strange Case of William Mumler, Spirit Photographer* (University of Minnesota Press, 2008); *American Exposures: Photography and Community in the Twentieth Century* (University of Minnesota Press, 2005); and *Laszlo Moholy-Nagy: Biographical Writings* (Duke University Press, 1995); and editor of *The Damned Universe of Charles Fort* (Autonomedia, 1993).

JEFFREY MINSON

Jeffrey Minson has written across the fields of political, legal, and cultural theory; on the political and ethical aspects of Michel Foucault's work; on ethics and the state; and on questions of citizenship from the ethical demands of democracy to sexual harassment and cultural policy. He is currently working on a comparative study of the styles of political civility associated with rival political and cultural theories.

DAVID ROBBINS

The work of David Robbins has been seen in numerous solo exhibitions in the US and Europe over the last 25 years. His books include *The Ice Cream Social*, a novella originally published in 1998 (republished by JRP|Ringier, 2007) and *The Velvet Grind: Selected Essays, Interviews, Satires 1983–2005* (JRP|Ringier, 2006). He is currently completing his magnum opus, *Concrete Comedy: An Alternative History of Twentieth Century Comedy*, after a decade's work.

MICHAEL SMITH

Michael Smith is a video/performance/installation artist known for his eponymous performance persona named Mike, the central figure in an ongoing series of large-scale narrative-based projects. Smith has shown his work extensively in the US, Canada, and Europe at a variety of venues including museums, galleries, universities, festivals, nightclubs, on television, and in the streets. *Mike: Solo and Collaborative Works by Michael Smith and Joshua White (and other collaborators)*, a survey exhibition of Smith's work 1980–2005, was at the Blanton Museum of Art in Austin (2007).

JAN TUMLIR

Jan Tumlir is an independent curator and writer based in Los Angeles. His articles have appeared in *Artforum*, *X-TRA*, *Art Issues*, *LA Weekly*, *Flash Art*, and *Frieze*; and his exhibitions include *Morbid Curiosity* (ACME, LA, 2001, and I-20, New York, 2002); *The Lateral Slip* (Sweeney Art Gallery, UC Riverside, 2004); and *Desertshore* (Luckman Gallery, Cal State, LA, 2008). He has also written catalogue essays on the work of Bas Jan Ader, Uta Barth, David Bunn, Jessica Bronson, De Rijke & De Rooij, Jorge Pardo, Pae White, and others. Tumlir has taught art and media history/theory at several LA-area schools, including Art Center, Pasadena; the University of Southern California, Los Angeles; and CalArts, Valencia.

JOHN C. WELCHMAN

Series editor and SoCCAS chair, John C. Welchman is Professor of Art History and Theory in the Visual Arts Department at the University of California, San Diego. His books on art include *Modernism Relocated: Towards a Cultural Studies of Visual Modernity* (Allen & Unwin, 1995), *Invisible Colours: A Visual History of Titles* (Yale UP, 1997), and *Art After Appropriation: Essays on Art in the 1990s* (Routledge, 2001); he is editor of *Rethinking Borders* (Minnesota UP, 1996); the collected writings of Mike Kelley, *Foul Perfection: Essays and Criticism* (MIT Press, 2003); *Minor Histories* (MIT Press, 2004); and *Mike Kelley: Interviews, Conversations, and Chit-Chat, 1988–2004* (JRP|Ringier, 2005). Recent and current projects include monographs on Vasco Araújo (ADIAC, 2006); Tony Oursler (JRP|Ringier, 2008); and Mike Kelley (Taschen, 2011).

JANET WHITMORE

Janet Whitmore is an art historian specializing in 19th- and 20th-century art and architecture. She has researched and written on the journals, graphics, and associated imagery of the Montmartre scene in the 1880s and 1890, and currently teaches at Harrington College of Design in Chicago.

GREGORY H. WILLIAMS

Gregory H. Williams is assistant professor of contemporary art at Boston University. A regular contributor to periodicals such as *Artforum International* and *Texte zur Kunst*, he has written essays for the retrospective exhibitions of Rosemarie Trockel at the Museum Ludwig in Cologne (2005) and Martin Kippenberger at Tate Modern in London (2006). His essay, "Jokes Interrupted: Martin Kippenberger's Receding Punch Line," first published as part of the Kippenberger retrospective at Tate, was reprinted in Jennifer Higgie, ed., *The Artist's Joke* (MIT Press, 2007). He is currently working on a book that explores art, humor, and politics in Germany from the 1960s to the present.

This book is the fourth volume of the Southern California Consortium of Art Schools [SoCCAS] symposia. It is expanded from a symposium at the Hammer Museum of Art, Los Angeles, in 2007.

EDITOR John C. Welchman
EDITORIAL COORDINATION Salome Schnetz
EDITING + PROOFREADING Clare Manchester
PICTURE EDITING Julia Dzwonkoski
RESEARCH ASSISTANT David Mather
COVER IMAGE Raymond Pettibon, *No Title*, 2009; Pen, ink, gouache, and acrylic on paper; 30 x 22 1/2 inches (76.2 x 57.2 cm)
DESIGN Nicola Todeschini for Gavillet & Rust, Geneva
TYPEFACES Hermes (www.optimo.ch), Guernica
PRINTING EBS Editoriale Bortolazzi-Stei, Verona

ACKNOWLEDGMENTS
The publication has received generous support from the founding member schools of SoCCAS: Art Center College of Art and Design, Pasadena; California Institute of the Arts, Valencia; Otis College of Art and Design; University of California, Irvine; University of California, Los Angeles; University of California, San Diego; University of California, Santa Barbara; and the University of Southern California; and from the University of California Institute for Research in the Arts (UCIRA); and the Center for the Humanities and the Visual Arts Department, University of California, San Diego.

Printed in Europe.

PUBLISHED BY
JRP|Ringier
Letzigraben 134
CH–8047 Zurich
T +41 (0) 43 311 27 50
F +41 (0) 43 311 27 51
info@jrp-ringier.com
www.jrp-ringier.com

ISBN 978-3-905770-96-4

JRP|Ringier books are available internationally at selected bookstores and from the following distribution partners:

SWITZERLAND
Buch 2000, AVA Verlagsauslieferung AG, Centralweg 16, CH-8910 Affoltern a.A.
buch2000@ava.ch, www.ava.ch

FRANCE
Les Presses du réel, 16 rue Quentin, F-21000 Dijon
info@lespressesdureel.com
www.lespressesdureel.com

GERMANY AND AUSTRIA
Vice Versa Vertrieb, Immanuelkirchstrasse 12, D-10405 Berlin
info@vice-versa-vertrieb.de
www.vice-versa-vertrieb.de

UK AND OTHER EUROPEAN COUNTRIES
Cornerhouse Publications, 70 Oxford Street, UK-Manchester M1 5NH
publications@cornerhouse.org
www.cornerhouse.org/books

USA, CANADA, ASIA, AND AUSTRALIA
D.A.P./Distributed Art Publishers, 155 Sixth Avenue, 2nd Floor, NY 10013, USA-New York
dap@dapinc.com, www.artbook.com

For a list of our partner bookshops or for any general questions, please contact JRP|Ringier directly at info@jrp-ringier.com, or visit our homepage www.jrp-ringier.com for further information about our program.

IN THE SAME SERIES:
The Aesthetics of Risk
(ISBN: 978-3-905770-55-1)
Institutional Critique and After
(ISBN: 978-3-905701-65-4)
Recent Pasts. Art in Southern California from the 90s to Now
(ISBN: 978-3-905701-20-3)